Starting Your Career in Academic Psychology

Starting Your Career in Academic Psychology

ROBERT J. STERNBERG

AMERICAN PSYCHOLOGICAL ASSOCIATION
WASHINGTON, DC

Copyright © 2017 by the American Psychological Association. All rights reserved. Except as permitted under the United States Copyright Act of 1976, no part of this publication may be reproduced or distributed in any form or by any means, including, but not limited to, the process of scanning and digitization, or stored in a database or retrieval system, without the prior written permission of the publisher.

Published by
American Psychological Association
750 First Street, NE
Washington, DC 20002
www.apa.org

To order
APA Order Department
P.O. Box 92984
Washington, DC 20090-2984
Tel: (800) 374-2721; Direct: (202) 336-5510
Fax: (202) 336-5502; TDD/TTY: (202) 336-6123
Online: www.apa.org/pubs/books
E-mail: order@apa.org

In the U.K., Europe, Africa, and the Middle East, copies may be ordered from
American Psychological Association
3 Henrietta Street
Covent Garden, London
WC2E 8LU England

Typeset in Goudy by Circle Graphics, Inc., Columbia, MD

Printer: Edwards Brothers, Inc., Lillington, NC
Cover Designer: Beth Schlenoff Design, Bethesda, MD

The opinions and statements published are the responsibility of the authors, and such opinions and statements do not necessarily represent the policies of the American Psychological Association.

Library of Congress Cataloging-in-Publication Data

Names: Sternberg, Robert J., author.
Title: Starting your career in academic psychology / Robert J. Sternberg.
Description: Washington, DC : American Psychological Association, [2017] | Includes bibliographical references and index.
Identifiers: LCCN 2016025385 | ISBN 9781433826382 | ISBN 1433826380
Subjects: LCSH: Psychology—Study and teaching (Higher) | Psychology teachers. | College teaching—Vocational guidance. | Psychology—Vocational guidance.
Classification: LCC BF77 .S683 2017 | DDC 150.23/73—dc23 LC record available at https://lccn.loc.gov/2016025385

British Library Cataloguing-in-Publication Data
A CIP record is available from the British Library.

Printed in the United States of America
First Edition

http://dx.doi.org/10.1037/0000013-000

CONTENTS

Introduction 3

Part I. In the Beginning 7

Chapter 1.   Before You Even Start 9

Chapter 2.   Getting Going 25

Part II. Teaching 37

Chapter 3.   Getting Started Teaching Your Courses 39

Chapter 4.   Collaborating With Students 59

Part III. Research 73

Chapter 5.   Forming Ideas for and Implementing Your Research 75

Chapter 6.   Setting Up a Lab 93

Chapter 7.	Forming Collaborations	105
Chapter 8.	Getting a Grant	117

Part IV. Service **141**

Chapter 9.	Service to Your Department and University	143
Chapter 10.	Service to Your Academic Field	159

Part V. Professional Advancement **167**

Chapter 11.	Networking	169
Chapter 12.	Giving Talks and Lectures	179
Chapter 13.	Writing Articles	189
Chapter 14.	Departmental and University Politics	201
Chapter 15.	Preparing for Tenure and Promotion	209
Chapter 16.	Resolving Conflicts	225
Chapter 17.	Twenty-One Common Mistakes Junior Faculty Make	237

Epilogue 249
References 251
Index 255
About the Author 265

Starting Your Career in Academic Psychology

INTRODUCTION

I got off the plane from California to New York—from graduate school to my first job—and there I was, an assistant professor supposed to start on a promising career. I did not bother to mention to anyone in my university that I was having deep feelings of insecurity and even fraudulence—I identified much more with the graduate students than I did with the professors. Sure, I had been a teaching assistant, but I'd never actually taught a course. Sure, I'd done research, but I'd never had to go on my own from the conception of an idea to a publication in a major journal. And sure, I knew I had to serve the department, but I had only the vaguest ideas about what I possibly could offer that would serve my department, or any other department, for that matter.

My start as an assistant professor revealed me to be exactly the novice—that would be a complimentary word—that I felt myself to be. It seemed like if there was a mistake to be made, I was there ready to make it.

One of my first tasks was to figure out what to do with the $5,000 start-up money I received. At the time, I was doing reaction-time experiments, so I

---

http://dx.doi.org/10.1037/0000013-001
Starting Your Career in Academic Psychology, by R. J. Sternberg
Copyright © 2017 by the American Psychological Association. All rights reserved.

invested, would you believe this, $4,500—90% of my start-up—in an Iconix tachistoscope, a device that provided rapid visual presentation of stimuli. This was mid-1975—just before computers were starting to make it big in the running of experiments—and I thought a fancy tachistoscope would serve me better. Iconix was even referred to as the "Cadillac" of tachistoscopes. But computers were making rapid inroads. When, rather soon after I got it, my tachistoscope went on the blink, I called Iconix, only to discover that they were going out of business. There went my $4,500. I had $500 left in my research account.

Things did not go much better in my teaching. I was teaching a course on theories of intelligence. I had this brilliant idea that I could write a book and prepare my lecture notes at the same time simply by turning the lecture notes into book format. I was a big hit. My first class session had about 50 students, my second class session about 25, my third about 12, and I ended up with about five. It was a nice example of a descending geometric progression, but it scarcely was what I had in mind to become a successful teacher. In the end, I think my overall course rating was about 3 out of 5, but only because the large majority of the class had dropped out.

I was asked to be department computer authority, meaning that I would do service by assigning money to people's mainframe computer accounts. But I did not keep careful records and soon lost track of how much money I had allocated, until I used up all the money assigned to the department for computer use early in the school year.

Well, I won't go on to describe my various and sundry miseries during my first few years as a faculty member, but this book is intended to make sure you don't have the kind of checkered start I had. You can and will do better. This chapter describes how the book is organized and how it will ensure you get off to the great start of which you are capable.

This book is written for graduate students and postdocs who are just about to start their careers as academic psychologists and also for academics who are just starting out in faculty positions, whether tenure track or adjunct, whether in a large university or a small one, and whether in a psychology department or in a related department. (I used to teach in a psychology department, for example, but now I am in a department of human development.)

A word about myself: I've dealt with starting careers in academia from many points of view. I've seen it myself as an assistant professor, of course, but also from the standpoint of being an acting chair, dean, provost, and president. I've taught at four different universities, and so I've seen that although some things are different about starting out, most things are the same. And, as a past president of the American Psychological Association, I've dealt with some of the issues in starting out that are peculiar to psychology. So I think I am in a pretty good position to author this book.

The book is organized into five main parts plus this Introduction. Here is how the book is laid out:

Part I, "In the Beginning," deals with opening issues. It consists of two chapters. Chapter 1, "Before You Even Start," presents advice on how to prepare for and live through a job interview. Chapter 2, "Getting Going," contains general suggestions for those who have gotten the position and are just starting out—what they need to do right away, up to and including their first days on the job.

Part II, "Teaching," explains how one can effectively prepare to start teaching and then succeed when one actually enters the classroom. This part consists of two chapters. Chapter 3 deals with "Getting Started Teaching Your Courses." It tells you how to prepare for teaching, before you even enter the classroom, and then how to be effective once you get into the classroom. Chapter 4, "Collaborating With Students," discusses specifically how to work with students.

Part III, "Research," contains four chapters that address how to get started with, and then be effective in, your research. Chapter 5, "Forming Ideas for and Implementing Your Research," discusses how you can get started on a systematic research program. How do you get ideas? How do you get going? How do you keep going once you've started? What are the obstacles you are likely to encounter? Chapter 6, "Setting Up a Lab," presents the steps in starting your lab, including getting space, making equipment purchases, hiring people, recruiting students, and the like. Chapter 7 is "Forming Collaborations." Much research, especially in modern times, is collaborative. This chapter discusses how to form, maintain, and, when necessary, end collaborations. It also discusses what tends to go right in collaborations and what kinds of things can go wrong. Chapter 8 discusses "Getting a Grant." It briefly surveys your options for getting funded and gives guidance for writing a successful grant proposal, as well as what to do when your proposal is accepted (or rejected).

Part IV deals with "Service." It contains two chapters. Chapter 9 covers "Service to Your Department and University." It talks about what kinds of service help your career and what kinds are dead ends. It also discusses both the benefits and drawbacks of service to your department and university. Chapter 10 covers "Service to Your Academic Field." Service to your field is evaluated differently than service to your college or university. This chapter explores what kinds of service you can do, how you can do it effectively, and how you can ensure that service work helps your career rather than wastes your time.

Part V covers the topic of "Professional Advancement." It contains six chapters. Chapter 11 is on "Networking"—how you can get to know other people in your field or related fields and use those connections to advance your career. Chapter 12, "Giving Talks and Lectures," explains how to give them effectively and for maximum impact. Chapter 13, "Writing Articles," explains how you can write them so that they best convey what you want them to communicate. Chapter 14 deals with "Departmental and University Politics." Most of us, especially at the junior level, want to stay out of departmental politics. But that is not always possible or even advisable. Good handling of sticky political situations can advance your career, whereas handling them poorly can set you back.

Chapter 15, "Preparing for Tenure and Promotion," covers what you need to do to build a case, what errors of commission and omission can hinder your case, and when you should come up for early, or later, promotion. Chapter 16 deals with "Resolving Conflicts." It is difficult to get through a career without professional and even personal conflicts, some of them serious. What do you do when you face such conflicts, and how do you ensure that you come out of them as well as you can? Chapter 17 identifies "Twenty-One Common Mistakes Junior Faculty Make." What are the mistakes people make that stymie them so much that, almost regardless of what else they do, they struggle to advance to the next steps? Finally, the Epilogue is a brief final note regarding the importance of other people to your career.

I hope you find this book useful and fun to read. Let me know. I can be reached at robert.sternberg@cornell.edu.

I
IN THE BEGINNING

1

BEFORE YOU EVEN START

This book is about maximizing your success early in your career. If you are an early career professional, this book is for you! And if you are a bit past the early-career point, you still may find the book useful.

This chapter is about what happens before you start your new job—you have to get the job in the first place! And that process starts while you are still in graduate school. You need to do the right things before you start your career—hence this chapter!

WHILE YOU ARE STILL IN GRADUATE SCHOOL

Getting to a job interview starts when you start graduate school. You need to build up a record that will attract institutions to you. Generally, building a record involves developing a serious research program and getting

http://dx.doi.org/10.1037/0000013-002
Starting Your Career in Academic Psychology, by R. J. Sternberg
Copyright © 2017 by the American Psychological Association. All rights reserved.

experience in teaching. How much research and teaching each will count will differ from one institution to another.

When you start graduate school, you likely will become involved in your primary adviser's research program. At some time during your graduate career, however, you need to make a transition to developing your own program of research. This transition often occurs around the third year. If by your fourth year it is not happening, you need seriously to consider why not. The research program may relate to your adviser's program, but it needs to be perceived by yourself and others as distinctively your own.

As you know, most institutions expect you to have published research, or at least to have research in press, by the time you apply for a job. If you have no research at least in press, you probably are better off either waiting another year or applying for postdoctoral study. In the past, postdoctoral study was the exception, but increasingly it is becoming the rule. Today's beginning assistant professors often have publishing records closer to what used to be the publishing record of an advanced assistant professor.

There is one other important issue to consider: Should you start a job hunt if you are going to be ABD (i.e., done with all but the dissertation)? I recommend not going on the job market until you are confident that you will either finish your dissertation or be done with it except for the most minor polishing. I once had a student who took an academic job—against my advice—with her dissertation incomplete. She immediately was hit with a heavy teaching load plus the expectation she would be doing new, postdissertation research. She found herself unable to find the time to complete her dissertation and after 2 years was let go. You have very few years go get reappointed, tenured, and promoted. You do not want to be spending your time doing work you were expected to have finished in graduate school.

If you are going to be ABD, consider completing another year of graduate school or applying for a postdoc. But if you apply for a postdoc, keep in mind that your postdoctoral adviser likely will expect you to work on the project for which you were hired. So you still will be short on time for completing your dissertation. If you apply for a postdoc, remember that most postdocs (except those that are independently funded) require you to work on a grant- or contract-funded project. Make sure your application shows enthusiasm for that project and for the project director.

Although the main coin of the realm in academic psychology is empirical papers, other kinds of papers also can help establish your credentials, including theory papers, literature reviews, or spinoffs such as book chapters that review your own and others' work. If your dissertation is particularly successful, you may even consider trying to contract for a book, although such a practice is much more common in the humanities than in the sciences.

If I were to comment on the most common mistake I see among graduate students, it is that they fail to set the stage for acquiring at least three strong letters of recommendation. In the past, a well-connected adviser single-handedly could get his or her most promising students a job. Those days and the networks they supported are long gone. You need at least two other individuals besides an adviser to write for you.

There are different ways you can get to know faculty members other than your main adviser. Here are some of the best ones.

One is to get to know faculty members on your committee (assuming you have a committee). Graduate students sometimes pay little attention to others on the committee beside the main adviser. This is a big mistake. The others can be important sources of recommendation letters.

A second possibility is to ask someone from whom you have taken a course to write a letter. Preferably this would be someone in whose course you excelled. If you did not excel in the course, do not hope for the best; ask someone else. I personally abhor the situation in which someone asks me for a letter of recommendation and I have either to suggest they seek someone else or to tell them that if I write, I cannot be strongly supportive. It will be even better if you have taken a couple of courses from the faculty member.

A third possibility is to seek to do research with a faculty member other than your adviser. This is an excellent way to get to know a faculty member, and when the faculty member writes, he or she will be able to comment on your research, which is generally viewed as more important than course performance.

A fourth possibility is to ask a faculty member for whom you have been a teaching assistant for a letter. It is a very good idea to have at least one recommender who knows your teaching. Institutions differ in the extent to which they use teaching skills as a criterion for hiring a new faculty member, but no institution wants a bad teacher. Most institutions want not just good but excellent teachers.

A fifth possibility is to ask a faculty member from your undergraduate institution to write a letter. I generally do not recommend this course of action unless your undergraduate teacher has stayed in touch with you throughout graduate school (or postdoctoral training) and can comment on your recent progress, not just what you accomplished as an undergraduate. Having an undergraduate recommender can send the message that you just cannot find anyone else. There is one other exception to the general rule of avoiding undergraduate teachers—if the teacher is extremely famous or is particularly well known to the hiring institution. In those cases, the letter may make a real positive difference.

A sixth possibility is, during the course of your graduate or postdoctoral training, to get to know someone at an institution at which you never have worked. You might meet a faculty member at a professional meeting or through your writing to the individual to express interest in or ask questions about his or her research. The challenge in such cases is to get to know the individual well enough so that he or she is in a good position to write a letter for you.

A seventh possibility is to ask someone, such as a director of graduate studies or a department chair, to write in an official capacity. I do not recommend such letters unless you are desperate. Even if the person has a respected position, if he or she does not know you well, it inevitably will come through in the letter.

There are two other common mistakes I should mention before moving on to job interviews. The first mistake is getting into a research area merely because it is "hot"—that is, because at the time there are a lot of jobs. First of all, what is hot can change over time, and you may find that an area that is red hot when you start your studies is ice cold when you finish. Second, you never do your best work in areas that are not truly of interest to you (Kaufman & Sternberg, 2010; Lubart & Sternberg, 1988). To do your best work, you have to be passionate about what you study and find a strategy in your work that fits you. Oddly, people often don't use the strategies that best fit their own patterns of abilities and interests (Sternberg & Weil, 1980). They may be smart in a traditional sense but not in the sense of knowing how best to leverage their strengths and weaknesses (Sternberg, 1984) or how to find a style of work that makes sense for them (Sternberg & Grigorenko, 2001).

The second mistake is working in an area you love but for which there is no market and no sign there ever will be. You need not only to be excited yourself—you need also to excite others. If you will not be able to do so, you may find yourself talking to yourself, an unenviable position for any academic. The fact that an area is not of great interest at one time does not mean that it will not be of great interest at a future time. But if you are going into an area with few colleagues, it may be incumbent on you, in the future, to show others why the area is worth their attention.

One final warning I would like to add if you are a minority-group member. There will always be people who believe that people of a sex or ethnicity or socially defined race different from their own are somehow less intelligent than they are. Such views are based on discredited theories of racial and other group differences in intelligence (Sternberg, Grigorenko, & Kidd, 2005). Never, ever let yourself fall into the trap of accepting their viewpoint, no matter how bad a period you may be going through or how belittled you may feel. Ultimately, you will be judged by your accomplishments, not by your race, your ethnicity, your gender, or other characteristics irrelevant to the quality of the work you do. And all of us, no matter our race or ethnicity, can improve our intelligence and other abilities (Detterman & Sternberg, 1982).

MATCHING YOURSELF WITH A JOB

When you apply for graduate school, typically every university in which you might be interested has some openings in any given year. When applying for a job, this is far from the case. Most institutions have no job openings in a given year. In some years, the jobs are very slim pickings indeed. Many PhDs end up as adjuncts, either through choice or because tenure track job openings for which they are suitable never become available.

Whether you go tenure track or adjunct, the most important thing in taking a job is fit—just as in a relationship with a significant other. If your first love is teaching, you need to think twice or three times about taking a job in an institution that will evaluate you primarily on your research. But if teaching is not your thing, you want to avoid like the plague colleges that emphasize teaching. Too often, people stress reputation above fit. Early in my career I gave a student really bad advice, suggesting she take the more prestigious of two job offers she got. She took that offer and was miserable. She later went to a smaller liberal arts institution that was a much better fit with her passion for teaching. Emphasize fit in seeking a job the same way you would in seeking a partner.

In seeking a job, please consider nonacademic as well as academic possibilities (Sternberg, 2007, 2017a). Of course, there is the academic path in a psychology department. But there are so many other possibilities, even in academia, such as a career as a faculty member in education, human development, business, law, medicine, criminal justice, or public policy. Moreover, there are many possible nonacademic tracks, such as clinical, counseling, health, forensic, military, school, sports, organizational, and consulting psychology. Some psychologists go into business as managers, and others use their skills in psychology in far-flung fields. There are very few jobs that do not require psychology in some way. So as you think about the future, keep your eyes open!

Even if you do go academic in a traditional psychology department, there are many possibilities. For example, your life will be very different as an adjunct versus tenure track faculty member or in a community college versus a comprehensive university. The full range of differences is beyond the scope of this book, but elsewhere I have discussed differences among various types of academic jobs (Sternberg, 2017b).

PREPARING FOR AND DOING THE INTERVIEW

The job interview isn't really the start of your career. It occurs before the start of your career. But if you don't get through the job interview successfully, your career probably never actually will get started!

Many interviews occur in person on location at the hiring institution. But more and more interviews are being done via teleconferencing or a similar electronic means. Some may even be done in person but at a convention. So here are some suggestions for optimizing your job interview!

Know the Institution as Well as You Know Your Own

Institutions of higher learning want to make job offers to candidates who are likely to accept their offer. If you show that you know little about the institution, you are advertising your lack of interest in the institution. The assumption often is that if you have not bothered to learn about the institution, you are unlikely to be serious about going there. For example, if you have to ask if the faculty is unionized or if there is a graduate program in your specialty area, it will be hard for the institution to take your candidacy seriously. Check out the website of the institution before you visit, and especially peruse the website of the department you are potentially interested in joining.

Learn About the Work of the Faculty in the Institution, Especially in Your Area of Expertise

Suppose you were interviewing two candidates. One knows and is excited about your work. The other knows nothing of your work—indeed, she seems hardly to know who you are. Which candidate would you prefer? Probably it is the same candidate almost any faculty member would prefer. The moral of the story is simple: Know about the work of faculty with whom you are likely to talk, show interest in it when you meet them, and ask questions that show your knowledge and interest. You might even express interest in future collaborations with them. Never, ever offer your suggestions for what they might have done better. Save that for another day—after you are hired!

Emphasize What You Can Do for Them, Not What They Can Do for You

When you consider a job, you probably consider carefully whether the job will help your career, and if so, how. The hiring institution is less interested than you are in how it will help you, but it is probably more interested in how you will help it. You need to think about what you have to contribute that the institution does not already have. Do you bring a new area of research? Why would the institution want your area of research? Can you teach courses no one else can or wants to teach? Do you have special expertise in computers or in methodology? Think about what you have that you think the department needs, and then emphasize it in the interview, especially in speaking with the chair of the department.

Know the Strengths and Weaknesses of Your Own Work

You may or may not be aware of your weaknesses, but at least some of the department members will be aware of them. They will have read your letters of recommendation and carefully examined your CV. The last thing you want is to be caught off guard when someone asks why you have not published more or in better places, or how you can expect to teach with such a lack of teaching experience. Ask your advisers in your home institution what kinds of weaknesses others are likely to perceive. Then be prepared to address those weaknesses when (and if) people bring them up.

A tricky wicket is the problem of what to do about weaknesses no one brings up. For example, if you know that your publication record is sparse but no one mentions it in the interview, should you say anything? There is no one right answer to this question. In general, I suggest use of the following guideline in deciding whether to bring something up: If the department knew about the something, might it change a decision that otherwise would be positive? Number of publications is easily observable on a CV. If the hiring institution does not bring it up, there is no reason why you need to bring it up.

But there are other issues you need to bring up. If, for example, you have an issue the department might care about but would not know about through your CV or letters of recommendation, you ought to bring it up. Such an issue might be a past felony conviction, an accusation of academic misconduct that is pending against you but that is not yet resolved, or an academic misconduct charge that was resolved against you; you should bring up such issues with the chair. It is much better to have an institution not hire you than to have one withdraw a job offer after it is made or to hire you and then believe the hire was done under false pretenses. In the latter instances, the situation may be written up in higher education publications, and once that happens, it may be hard to get a job anywhere.

Have a Super-Duper 1-Minute Elevator Speech

Once you arrive at the interview, chances are some people will tell you all the reasons they just cannot attend your talk. They have class; they have child care they have to do; they have the most important appointment since the beginning of time; they are just leaving for a trip. Maybe they just want to play golf, but they probably will not tell you that. You need a 1-minute elevator speech (which can go to 90 seconds, but no more) on what they would have heard if they had gone to your talk.

The elevator speech is really important. For some people, that's all they will know of what you do. It should state the problem that interests you, why the problem that interests you should interest them or anyone in his or her right mind, how you went about addressing the problem, what you found, and why what you found is important scientifically and, if possible, important to the world. Do not assume that people can see for themselves why your work is significant. You have to show them. And don't assume that because you think your work is superb, other people will see that as well. It's up to you to show the work is superb, without actually saying so. Give them all the evidence and let them figure it out for themselves.

Do Not Assume You Know the Power Structure in the Department or Institution

The power structure of a department matters greatly to you because in some departments, powerful people often have an especially loud voice in deciding who gets hired, who gets to stay, and how people are treated. The problem is that when you go for an interview, you are unlikely to know who these people are. Moreover, members of the department are likely to be reluctant to tell you who the people are; junior faculty—the ones most likely to open up to you—may not even know. Therefore, you should assume that anyone you talk to might be a powerful person in the department and treat each individual as such.

Present a Talk That Would Interest Your Grandparents

You may be tempted to present a talk that will wow the aficionados of your particular area of research—one that will show your supreme technical or data analytic or other skills. Don't give that talk—unless you are invited to give a separate talk only to people in your area of specialization. For a department talk, the most important thing is to give a talk that will interest and impress as many people as possible. Leave the displays of advanced statistics or technical skills to your papers or to one-on-one conversations with experts in your field. Give a talk that will make everyone in the department want to hire you, not just those in your area.

In most departments, hiring is a multistep process. The first step is the search committee. Even the search committee may—indeed is likely to—have some members who are not experts in your area. You cannot get a job just by appealing to narrow experts. The second step is the department. Usually, everyone gets to vote. That means you have to appeal to people who know little or nothing about your area, not just those who are experts. Then the decision goes to higher levels of administration. The bottom line is that if you want to impress as many people as possible, speak to all of them when you give your talk, not just to those who share your expertise.

Be Ready for the Technology to Fail

Technology fails regularly. It often is interesting to see how people handle failed technology. The way you should handle it is to be ready with a backup. Be able to speak without PowerPoints or slides or whatever you are using. The best way to impress an audience when technology fails is to be able to keep going, not to stand there waiting and hoping it later begins to work. You cannot afford the lost time or the possibility that you are waiting for a fix that will never happen.

Be Ready for Annoying Questioners

Too often, especially in a job talk, there is someone in the audience whose fervent goal in life is to show that he or she is smarter than you are. Such people often are smart but, at the same time, foolish (Sternberg, 2002). The blabbermouth will spend some time trying to come up with a killer question that shows how smart he or she is and how pathetically incompetent you are. If you get a question you cannot answer, say you do not know the answer but are willing to get back to the questioner later. Or say that the question is extremely complex and that there just is not time to go into a detailed answer. Give a short answer and move on. Sometimes a questioner will persist and want to monopolize the question period or, worse, the time allotted for your main talk. In that case, feel free to say politely that you need to move on in your talk or to another questioner. Do not let a showoff ruin your presentation.

Present the Talk That Best Shows What You Have to Offer the Institution

You may be one of those fortunate people who can choose between two or even more talks to present at a job interview. You may then wonder how to choose between the talks. Present the talk that best shows what you can add to the institution. That is, think of the talk from the institutional perspective, rather than your own. What does the institution need most that you have to offer? If you are not sure, you might ask the individual who invites you what he or she thinks the department or institution needs. Or if you have other contacts in the host department, ask them. A little research can go a long way. And be sure to say not only what you have done in research, but what you hope to do. The department wants to know where you are planning to go with your research program.

One way to show you have a lot to offer the institution is to be a great teacher during your job interview. The department probably is looking for strong teachers, not just strong researchers. Some departments even have a separate teaching lecture. Those departments may value teaching more than research. Whatever you speak about, speak about it as if you were trying to give the best lecture you possibly could to students who are possibly interested in what you do.

Remember, the Dinner Is Part of the Interview

Chances are that members of the department in which you are interested will invite you out to dinner. The dinner is very unlikely to get you the job, but it sure can blow your chances. The advice I have is the obvious stuff. Don't get drunk or even tipsy. Don't be rude. Don't gossip. Don't order the most expensive dish on the menu. Don't insult anyone. Be careful about your jokes. Don't eat messily. Don't make any comments that could be interpreted as racist, sexist, or any -ist. Be engaging, but let others talk, too—they want a good listener at least as much as they want a good talker.

In One-on-One Meetings, Show Your Knowledge About and Interest in the Work of the Faculty Members With Whom You Are Speaking

It is tempting to use one-on-one meetings as a chance to talk about yourself, your interests, what you will be doing in the future, and so on. You need to remember that the meetings are at least as much of a chance for you to listen as to speak. Try to find out what your conversational partner is interested in, and then relate your interests to his or hers. Faculty want to know how you will help them, and the one-on-one meeting is a chance to show them!

Announce at the Beginning of Your Talk That You Will Take Clarification Questions During the Talk and Other Questions Afterward

There are basically two kinds of questions that come up in job talks—clarification questions and probing questions. The latter can take a long time to answer. You want to finish your talk, so save those questions for the end to ensure that you can do so.

When calling on people, try to avoid any pattern of selecting people that may appear to show a bias. Do not appear to favor men or women, or people of one ethnicity or another, or even people on one side of the room or another. It is easy to make a mistake in this regard. People may notice.

Also, give answers that are concise and to the point. Question periods are usually of very limited duration, and people with questions want to have their questions answered. If you give very long answers, you will have less opportunity to call on people. Moreover, you may appear to be verbose or to lack focus.

Emphasize in Your Interactions With People How Much You Want to Go to the Institution

If you want to play hard to get, save it for a potential romantic partner, but even then, don't expect great results from this strategy (Sternberg, 1998a)! If you are very senior, perhaps you can play hard to get. But if you are early in your career, you need to show people in the institution that you are excited about the possibility of taking a job with the institution. Just as you want them to be excited about you, you need to be excited about them.

You do not want to be fawning or appear to be a suck-up. Rather, you should emphasize your compatibility with the goals and culture of the institution. If, however, you interview and find that you are not compatible with the goals and culture of the institution, go home and withdraw from consideration for the job, or at the very least, do not take it if it is offered to you. You will be miserable, and you will feel underappreciated. One of the worst things that can happen in an academic career is to work in an institution that does not appreciate what one has to offer or that works in a way that one finds foreign to one's nature.

In interpersonal relationships, we tend to be attracted to persons who are like us (Sternberg, 1987). Similarly, we are attracted to, and institutions are attracted to, others like ourselves. Find an institution that is like you!

Show Flexibility in Your Willingness to Teach Diverse Courses

You may have listed on your CV the courses you are prepared to teach. View those as a starting pitch, not as a final list representing what you can or are willing to do. You just cannot know in advance what courses institutions will need you to teach. For example, it may never have occurred to you to teach intro psych, but you may be needed. Or you may be needed for stats. New faculty members usually do not get the plum teaching assignments. Over time, you can develop the courses you most want to teach. As the newbie, accept what you are asked to teach, unless you feel you just totally are incompetent to teach it. That said, I was asked to teach courses about which I knew little. I was amazed at how quickly I could learn the material. Moreover, some of those were my best courses precisely because I did not know that much about the material and thus did not teach over the level of the students in the class.

Don't Talk About Your Expectations for the Job and What It Pays

If you get a job offer, you will have plenty of time later to talk about pay, benefits, teaching loads, and the like. The job interview is not the place to bring up these issues. If the chair brings them up with you, then you should discuss them, but do not put yourself in a position where you are or seem to be making demands. If anyone else brings up these issues with you, try to change the subject. You do not want to lose a job because you are perceived as making unreasonable demands. Get the job first; then worry about the details of the offer. The next chapter deals with how to negotiate these issues.

Take Meetings With Students and Staff Very Seriously

Probably the most important meetings you will have are with members of the selection committee. Closely following are meetings with the chair. The meetings with students and possibly with staff may appear to be the least important meetings, but this appearance is deceptive. Often everyone in the department is asked to comment on each candidate, and in most departments, students' views are taken seriously, especially for entry-level appointments. The department usually wants someone who will be responsive to and work well with students. What they really do not want is someone who will have troubled relations with students. Such people take up an inordinate amount of time and resources. You do not have to have perfect interactions with students. But if your interactions are less than good, it will be harder for you to get the job. Also, if you are viewed as someone who sucks up to superiors but then is arrogant with or dismissive of those lower on the totem pole, you will not be viewed as an attractive candidate. Treat the meetings with students and staff as in every way equal in importance to the meetings with faculty.

You may meet with a dean. The dean will probably know little or nothing about your research or even your field. Such visits may be a courtesy, but keep in mind that a dean usually can veto an appointment. Thus, at worst, make a neutral impression. Don't say anything you might later regret.

Be Ready to Explain Weak Aspects of Your CV

I discussed earlier whether you should bring up weak aspects in your record. But what if someone else does? What do you do?

The best thing to do is to acknowledge the weakness and explain it as best you can. Don't make excuses, and don't try somehow to turn it into a source of pride (e.g., "I may not publish much, but that's because I have exceedingly high standards, for myself as for everyone else"). If you have too few publications, say why. Did you have trouble gaining access to participants? Did you have computer troubles? Did you switch areas of research? Or what? Sooner or later, people will want to understand your weaknesses, and there is nothing more disarming than acknowledging those weaknesses and indicating how you plan to improve in the future.

Never Lie

You, like everyone else, will be tempted in the course of a job interview to lie. It may be to slightly exaggerate your credentials, or to hide flaws, or to create an impression that you know is false. Never lie. There are three reasons. First, it is unethical, and if you act unethically or people think you are unethical, you will have a limited and probably short future in your chosen career. Second, a lie is enough to lose a job. Who wants to hire a liar? Third, in this age of the Internet and global communications, it often is very easy to verify whether what someone says is true. So why invite scrutiny you don't need or want? Even if you have something to say that is not likely to help your case, get it over with quickly and move on.

There is one other thing. Sometimes we feel that the lie we tell is just a wee one. But once you start lying at all, you start sliding down the ethical slippery slope (Sternberg, 2012). Liars often start with small fibs and then work their way up to major falsehoods. You just don't want to go down that path.

If You Need Partner Accommodations, Mention It Early

No department wants to hear, after you get an offer, that by the way you have a spouse for whom you need a job or else you will not take the job that has been offered. Not mentioning that you have a spouse or other partner before the offer comes pretty close to lying by omission. You want institutions to level with you; you should do the same with them.

The situation is different if you would like a job for your partner but the job is not a deal breaker. In this case, you might mention this fact during the selection process, but you do not have to, as it does not affect whether you will accept the job, or so you think. The problem with saying nothing is that later, it may actually be a, if not the, deciding factor. If you mention the job issue after you get the job offer, and if another institution offers you a job and your partner one as well, you may be more likely to take the other job. In that case, your not mentioning your partner's need for a job may seem two-faced to the hiring institution that offered you a job in good faith, not realizing that there would be a partner who had to be placed as well.

Discuss Competitive Offers if You Are Asked

You may be asked at an interview if you have competitive offers. If you are asked, you should say where they are from and what they are. Trickier to deal with is the case in which you are not asked. If it were me, I would bring it up. An institution expects to know whether it is competing with another institution. You can bring it up in the context that, nevertheless, you still are very interested in the institution you are now visiting; otherwise, you never would have come for the interview. You do not have to mention other institutions to which you are applying but from which you do not have offers. If you are asked, however, you should just answer the question.

AFTER THE INTERVIEW

Write a Thank-You Note

It can be amazing how much difference showing common courtesy can make. If you bombed your interview, writing a thank-you note is going to make no difference, other than to show that you are a courteous person. But if the interview went reasonably well, your thank-you note will show you are courteous, still interested in the job, and hoping to engage further with the institution.

Sometimes you may decide that the institution at which you interviewed is not for you. If you do, don't go through the farce of having the institution make you an offer and then turning them down. Send a note after the interview withdrawing from consideration.

Reply to Offers Promptly

If an institution makes you an offer, show the courtesy of responding promptly. And remember that institutions hate being turned down, so if you are going to do it, get it over with and let them—and you—move on. There are several reasons institutions greatly fear being turned down. First, it is embarrassing to the institution. Second, the institution has kept other candidates waiting, and those candidates may accept another job while waiting to hear from the institution waiting on its first choice. Third, if the institution is unable to fill the slot, for one reason or another, it may not get the slot again in a future year, so the institution does not want to risk losing all its candidates and then the slot for which they hoped to hire someone.

Sometimes it is difficult to reply within the time limit you are given. Usually, this is because you are waiting or at least hoping for another offer or because issues with your spouse need to be worked out. You always can ask for an extension. It may be or may not be granted, as the institution is likely to have backup candidates waiting to hear. It sometimes is possible even to get the extension. But whatever you do, be reasonable in what you ask for, and after getting one extension, do not ask for another one. Make your decision and move on, whatever way you go.

Remember That Academia Is a Very Small World

Academia is a very small world. What happens during your interview will get around the department but also may leak through a variety of sources to the outside. Therefore, do not say anything that you would not want people at another institution to hear. For example, don't denigrate another institution to which you are applying ("Well, that's only my fallback application" or "I know it's not a fit for me, but I wanted to keep my options open"). You just do not know what will get back to people.

* * *

Well, hopefully you will have a successful interview and be ready to move on. The next chapter discusses how you can do so.

2
GETTING GOING

How you start affects how you end up. So starting off right is crucial for your success in academia. Starting off involves many different things, such as responding to an offer, meeting the right people, setting up a lab, and so forth. I discuss some of these issues in this chapter.

THE OFFER

Employment starts on the first day of a contract, but there is one crucial aspect of employment that starts before the critical first day on the job. This crucial aspect is the offer.

Salary

The good news is that if, someday, you are moving to start a job as a full professor, there probably will be substantial room for negotiating your precise

---

http://dx.doi.org/10.1037/0000013-003
Starting Your Career in Academic Psychology, by R. J. Sternberg
Copyright © 2017 by the American Psychological Association. All rights reserved.

starting salary. The not-as-good news is that when you start as an instructor, lecturer, assistant professor, or adjunct assistant professor, there usually is little room for negotiating. Generally, you are expected to take the salary you are offered, within small negotiating limits. You can try asking for a higher salary, but keep it low key because chairs generally expect you to take the salary you are offered.

There are two exceptions. One is if you are not actually starting—that is, if you have been a faculty member elsewhere and just are restarting in a new position. If you have past experience, you may have more room for negotiation. But again, at the lower levels of the academic ladder, negotiating room on salary is highly limited.

The second exception is if you have a higher competitive offer. You simply can point out that Institution X is offering you more money and offer to show the institution the letter if they want to see it. If the difference is small, the institution may raise your offer. If the difference is large, they may tell you to take the other offer!

You are better off saving whatever bargaining chips you have for other aspects of the contract. If it makes you feel any better, my starting salary was $12,500. I bet yours is higher than that. My graduate adviser's was $4,500, I believe. So at least salaries have been going up (along with inflation). One important thing to check with regard to salary is how many months it is for. Academic salaries are typically 9 months but may be 10, 11, or 12 months. You also need to check who is paying the salary. In most psychology jobs, term-time salary (excluding summer salary) is paid for by the institution. But in some jobs, you may be expected to fund some or even all of your salary by external grants, if not initially, after a period of time.

Summer Salary

Many, but not all, academic salaries are for 9 months, paid over 12 months. Sometimes starting offers for those on 9- (or 10- or 11-) month salaries include some kind of allocation for summer salary. This is by no means a standard deal. It depends on the place. For an assistant professor, a good offer will include 1 year of summer salary, and an excellent offer will include 2 years of summer salary. It is rare for the offer to go beyond 2 years. Many places won't offer any summer salary, expecting you to get a grant to cover any additional months for which you want to be paid. Actually, most places will expect, or at least hope, that you get a grant sooner or later to cover summer salary and other things.

Starting Teaching Load

Many universities will give new assistant professors a reduction in teaching load during the first year. (Such offers are much less common for lecturers, and if they are paid by the course, essentially nonexistent.) Typically, the reduction, if there is one, is one course. If, as a new assistant professor, you have not been offered a reduction, it is reasonable to ask for one. Such a reduction is unlikely to be granted at levels lower than assistant professor.

What Courses You Will Teach

Typically, the courses you teach will not be part of your contract but will be decided through conversations with the department chair (or in some cases, the dean). Sometimes you are told you are expected to teach certain courses and have an option to choose other courses. In many cases, however, the identities of the courses for you to teach are negotiable. Thus, you may be expected to teach a large service course, but there may be room to negotiate which one. You may be told you are expected to teach an upper level seminar but be given flexibility as to which one it is. In some cases, you even may be able to invent your own new course. If, however, you are the only person in the department available to teach a certain service course (either because no one else can or no one else wants to), you can expect that, as the person with the least seniority, you will not be able to negotiate yourself out of it.

Regular Teaching Load

Teaching loads tend to be more or less standard within a department. Sometimes reductions are made for people who come in with a grant or contract, but relatively few first-year faculty members have grants unless perhaps they previously were postdoctoral fellows. You also might get a reduction if you take on some kind of major administrative responsibility, which is not typical or particularly wise if you are just starting out. In general, for new faculty at the starting level, there is not much room for negotiation of teaching load, unless you want to increase your load for some reason. (I actually took on an extra course my first year because there was so much demand for a particular course, multivariate analysis, and there was no one else in the department who could or wanted to teach it at the time. I do not recommend taking on extra teaching responsibilities during the first year, even for extra pay. You will have enough to do without them.)

Starting Date

Generally, you are expected to start in the fall of the academic year following the offer. Occasionally, exceptions will be made that will allow you to start in the next calendar year (usually the beginning of the second semester). Senior faculty who are given offers have more flexibility and often start 1 year later. This delay gives them flexibility in completing their work at their current institution.

There are exceptional circumstances that can lead to a delay in the start date, even at the entry level. One is a pregnancy or the very recent birth of a child. In general, departments are not thrilled to learn after an offer is made that you are pregnant, as it means you will in all likelihood be taking significant leave shortly after beginning your job. However, under federal law, pregnant women are not obligated to disclose their pregnancy to potential employers when they apply and interview for jobs, and employers are prohibited from asking about, or discriminating on the basis of, a job applicant's pregnancy. Whether to disclose is a complicated decision that requires careful consideration.

A second exceptional circumstance is a serious unexpected illness or injury. Obviously, employers do not bank on unexpected illnesses, but they can happen. If this circumstance comes up, the new employer will want to be assured, if possible, that this is a one-time occurrence. A third circumstance is a grant that needs to be finished and cannot be transferred to the new institution. There also may be other circumstances. You need to use good judgment in asking for a delay in start date, as the hiring department may be counting on your prompt arrival.

Start-up Grant

The start-up grant is often where you have the most room for negotiation. Many departments, if they have the resources, will give some amount of money to get you going in your research. Sometimes the department will state an amount and then ask you to prepare a budget that falls within that amount. Less often the department will ask you first to prepare a budget and then will give you what it can afford. If the start-up grant is inadequate for your needs, then you may want to negotiate for a higher grant, explaining why it would be useful for you to receive a larger budget. If you ask for more money, make sure you can justify your request in a compelling way. Don't ask for more money just for the sake of having more money.

Start-up grants often are not uniform within a department but rather depend on the area in which you are doing research. For example, a new faculty member in cognitive neuroscience may receive a larger grant than a new faculty member in mathematical psychology. One way to increase your start-up is to show that your research funding needs are higher than what might be typical for other faculty members in your area of research.

There is one aspect of a start-up grant that new faculty often pay too little attention to but that is almost as important as the amount of the grant—namely, the expiration of the grant. If the grant has no expiration date, then you are fortunate. But grants often have expiration dates, which can be as early as 1 year from the date of the allocation of the funds (but more typically, 2 or 3 years later). You should try to get as late an expiration date as possible because you do not want to be in a position where, at some point, you are spending the money just to use it up, or worse, you are expecting to use the money and find out that it has expired.

Office Space

If you are a new assistant professor, typically you are assigned an office from available space. If you are an instructor, lecturer, or adjunct, you may be asked to share office space, or you may be given no office space at all. There usually is little or no room for negotiation on office space. An exception would be if you have a disability and need a first-floor office or some other special accommodation.

Lab Space

You ought to be crystal clear in your negotiations, before you ever are offered a contract, about what you need in terms of lab space. Lab space is usually at a premium, and you should not be surprised if you are asked to share space. In negotiating for lab space, you also should make clear what furniture and equipment you need. Such furniture and equipment may be supplied from college or university surplus rather than being bought new.

Service Requirements

When you are just starting out, you want to try to minimize your service requirements. On the one hand, you may want to show that you are a good departmental citizen. On the other hand, your first year of teaching is likely to be pretty overwhelming, and you are unlikely to be looking for lots of extra things to do. If you are asked to be on a task force or committee, you probably should accept, but try to limit it to one.

An additional problem is faced by members of minority groups and sometimes by women, who often are asked to serve on task forces and committees so that the college or university can trumpet that its task force or committee membership was "diverse." Avoid becoming a token on numerous committees. You easily can find all your time being sucked up in being a showcase for diversity.

Spousal Accommodations

In most instances, new faculty members arrive and, if they have a spouse who wants to work, hope that their spouse will find employment in the new setting. Sometimes spouses are able to find employment before the move. You can ask the college or university for help, but at the junior level, few faculty members have the leverage to ensure that the institution will find a job for the spouse. In cases of dual-career academic couples, if you want your spouse to have an academic position as well, you can either try to negotiate this upon hiring or, more likely, hope something opens up.

Whatever It Is, Get It in Writing

Most important, get all agreements in writing. The institution may imply or even state that you should trust them. It's not about trust. When agreements are only oral, many things can go wrong. Different parties may have different understandings of what was agreed to; the personnel at the institution may change, with the new personnel unaware of what was agreed to orally in the past; institutional finances may change and the institution may want to revisit agreements in which it is not totally clear what was agreed to; people may just forget. Whatever it is, *get it in writing!*

THE INTERIM

You probably won't be moving to your new job right away—assuming you indeed need to move. Here are some things to attend to in the interim while you are waiting to start your job.

Finish Your Dissertation if You Haven't Already

Some scholars are hired with their dissertation not yet complete on the understanding that they will finish it expeditiously (sometimes defined as by the end of the first year of employment). If at all possible, do not start your new job planning to finish your dissertation once you arrive. I have seen too many scholars who either lose their valuable first year of employment finishing their dissertation—when they should be doing the work that will lead them to tenure—or don't finish the dissertation in the required time period and lose their jobs. (It happened to one of my own graduate students.) You want to start your new job doing new stuff, including, if you have not done so already, preparing your dissertation for publication. You don't want to spend the year finishing the work you should have done in graduate school.

Join Relevant Professional Associations

Later in the book, I will devote a whole chapter to the importance of networking (see Chapter 11). One of the best ways to network is through professional associations. So join them now and get a head start on familiarizing yourself with and getting to know the other scholars, in whose hands much of your future will lie.

Prepare Your First-Term Courses Now

Now, here is a piece of advice I learned through the School of Hard Knocks. I didn't prepare my courses in advance. I didn't even have a sense of how much work it was to prepare for courses. I got to my job facing a two-course teaching load the first semester and found that I could not keep up with preparing the lectures for both of them. In one of them, I started winging it class by class, and wow, it sure did show. My teaching ratings for that course were bargain-basement level. It typically takes two to three times as long to prepare for a class as the class itself takes. If you can get a head start, you will have a much better first year.

Read Up on the College or University

Much of what you learn about your future institution will be tacit knowledge—the kind of informal, unspoken knowledge you have to be there to absorb. But you should know as much as you can at least about who the students are, who the faculty are, what the town or city the institution is in is like, what the regulations are, and so forth. Every institution is different. Know about these differences. For example, what range of preparation levels will students have when they start at the college? Without that knowledge, you really can't prepare to teach your courses. What are the expectations for faculty members? Especially read any faculty handbook that may exist. It will tell you the expectations for faculty members and also the penalties for not meeting them.

Find Living Quarters

In many instances, finding living quarters can be much more frustrating than you ever would expect. I have held five academic positions, each in a different state, and in every one, finding a place to live was more challenging than I had anticipated. Many colleges and universities are in "college towns," where there is a premium on both rental and for-sale properties. In addition, prices in college towns often tend to be higher than one would hope because the landlords and existing owners have a captive audience. Moreover, you are competing not only with other faculty members, but also with students who are in your segment of the real estate market. Do not wait until late to look for housing because the choice locations are likely to have been snapped up by then. Real estate markets in college towns tend to be seasonal, so if you are looking to start work in late August or early September, you probably want to be looking for a place to live in mid- to late May or early June, but certainly no later than the beginning of July. And if you are buying, remember it easily can take 6 weeks to close on a property.

Move Early Enough to Give You Time to Set Up

You don't want to spend the first couple of months on the job doing all your move-in stuff. Get to your new location early so you can be done moving in when you start teaching.

Plan Out Your Research

Research plans tend to be like life plans, for which there is the saying, "God laughs at our plans." Nevertheless, it is important to have a plan, even if you are unable to fulfill every aspect of the plan, or end up deciding that something else looks more appealing. Some days, over the summer before you start, you may have full days when you can sketch out your research plans. Once you start teaching, full days like that will be a luxury, possibly an unattainable one.

Write or at Least Start a Grant Proposal

If you can write or at last start a grant proposal before you start work, you will have an incredible leg up on your work. There are so many reasons to get a grant quickly—money to pay students, money to pay other hired help, money to buy additional equipment, summer salary, and the demonstration to your department that your research is viewed as serious enough by granting agencies to merit funding. You probably won't be able to finish all aspects of the grant proposal. Generally, you will need the help of your department to prepare the budget showing the correct rates of overhead (indirect costs) and fringe benefits. I got funded by May of my first academic year, and it was a total blessing. That was very early, so I was lucky. Try at least to have funding in place, if possible, sometime during your second or third year—but if at all possible, before you are considered for tenure.

There may be some institutions that do not expect you to write grant proposals—for example, many community colleges, any place where you are an adjunct, business schools, and the like. But if you are expected to get grants, get one as soon as you can.

Say Your Goodbyes

This may sound like an odd piece of advice. But what sometimes happens is that people wait until the last moment to say goodbyes, and then never get to say them to some people or do so only in an abbreviated fashion to others. Goodbyes are important for three reasons. First, they give you and your colleagues in what is soon to be your former institution a sense of closure. Second, they are opportunities to receive parting advice from senior colleagues that you might otherwise never receive. And third, academia is a very small world. Many of the people you are leaving behind will continue to be important to your career after you leave, so you may as well show them you care about them—if you want them to care about you.

Read a Book for Pleasure or See Some Movies You Really Want to See

During your first year on the job, you may have zero time to read zero books for pleasure. Time for movies may be a luxury, too. So use the time before you start to do things, like reading a book or seeing movies, that you may not be able to do again for another year or maybe even more.

WHEN YOU FIRST ARRIVE

Once you move to your new institution, you will need time to set up before classes begin. Here are some key matters to attend to during this initial period on the job.

Set Up Your Office and Organize Your Books

Set up your office (or portion of office, if you have even that) as soon as you arrive. That means getting your computer installed, phone connections activated, bookshelves filled, and supplies such as pens, paper, and paperclips in place. If you have a lot of books, organize them right away. Any time I have gone into a new situation and just slopped the books on the shelves, promising to organize them later, I never have gotten around to the "organizing them later." In the meantime, if the books are not organized, it will always be a total pain to find the ones you need. Also, make sure your computer has antivirus and antiadware protection, an appropriate spam filter, and a backup service in case your computer crashes and you lose your files. In years past, scholars would regularly lose files when computers crashed. Today, with the existence of backup services, there is no excuse for losing your files. You also can use a flash drive for backup, but then you absolutely must remember to do backups on a daily basis. People tend to believe in such backups in principle but not to do them in practice. Backup services where your documents are stored in the cloud are better!

Immediately Get to Know the People Who Matter the Most— the Departmental Clerical and Technical Assistants

Probably no one will be more important to you, at least initially, than departmental clerical and technical staff—the people who are in charge of the central departmental facilities. They are the ones who often can help you with grant budgets and submissions, copying and other forms of printing, mailing, burned-out lightbulbs, and the like. If you are nice to anyone, be nice to them, because they can make your life very easy or very hard.

Introduce Yourself to the Department Computer Tech, if There Is One

Sooner or later, your computer is going to go on the blink. Most likely, it will be exactly when you need it most (which is, to a first approximation, always). Computer techs tend to be harried people. Their services are continually in demand, and many institutions, to save money, have reduced the number of techs to a bare minimum. For the most part, computer techs take requests for service as they come, in the order received. But having a good relationship with your computer tech can never hurt and may get you quicker and even more careful service when you need it most.

Arrange to Meet Other Faculty; Don't Wait for Them to Come to You

Whenever I have started a new job, I've waited for the inevitable parade of old-timers who come to introduce themselves and to wish me luck. The problem is that I'm getting old and, for the most part, I am still waiting for them. Don't wait for people to come to you. They may or may not come. All are busy, or they may think you are too busy. Make a point of introducing yourself to them, one at a time. Personal relationships are very important in a department and can make the difference between success and failure in almost any institutional environment.

Find Out Where the Important Places Are Within the University

Figure out where the important places are in the university where you will need to go. The other places you can find as you need them. In particular, make sure you know where you will be teaching well before you need to be there for your first class. I know that sounds obvious, but many of us make the mistake of thinking we know where our first class is, getting there, and then discovering that we have the wrong building—with 5 minutes left until the class begins.

Find Out Where the Important Places Are in the Town

Figure out where the important stores and offices are—supermarket, bank, pharmacy, physician's office, dentist's office, children's school (if relevant), and so forth. Also, check routes so you know about how long it will take you to get from one place to another.

Set Up Your Lab and Check That Furniture and Equipment All Function Properly

There are few annoyances greater than finding out that your new lab equipment does not work or that your desk chair is scientifically designed to ruin your back in the most painful way possible. Don't wait to check these things out, because getting lab equipment repaired or replaced, or even getting new furniture, can take a maddeningly long time. You don't want to be moved for a month, only to discover the day the term begins that your precious lab equipment will not be able to run those experiments you were all set to start early in the fall. If you are a scholar who does not need a lab, congratulations: That's one problem you won't have!

Meet the Chair (or Head) and the Dean

The chair is the person who will have the most power to make your life easy or hard (except perhaps for the department assistants). Get to know the chair well, and do what you can to make a good impression. In the unfortunate case that you don't get along with the chair or head, keep in mind that these positions usually are not permanent. If you can weather the current chair or head, you can try again with the next one. I have had any number of chairs with whom I did not have the best relations. I always survived until the next one!

Make Sure Arrangements Are Made for Paying Your Salary, Receiving Health Benefits, Investing Retirement Funds, and so Forth

Usually, there is some kind of onboarding procedure when you first arrive. Take it seriously. Although these sessions can be boring, they also can be very important for your future. Make sure you study up on health care options and options for investing any retirement earnings you may make. Most important, perhaps, arrange for payment of your salary, whether by check or direct deposit in your bank account.

If You Have Children, Settle Any Day Care Issues

Arranging day care, at least in the United States, tends to be a torturous process. It is difficult to arrange, and it is not atypical that whatever arrangements you make fall through within short order. Explore all the options and find what is right for you. Have a backup: You may need it sooner than you ever would have thought possible.

* * *

Now that you have gotten going, it's time to get ready to teach.

II
TEACHING

3

GETTING STARTED TEACHING YOUR COURSES

It's time to start preparing for and teaching your courses. If you have never done this before, it's a daunting task. If you have done it for 40 years, as I have, it's still a daunting task! How can you make it easier?

DEVELOPING A COURSE

Know the Size of Your Class

You absolutely need to know the size of your class in advance. Not knowing can lead you to prepare in ways that are inappropriate. Even after all my years of teaching, I almost made a mistake this year. I was led to believe that a course I was to teach for the first time (and that had not previously been offered in our department) on lifespan development could have very large numbers, perhaps close to 200. I started to prepare lectures. I then decided to check the actual enrollment figures, and discovered that the class would have just 25 students in it. I immediately switched to my preferred format for this number of students, a discussion seminar. Of course, it could have gone the other way. I could have spent a lot of time preparing discussion questions and then discovered that I had close to 200 students in the class. How you teach inevitably depends on the number of students, so you need to know well in advance the size of your class—if not the exact number, at least an approximation that will enable you to decide how to teach.

Know Who Your Students Are

You need to know who your students are. Are they academically well prepared or not so well prepared? Do they have solid background for the course they are taking with you, or are they coming in with little or no background? Are they taking the course as an elective, so they are likely to be motivated, or as a requirement, so their motivation is likely to be mixed? I have taught at universities ranging from extremely highly selective to moderately selective, and the students were quite different in how they could handle the material for a given course.

Perhaps the worst experience I've had was when I guest taught a series of lectures in another university. I was given no clear advance information on the prior knowledge of the students, even though I asked for it. After the first set of lectures, some students came to me and said my lectures were insultingly easy—it was as though I thought they came into the course knowing nothing. So I raised the level of the lectures, only to be told by the professor who invited me that the level of my teaching was now too high—the students were not understanding what I was saying. I am not sure what I could have done differently in that case, as I had asked for information on their background, but my experience highlighted to me the importance of understanding the background knowledge of the students I am teaching.

From the start, get a sense of how conscientious the students you are teaching are likely to be in your class, because conscientiousness is an excellent predictor of how students will do (Komarraju, Karau, Schmeck, & Avdic, 2011). If they are not conscientious, ask yourself whether there is any way you can relate your teaching more to their lives so that they will be incentivized to be more conscientious.

Before Anything Else, Figure Out Your Course and Learning Goals

You will be busy when you start out. You may quickly choose a textbook and then start out organizing your course to fit the textbook. This is exactly the wrong way to plan for a course. Always start with your course and learning goals. What do you want students to learn? How will you ensure they learn it? How will you know whether they learned what you hoped they would learn? Then choose a textbook or other readings that fit your learning goals. Never let a textbook or your readings drive your course. Let your ideas about what the course should accomplish drive your course.

Choose Your Readings to Fit Both Your Course and Your Students

Choosing the readings for your course is one of the most important things you will do. It sometimes is tempting to choose readings based on hearsay. For example, you might know that such-and-such is the best-selling text for the course you are teaching, or someone might tell you that so-and-so really worked for her when she taught the same course. All I can say about these methods of choosing books is: "No, no, no!" The leading text may be too hard or too easy for your students, or the material it covers may not be the material you want to cover. The textbook that works for your colleague may be based on a teaching philosophy different from your own. You owe it to your students to examine the potentially relevant books for your course and choose the ones that work for you in the course and for the students you teach.

Order Examination Copies of Relevant Texts, but Don't Cheat

Unfortunately, textbooks are so expensive today that it is not practical to order a bunch of them to compare—unless you order examination copies. So be sure to order your examination copies well in advance so you can decide which textbook or other books will work best for you.

Don't order texts you would not consider adopting just to have them on your shelf (perhaps to help with lecture notes). When you get a free copy of a book, the book is free to you, but nothing in the textbook industry actually is ever free. Students pay for examination copies in the sense that the price they pay for the book reflects the publisher's loss in providing examination copies. Textbooks already are expensive enough: Don't contribute to their high cost by cheating and ordering textbooks you never would consider adopting.

Never Sell Your Examination Copies

Selling examination copies as used books not only contributes to the high cost of books, it also is unethical. You are selling something you got for free. Just don't do it.

Prepare Your Syllabus

The syllabus is probably the single most important document you will prepare for any course. Some professors skimp on the syllabus, but this is a mistake. If you get into a dispute with a student over course expectations or requirements, you want to be able to go back to the syllabus and show that the expectations and requirements were clear before the course began—that is, that you didn't make up stuff as you went along.

The syllabus should give the basic information about yourself, the course, its requirements, the texts, and so on. But beyond the basics, it should make clear your rules for questioning during class; make clear your rules for use of computers, tablets, and cell phones; tell students in advance whether you plan sometimes to argue with what students say just to teach them how to think and defend their positions; and make clear your expectations for language and behavior.

Specifically, make sure the syllabus covers all major points, including the following, at minimum:

- your name
- your office building and number
- your office hours

When you state your office hours, indicate whether you also are available by appointment outside of your office hours.

- your phone number
- your e-mail address
- the same information for teaching assistants, if any
- meeting times and place
- the goals of your course
- any further information about the approach of the course
- required (and optional) readings
- required and any optional assignments for the course
- all relevant deadlines
- penalties for late work

Some students take deadlines seriously; others view them as starting points for a negotiation. You need to decide what your attitudes are toward deadlines and make them clear in the syllabus. What kinds of excuses will you accept, if any? What penalties will you impose for late work, or will you accept late work at all?

- how grading will be done

For better or worse, there are few things students care more about than grading. I have found that the simpler and more transparent I can make my grading system, the fewer the number of complaints I receive later. I am very explicit about grading. I state what counts, how especially it counts, and how the various sources of information are put together.

- extra credit, if relevant

Extra credit can become a sticky wicket, especially when the term is well under way and some students are finding that they are not doing as well as they thought they would. At that point, you may get requests for extra credit. It is very important, I believe, that all students get exactly the same opportunities for extra credit—that is, that you do not award opportunities to some students that are not awarded to others. You do not want to penalize the students who never bothered to speak up, much as they also might have wanted the opportunity for extra credit.

- standards of academic integrity

I refer students to the university website for rules on academic integrity. The rules are complex, and I do not want to make the mistake of putting some of them in my syllabus and leaving others out, as though the others that I happen to leave out do not apply.

From time to time, I get students who cheat, one way or another. Realistically, there probably are many more students who cheat than I ever catch. If I ever do catch them, I *always* report them to the proper university authority (usually the dean of students). I never just decide on a penalty and leave it at that. The reason is that unless you report the cheating, you have no way of knowing whether this is the student's first time or fifth. Some students may be on the verge of expulsion and deservedly so. There needs to be a central record of cheating so that students can be treated according not only to what they did in your class but also to what they did in all their other classes.

- calendar—what will happen when
- accommodations for students with disabilities

Accommodations are a matter of college or university policy. You should make sure you are in touch with the college or university office that handles policies for students with disabilities. Improper accommodations can lead to legal action. You don't want to get caught in that.

PLANNING INDIVIDUAL LESSONS

If You Are Teaching a Lecture Course, Prepare Your Lectures as Much in Advance as Possible

Academics have so much to do, and in some institutions, research counts more than teaching toward the attainment of tenure. Therefore, especially if one is in a research-oriented institution, one sometimes finds an incentive to spend more and more time on research and less and less time on teaching. You may figure that you can prepare your lectures in the few days before you need to give them, or even on the day you plan to teach. These are really bad strategies. Lectures take a long time to prepare. Although you may not think your students notice when you are winging it, they will notice (just as you will notice when they are winging it, even if they think you don't). Prepare well in advance so you don't fall behind and find yourself having trouble keeping up with your teaching.

Use Attractive PowerPoints for Main Points, Not Details

PowerPoints work best when they attractively present main points, not when they obsess over little details. No one wants to read a bunch of fine print on a PowerPoint, and many people will be unable to read that fine print. Stick to the main points.

Don't Overdo the Technology

I once heard a job talk by a candidate who was very proud of his prowess with the technology of giving a presentation. During his talk, he got so involved in the technology of his presentation that the substantive message seemed to get lost. He didn't get the job. It is nice to have an attractive PowerPoint or other technology-based presentation. But don't get so caught up in the beauty of the technology that the substance of the lecture gets submerged by its fancy technology.

Have a Backup Plan in Case Your Technology Fails

Sooner or later, you are going to give a lecture during which the technology fails. Be ready for it. When I've downloaded PowerPoint talks from the Internet, I've tried to have a backup on a memory stick. When I've used a memory stick, I've tried to have a copy of my lecture online.

I remember two notable cases in which the technology failed for important lectures. Both instances were during job interviews. In the first case, the technology failed and the speaker managed nevertheless to give an excellent talk. She was hired for the job. In the second case, the speaker refused to speak until the technology was fixed. She didn't get hired. The point is that whether you are speaking to a class or giving a job talk, you need to be prepared in case the technology fails. I remember commenting, only half in jest, that a department always should arrange for the technology to fail for job candidates, and if they cannot show the flexibility to give their talk without it, we should never hire them. So be prepared for the possibility that anything that can fail, sooner or later, will.

Review Your Lecture Notes the Night Before or the Morning You Teach

Of course, you want to prepare your lectures in advance, but then make sure that you review your notes shortly before you are to lecture. I have been amazed at how I can prepare lecture notes and then, when the time comes, look at them and feel like they were prepared by someone else. With all the things on my mind, I just don't remember what I prepared to say. It's no fun to work hard to prepare a lecture and then look unprepared because you failed to review your notes. So review those notes before you speak to ensure you sound as well prepared as you should be.

If You Are Teaching a Discussion Course, Prepare Discussion Questions in Advance

Here is what every teacher would like to do: Walk into a classroom, ask a question or two, and then watch 50 minutes of productive, engaging discussion follow with unimaginable ease. The only problem is that such discussions almost never happen. More likely, students will sit in their seats saying nothing, waiting for more cues, or they will answer your question and then wait for further cues.

The best way to ensure that a discussion is focused and productive rather than rambling and degenerative is to prepare discussion questions in advance. The discussion questions should cover all the topics you believe are important for the class to consider. If you don't need all or even any of your questions, consider yourself fortunate. But by preparing questions in advance, you foreclose the possibility that you will lack meaningful things to talk about.

If You Use Student-Generated Discussion Questions, Prescreen Them Before the Class

As a believer in active learning, I always have tried to have students learn by doing. One way for them to learn by doing is to have students participate in discussions, but another way is to have them prepare the discussion questions. I have done this many times. The good news is that preparing discussion questions really does force students to engage with the material and think about what is important. The not-as-good news is that the discussion questions students generate are, at least in my experience, highly variable in quality. They range from "Why didn't I think of that?" (not so many) to "How could anyone come up with that question?" (more frequently). You do not want to spend your time in class screening questions. Therefore, I have students prepare the questions in advance, and I screen them before I ever enter the classroom with them.

MAKE SURE DISCUSSION QUESTIONS COVER THE TOPICS YOU THINK ARE MOST IMPORTANT

You want to make sure you cover the scope of the issues that need class discussion. Don't just hope topics come up; make them come up if you think they are important.

Make Sure Discussion Questions Require Critical and Creative Thinking and, Where Relevant, Practical Thinking as Well as Recall

My colleague Louise Spear-Swerling and I once surveyed classrooms to analyze the kinds of questions teachers were asking (Spear & Sternberg, 1987). We found that the overwhelming majority of questions asked were straight factual questions—for example, "Who did this study?" "What did they find?" Such questions may keep students on their toes, but they do not generate reflective appraisal of what is being learned. There is nothing wrong with asking factual questions, but such questions rarely generate genuine class discussion.

A better strategy is to ask questions that generate a variety of kinds of thinking, such as analytical, creative, practical, and wise thinking (Sternberg, 2003; Sternberg & Grigorenko, 2007). An analytical question might be, "What errors were there in the experimental design, if any?" or "Compare and contrast the two theories being tested against each other in this experiment." A creative question might be, "How could the investigator have designed the experiment better?" or "What do you think would have happened had the investigator done the study with rural Alaskan Eskimo children rather than urban, Midwestern, mostly White children?" A practical question might be, "What is the relevance of the experiment for people's everyday lives?" or "How could the experiment have been conducted if a computer were not available for presentation of the stimuli?" And a wisdom-based question might be, "How could the experimental results be used to make people's lives better?"

THROUGHOUT THE COURSE

Show Why What You Are Teaching Should Matter to Your Students

When you choose material to read, and the material is truly what you want to read, you probably choose the reading material because you are interested in it—because it matters to you in some way. Students learn much better when they can see some kind of personal relevance of what they are learning. If the material fails to connect to them or their lives, it often seems abstract and not very meaningful personally. You want to teach so that what the students learn matters to them. They then are more likely to be motivated to learn, and retain, what you are teaching.

Don't Read Your Lecture From Lecture Notes

Did you ever look at a printed transcript of what you say in a lecture? It probably is difficult to understand. Similarly, written text is hard to understand when presented orally. We speak in a register different from the one in which we write. As a result, spoken lectures sound disorganized and sometimes barely comprehensible when they are read, and written materials sound stilted and boring when they are spoken. It is best to speak from notes or, if you have a terrific memory, extemporaneously. However, don't speak extemporaneously unless you *know* you have a great memory and won't forget what you wanted to say at the time you lecture.

Keep in mind that if you are going to read your lecture, students don't really need to be there in any case. They could just as well read the lecture on Blackboard or some other medium. Why waste their time repeating what they could read in half the time?

Don't Read Your Lecture Off PowerPoints, Either

Reading off PowerPoint slides is no better than reading off paper. Sometimes it is worse, because often the PowerPoint projection is in back of you, so if you read from slides, you actually are placing your back to the audience. No one wants to listen to you while your back is turned. It is always a good idea either to ensure that there will be a podium display of PowerPoint slides, or to have your own set visible to you on your computer, or to have paper versions of the slides in front of you while you talk. What you don't want is to have your back to your audience while you speak. Rear views are usually not super attractive, they make you harder to hear, and they can come across as discourteous to your audience.

Be and Sound Enthusiastic

Years ago, there was a professor in my department who did truly exciting work. It was not exactly in my area of interest, but when I read about her work, I have to say that I thought that this was a woman who really thought profoundly about psychological issues. I expected her career to take off like a rocket. It didn't. I'm quite sure that the reason why was that when she spoke about her work, she bored her audiences to tears. In her classes, I bet you could see students' eyes glaze over. I don't know why she was such a crashing bore. Because she was junior to me and I wanted her to succeed, I even spoke to her about it. The conversation made no difference at all. She bored her audiences because she sounded bored—and boring.

The young scholar might have been truly excited about her work, but she could not convey her enthusiasm. What she conveyed was a profound sense of ennui. If you cannot show your students why you are enthusiastic about what you are teaching, you cannot expect your students to acquire any enthusiasm. Two of my colleagues at Cornell, Wendy Williams and Stephen Ceci (1997), did a study in which they taught a course in two ways, one with enthusiasm and one without it. They found that the students in the course taught with enthusiasm learned more than the students in the course taught in a less enthusiastic way. Keep it in mind: If you want to motivate your students and excite them about learning what you teach, you need to show your own excitement first.

If You Are Teaching Online, Look at the Camera, Not at Yourself

When you are on camera, whether the camera is at a distance or on a nearby computer screen, it is tempting to look at the displayed picture of yourself. But you should not be talking to yourself, but rather to your viewers. The way to have eye contact with your viewers is to look at the camera, not at yourself.

Be Sensitive to Nonverbal Feedback

It is rare that a student will raise his or her hand to tell you what a bore you are and to ask you whatever gave you the crazy idea to go into teaching. If you are waiting for it to happen, you may have to wait a long time. Nevertheless, students know which courses they like and which they don't. They typically won't spontaneously tell you; they'll tell Ratemyprofessor.com or some other website or source of course evaluation.

The next best source of information is their nonverbal cues. Do they lean forward or backward? Are their eyes on you or on their computer screens? Do they engage in class discussions or withdraw from them? Do their eyes sparkle or cloud over? Do they engage with you or with their neighbors in attempts at covert conversations? Nonverbal cues can be just as revealing as, or more revealing than, verbal cues. Take advantage of them!

Be Prepared to Change Your Game

If the nonverbal cues of the students, or early course evaluations you give to the class, are not going the way you would hope, don't wait until the next time you teach the course to make changes. Plan to make whatever changes you can as soon as possible. Using formative course evaluations early during the term and just talking to students may give you a sense of what is and what is not working. Then change what is not working. Rigidity is always the enemy of good instruction. Don't get stuck in however you are doing things. Prepare to change them as soon as you need to.

Don't Go Overtime

You and even some or many of your students may be very excited about a particular class, or even every class. When you see such excitement, you may be tempted to go overtime. Don't. First, you are putting an unacceptable burden on students who have another commitment right after your class. Second, another teacher may need the classroom and may not appreciate having no time to prepare in the classroom or even having to start late. Third, some students may be less interested than others, and you are holding them against their will. Of course, you could offer students who have to leave to go ahead and leave. But those students, perhaps rightfully, will feel that you are placing a substantial burden on them because they will have to identify themselves as early leavers and probably will not be able to or even want to say why they are leaving early. Prepare to fill the whole class but nothing more.

Don't End Up Lecturing in Discussion Classes

Professors often come to view themselves as founts of knowledge and perhaps even wisdom. Moreover, they often are so used to lecturing that it becomes their default modus operandi. You may be tempted to start lecturing in your discussion class. Although periodic short lectures may be fine to clarify points, if you start lecturing regularly, students will get the message, and they are likely to stop contributing to the discussion. They may even set up a reinforcement system that encourages you to lecture. By not saying anything, they may create uncomfortable gaps in the class, which you then proceed to fill with lecture. After all, it is generally easier for students to sit passively in a lecture hall than actively to discuss what they have read (or perhaps have not read). You don't want to be in the position of creating a reinforcement system that leads to your lecturing in a discussion class. Let the students do the talking and you serve as a guide, not a lecturer.

Give Students Enough Time to Answer Questions

You ask a question. You wait for someone in the class to answer. No one does. You get impatient. The silence is deafening. You answer your own question. At one point, Rowe (1972) found that teachers tend to answer their own questions after just 3 seconds of silence. Students may even try to get you to answer your own questions by staying silent after you ask something. That is, they may learn that the best way to hide their ignorance of the answers to your questions is to let you answer your own questions!

Make Sure You Show No Bias in Calling on People

When you are in front of a class, you are in a position not unlike conducting an orchestra. You have many things on your mind. When you go to call on people, you are likely to call on the hands you see. But teachers can and often do have inadvertent biases. These biases could be a function of the gender of the student, the ethnicity of the student, the position in which the teacher sits in the room, or whatever. Position can be especially important: We sometimes tend to focus on certain areas of the classroom, ignoring others. Make sure you are fair in calling on your students, and don't let any one or a few students monopolize the discussion.

Never Give a Snide, Sarcastic, or Demeaning Response to a Question or Answer a Student Provides

Someday, sometime, a student will ask you what sounds like a really stupid question or will give you a really stupid answer to your question. It may be that the answer advertises loudly that the student did not do the reading, or listen to the lecture, or understand the material even at a rudimentary level. A sarcastic response may come to mind before you even have time to wonder how you thought of it. You cannot keep it from coming to mind, but you can keep yourself from saying it. If you act in a demeaning way toward students, they quickly will become fearful of saying anything. Even students who normally would be talkative may choose to stay quiet for fear of incurring your wrath or, worse, your sarcasm. You need to accept every response at face value. You gently can point out that the answer is not correct or does not take into account one fact or another. You do not want to create a hostile or intimidating atmosphere in your classroom that discourages students from opening their mouths.

Speak to Disrupters After Class or, Better, in Your Office

If you teach long enough, and sometimes not for very long, you will encounter students who are disrupters—who try to get attention in class by their negative contribution to it. You do not want to let such behavior go. Doing nothing may only make it worse when the disrupter sees that he or she is getting away with it. Therefore, you need to speak to the disrupter. Don't do it over e-mail. E-mail does not work well for corrective communications. Arrange to see the student after class or, better, during your office hours, when other students are not present, and make clear to the student the behavioral change you expect. If you do not then get the behavioral change you expect, speak to the student again, and this time make clear the consequences that will follow if the student does not change his or her behavior.

You may ask what kinds of negative consequences you can offer to students who disrupt your class. There are different ones. They include (a) lowering the student's grade for poor class participation (if class participation is explicitly part of the grading system for the class), (b) reporting the student to a director of undergraduate or graduate studies, (c) reporting the student to the chair, (d) reporting the student to the dean of students, or even (e) recommending that the student drop your course. What is appropriate depends on the exact situation in which you and the student find yourselves.

Make Clear Your Rules for Questioning During Class

If you are teaching a seminar, you probably will want to encourage questions during class. If, however, you are teaching a lecture class, you need to be explicit with students about your rules for questioning. In a large lecture course, allowing too many questions can result in your getting through little of the material you planned to get through. Even in a small lecture course, questioning can slow you down. At the same time, there is no sense in continuing to lecture if students do not understand what you are saying, or what you think you are saying. Generally, the way I handle this conundrum in large lectures is to say that I welcome questions of clarification during the lecture but I would appreciate students waiting until the end of the lecture with questions that range more widely, such as about interpretations or critiques.

If You Don't Know the Answer to a Question, Say So, and Say How You Will Get the Answer

Inevitably, you will be asked questions whose answers you do not know. Say you don't know. If you start faking it, students will catch on quickly and you will lose your credibility. Admitting you do not know the answers to questions does not undermine your credibility; it enhances it. If you do not know an answer, then you probably either should say that you will make every effort to find out the answer for the next class, or else encourage students to find the answer and report back to the class. Either way, you should provide a way to ensure that the question will be answered as soon as possible. If the question really has no clear answer ("What is the meaning of life?"), explain why and then move on.

Make Clear Your Rules for Use of Computers, Tablets, and Cell Phones

Electronic devices in a classroom can be a blessing or a curse. In my experience, they are a little of both. I just taught a class in which it was totally obvious that a student in the back row was doing his e-mail on his cell phone while the class was engaged in a discussion. He did this despite my having said, from the outset, that I would appreciate students not doing e-mail, shopping, or personal communications during the class. My response was to remind the class of my original request. If the student then kept using his phone inappropriately, I would ask him after class or during office hours to stop it. If he kept it up, I would tell him he was no longer allowed to use his phone. As I do count class work toward the grade, I also would tell him that he was hurting his grade for the course by engaging with his phone rather than the class discussion.

Make the Frequency and Difficulty of the Assignments You Give Reasonable

When we give assignments, we tend to think in terms of how long they would take us to do. After all, how can we know how long it would take students to complete the assignment? For most of us, it has been a bit of time since we did this kind of work with the mind-set of a student. Yet, students typically take longer to do assignments than we would. Even if we try to control for the difference, we still are likely to underestimate it because it is hard to remember what our mind-set was like when we were students. So when you estimate how long students would take, assume that your initial estimate is an underestimate, especially if the course requires quantitative work or a lot of reading.

Test What You Teach

More than once during college, I remember walking into a test and coming out wondering where the questions came from. They seemed to have little or nothing to do with what I thought we had covered in our textbooks and class. Well, one of those times was in a mathematics class—real analysis—and I dropped that class in a hurry. But it happened occasionally in psychology courses as well when the level of detail in the test was far beyond what I thought would be tested. And I have to admit that I have been caught giving tests to which students had the same reaction I did when I was a student. Therefore, make sure that students know what to expect when you test them, and that what they expect corresponds to what you thought was important when you taught them.

If Possible, Test in Various Ways

If you have a very large class, as I did last year (more than 250 students), you may find that your options for assessment are limited. Although I am no great fan of multiple-choice testing, I found myself having to use multiple-choice tests because of the sheer number of students in the class. If, however, your numbers are more manageable, try to use a variety of formats for testing students—multiple choice if you wish, but also short answer, short essay, and perhaps even longer essay if the time allows. Some teachers like true–false questions. I don't because they are very subject to error of measurement due to guessing and because they often are at least somewhat ambiguous, making it difficult for students to be certain of exactly what is meant in the statement. I also try to include questions that encourage students to think in a variety of ways—namely, critically, creatively, practically, and, where relevant, wisely.

Do Formative Course Assessments Throughout the Term in Addition to a Summative Assessment at the End of the Term

When I was in college, I never much liked taking tests. I still am no fan of taking tests. Like everyone else, I would rather give tests than take them! But frequent testing improves learning (Brown, Roediger, & McDaniel, 2014). By giving your students frequent quizzes and tests, you are helping those students learn better. In the lifespan development course I am teaching this semester, I am giving five quizzes. I never would have done that in past years. But I am taking into account the psychological research literature that shows that preparing for tests is one of the best ways for students to consolidate the material they have learned in the course. By making the quizzes frequent, I ensure that the students have to deal with manageable amounts of learning material, rather than everything at once.

Make Sure Your Grading Reflects Students' Knowledge and Thought, Not Agreement With Your Point of View

Students rather quickly become experts at figuring out what we as professors want to hear. They want to get a good grade in a course, and for the most part, that means giving teachers what they think the teachers want to hear. So if you have a discernible point of view on the material you are teaching, you may find the students reflecting back that point of view in the assessments you give them.

Inevitably, however, there will be some students who take a point of view different from your own, either because they disagree with you and have a different point of view, or because they are that kind of student who likes to challenge the teacher, regardless of what the teacher thinks. When grading is at all subjective, you always have to be alert as to how you are grading. In particular, you need to ensure that you truly are grading for the quality of the responses and not for the extent to which the responses agree with your own point of view.

As we acquire greater expertise, we sometimes become more rigid in our thinking, not more flexible (Frensch & Sternberg, 1989; Sternberg & Lubart, 1995). So the older and more expert we are, the more (not the less) we need to be on guard that we are not penalizing students for expressing points of view other than our own.

Try to Teach and Assess in Diverse Ways That Meet Diverse Learning Needs

Use a variety of teaching methods to meet students' learning needs, including the following:

- *Memory*: Ask questions that address the who, what, where, when, why, and how of what you are teaching.
- *Analytic*: Ask questions that encourage students to analyze, evaluate, critique, compare and contrast, and judge.
- *Creative*: Ask questions that encourage students to create, imagine, invent, discover, and suppose.
- *Practical*: Ask questions that encourage students to apply, put into practice, execute, use, and implement.
- *Wisdom*: Ask questions that encourage students to reflect on the common good, and especially how what they are learning could be used to achieve such a good, over the long and short terms, by balancing their own interests with those of others and with larger interests through the use of positive ethical values.

If You Make a Mistake, Admit It

Sometimes, while teaching a class, you will misspeak. Or, worse, you will downright make a mistake. At best, you will discover the mistake yourself.

At worst, a student will discover the mistake. It is tempting to downplay the mistake, to try to explain why you really were correct, or just to brush the whole thing off.

There are three problems with these solutions. First, you may leave students with misinformation. Second, you have served as a terrible role model for the students, for whom you are supposed to be a good role model. And third, you will have made it hard to live with yourself. If you make a mistake, admit it, correct it, and move on. In the process, you may even be able to convey to students the important lesson that even experts make mistakes. That's a valuable lesson for them to learn. Many students, especially from less educated backgrounds, come to college thinking that the professors always know what they are talking about. We who are professors know how wrong this is. Students should know it as well.

Don't Embarrass Students in Front of Other Students

Sometimes students say or do things in class that totally take you off guard—as in, "How could anyone say or do that?" You may generate, almost automatically, a response that puts the student in his or her place. Sometimes we all have a tendency, if someone says or does something stupid, to make sure that that person knows we know what just happened. Nevertheless, it is important to restrain yourself from the impulse to put down a student publicly. You are the authority in the class, and your put-down may permanently relegate the student to the lower ranks of esteem from others. Or, worse, your comment may place the student in a position of high esteem for others—for example, because the student stood up to you. There is no particularly good result of putting down a student in front of other students (or at any time). Your best bet always is to cool it and, if the behavior persists, talk to the student in a setting where other students are not around to see the interaction.

Don't Lose Your Temper

Some days work out exceptionally poorly. It may be because the class is going poorly. It may be because you had a lousy day at home before coming in to teach. It may be just the weather or an inexplicable mood. You never, ever want to lose your temper in front of a class, for any reason. If you do, you will lose your legitimate appearance of authority. You still may have the statutory authority of a teacher, but losing your temper will do little more than contributing to the loss of respect for you on the part of your students. So never lose it in front of your students (whether in a class or even a one-on-one meeting). You will lose respect, and you will show yourself to be an unenviable role model.

If You Are Going to Argue With What Students Say, Tell Them in Advance That That Is Part of the Course

Some instructors have a policy, perhaps implicit, that they will not argue with students. They may correct students' wrong answers, but they do not argue with them. Other instructors like to argue with their students to encourage the students to think critically. Whatever your policy is, make sure the students know it in advance. You do not want any of them to think that you singled them out for argument.

On a related matter, if sometimes you make up hypothetical situations, make sure the students know the situations are hypothetical. I've sometimes said things that I thought students would understand to be hypothetical. They didn't.

Be Really Careful With Jokes

When I teach, I tell a lot of jokes. It's just who I am as a person; I joke a lot, pretty much with whomever I am with. At the same time, I know that jokes can be really hazardous. Many things can go wrong when you joke. Some students may think you are serious. Other students may think your jokes are not funny. Other students may think you are being disrespectful or even offensive. And still other students may think that you are wasting valuable instructional time.

Joke if you wish, but keep in mind that there are very few jokes that everyone finds funny. Senses of humor vary, and you may tell a joke here and there that elicits blank stares that remind you just how difficult it is to joke successfully when you are teaching. Styles of jokes also vary generationally, and your sense of humor may reflect your age (as mine almost certainly does).

If You Are Observed in Your Teaching, Speak to the Students, Not the Observers

Sometimes one or more observers may come into your classroom, especially if you are approaching tenure time. If you have an observer, especially one whose observations are high stakes to you, you may be tempted to address your teaching, or at least much of it, to the observer. Avoid the temptation! You have a responsibility to teach your students. The observer is in the classroom to see how you teach students, not how you teach him or her. So pay attention to the students, and to the extent possible, act as though the observer were not there.

In Your First Class, Tell Your Students a Little About Yourself, Including Something That Is Not on Your CV

Students want to know who is teaching them. You don't have to make a big deal of who you are or where you came from. But it's a nice gesture to say a little about yourself so that students know who you are and a little bit about your background for teaching the course.

* * *

This book can only scratch the surface in terms of how you can prepare for teaching your courses. There are many excellent sources available that can provide many more details (e.g., Borich, 2013; Buskist & Davis, 2005; Landrum & McCarthy, 2012; Marzano, 2007; Sternberg, 1987; Svinicki & McKeachie, 2013).

Now that we have discussed what you need to do to prepare for teaching, let's talk about getting started in collaborating with students on research.

4

COLLABORATING WITH STUDENTS

When you work with students, you create for those students opportunities that may be, for them, chances that come just once in a lifetime. So although you may have, in the course of a career, many students whom you mentor, the students with whom you work may have only you as a mentor, or only you and one or two other mentors. It's therefore important to create for students the very best opportunity you can. Keep in mind that students often report that the aspect of their college career that matters most, at least educationally, is having a mentor who shows an interest in, cares about, and works collaboratively with them (Ray & Kafka, 2014; Rogers, 2015).

If you view collaborating with students primarily as a way to advance your research, you have it wrong. The primary reason to collaborate with students is to provide them with an educational experience second to none. There is no better way for students to learn than through research. An added benefit will be that your research will prosper, and so will theirs.

---

http://dx.doi.org/10.1037/0000013-005
Starting Your Career in Academic Psychology, by R. J. Sternberg
Copyright © 2017 by the American Psychological Association. All rights reserved.

CREATE A WIN–WIN SITUATION

Collaborating with students can and should be a win–win situation. Because the faculty member is the more powerful member of the teacher–student dyad, she or he is the one more responsible for making sure both parties win. For the faculty member, it is a chance to shape a future generation, to convey knowledge, to meet his or her teaching requirements, and sometimes to get research done. For the student, it is a chance to acquire knowledge about the field, to learn how to think about the field, to learn how to work collaboratively, to gain research credit, and in some cases to gain course credit as well if a joint project is being done for academic credit.

Teacher–student relationships fail when either the teacher or the student starts to see the collaboration, whatever form it may take, as a zero-sum game. In contrast, teacher–student relationships work best if both teacher and student think that if they advance the other's interest, they also advance their own. For example, a junior faculty member may view a research collaboration primarily as a step toward attaining tenure, whereas a student may view the collaboration primarily as a vehicle for getting academic credit or a job.

BE AUTHORITATIVE, NOT AUTHORITARIAN OR LAISSEZ-FAIRE

When we study parenting, we learn that there are three primary parenting styles—authoritative, authoritarian, and laissez-faire (Baumrind, 1991). The same styles, I believe, apply to mentorship. The authoritative mentor shows a moderate amount of control but a high level of warmth and responsiveness to students. The authoritarian mentor shows a high level of control and low levels of warmth and responsiveness. And the laissez-faire mentor is hands-off and pretty much leaves students to their own devices. As psychologists, we know that authoritative parenting, on the whole, is the most effective style of parenting. The question is whether we can generalize this lesson to mentoring.

An authoritative style develops knowledge, independence, and goodwill. An authoritative style on your part is what transforms students from dependent, often anxious learners to independent, self-sufficient, and self-efficacious learners. Why wouldn't all advisers be authoritative? Because they may let their own, perhaps selfish interests get the better of them. Consider the alternatives and their consequences.

Maybe they believe that with an authoritarian style, they can get more of their own research done through students. They may even see themselves not as authoritarian but as helping hapless students learn the right and wrong ways to do things. There are problems with an authoritarian style, however. First, students may come to resent it. Second, it is not ideal for helping students develop independence. Third, it may propagate the authoritarian style to the next generation of students, as students become teachers and imitate what they are familiar with. Finally, it encourages faculty members to delude themselves about how they are helping students when in fact what they are doing is advancing their own selfish interests.

The laissez-faire style, like the authoritarian one, is not maximally effective. First, students generally do not receive adequate guidance and are susceptible to floundering. Second, students do not learn as much as they could because their teacher is insufficiently available to them. Third, the teacher may pass this style on to future generations as their students themselves become laissez-faire mentors. Finally, the style encourages teachers to believe that it is enough to promise guidance and then not deliver it.

CHALLENGE STUDENTS IN THEIR ZONE OF PROXIMAL DEVELOPMENT

When I was a graduate student, I worked with a faculty member on a particular research project. I knew it was a good project. The problem was, I had no idea what I was doing. It was way beyond where I was in terms of my quantitative skills. When I tried to get further guidance from the faculty member, I could not understand what he was trying to tell me. I tried to learn the math I would need to do the project, but it was so far ahead of where I was that I couldn't make it work, and eventually I dropped the project. In Vygotskian terms, the project was way beyond my zone of proximal development (Vygotsky, 1978).

Most of us hope not to be in a position where we have to tell a senior PhD student exactly what to do and how to do it, expecting such explicit instruction to be below the student's zone of proximal development. I have had advanced graduate students ask me for such detailed suggestions, but I have refused to give them. If they cannot figure out what to do by that stage of their career, they are better off finding something else to do with their lives.

The challenge, therefore, is how one can provide just the right amount of guidance to students—not so much that it stifles them nor so little that they become lost and possibly experience a sense of despair. Figuring out how to relate to students in their zone of proximal development is a skill one acquires over a long period of time by supervising students and learning from one's own mistakes. But faculty members who can adjust their advising just to students' right level will gain by seeing the students thrive and be in a position in which they can get done whatever it is they are asked to do.

REMEMBER THAT WORKING WITH UNDERGRADUATE STUDENTS IS VERY DIFFERENT FROM WORKING WITH GRADUATE STUDENTS

Typically, working with undergraduate students is very different from working with graduate students. Undergraduates usually need much more direction, guidance, and supervision than graduate students, especially advanced graduate students. Faculty members who are used to working with undergraduates know that they cannot just leave the undergraduates to get the work done. The faculty members need to monitor the work quite closely, either directly or with the help of graduate students or postdocs. In my experience, even if graduate students or postdocs are available, faculty mentors need to be actively involved rather than just leaving the supervision to their advanced students.

SET BOUNDARIES

Therapists think a lot about boundary setting. Teachers of students in colleges and universities may give the matter less thought, even though it is no less important for them. Proper boundaries help students develop academically and personally. Ill-conceived boundaries can lead to development that goes off track and, in extreme cases, can lead to disciplinary action or even a lawsuit against a faculty member.

You want to help a student solve his or her academic problems, at the very least as they relate to you and the work you are doing with the student. Where things get tricky is when the student—or faculty member—wades too deeply into the personal arena. There are obvious boundaries that should not be crossed. These days, faculty members generally are not allowed to have romantic relationships with their students, and they probably are well advised to refrain from becoming "friends," at least while the students are under their mentorship. But other kinds of problems can develop as well, such as when a faculty member gets too close emotionally to a student and the faculty member or student then has trouble letting go.

Boundary setting can fail at the other extreme as well. If a student perceives a faculty mentor as uninterested in him or her personally, he or she may feel that the mentor is interested in the student only as a means to some kind of professional end. The student also may not put forth a best effort when a faculty mentor seems distant and personally remote. As with so many things, faculty members need to hit just the right middle ground of caring but not caring in a way that impedes rather than fosters the student's professional and personal development.

BE GENEROUS WITH YOUR TIME

As a faculty member, you are busy. You have too much to do and not enough time to do it. Meetings with students are sometimes productive, but let's face it—other times they are a waste of time, not only for you but also for the student. Moreover, the time you spent meeting with that student could have been time you spent preparing for class, or working on a grant proposal, or getting an article out. So it can be tempting to cut down on student face-to-face time.

Yet, many of us, looking back on our careers, would say that the best instructional time we spent was the face-to-face time with our mentors. That certainly is true for me. Even if not every meeting is a treasure, the cumulative effect of those meetings often results in a whole whose sum exceeds its parts. Moreover, such meetings often can help students from going seriously astray in their research projects. If you are generous with your time, it will come back to you through your knowledge that you have been a good mentor and through your students' increased productivity—and maybe your own as well.

BE OPEN TO IDEAS THAT MAY CONFLICT WITH YOUR OWN

We usually think of the teacher–student relationship as one in which the student learns from the teacher. And of course, if students are not learning from us, we are doing something horribly wrong. But interactions with students should be a two-way street. I often have felt that I learn as much from my students as they learn from me. At least in my case, many of the ideas in joint publications with students have come from the students, not from me.

Moreover, the increased expertise we have as instructors does not guarantee that we are more creative than our students in coming up with new ideas. A cost of expertise is greater risk for entrenchment—getting stuck (Sternberg & Lubart, 1995). As a result, it is often the students who have the more creative ideas because they are not yet stuck in any particular way of seeing things. What we have in expertise they may more than make up for in flexibility of thinking. So when your students see things a different way than the way you do, keep in mind that they may have generative ideas that you just would not think of. My own graduate adviser, Gordon Bower, made a career of following his students, and few psychologists of his generation had more success in their careers than he did.

FIND A PROJECT THEY ARE ENTHUSIASTIC ABOUT

I often have several projects about which I am enthusiastic. When a student comes to work with me, he or she most likely will have no projects about which he or she is enthusiastic. It's tempting to assume that if I am excited about a project, a student will be, too. But it is also wrong. The very projects that most excite you may excite your students not at all. And we know that scientists do their most creative work on projects about which they feel very enthusiastic (Sternberg & Lubart, 1995).

In working with students, therefore, our greatest challenge is not to find projects we are excited about, but rather to find projects they are excited about. They will not do great work in projects that do not particularly interest them, nor will they, most likely, give those projects their all. If you can work with a student to develop a mutually exciting project, both you and the student will benefit greatly.

DO A BACKGROUND CHECK

Show me a faculty member who has never had an advisee who was a "problem advisee," and I'll point out to you a faculty member who has never had an advisee, period. Sooner or later, usually sooner, we all end up with problem advisees. Usually, we have these earlier more often than later in our careers because students who could not work successfully with faculty members already in a department often gravitate to new faculty members who have not been previously in the department.

When I have advised students who have not worked out, I would say that more times than not I could have avoided these unproductive relationships if I had taken the time to do a background check on the students. Students likely will do a background check on you. You should do the same on them. I am not talking, of course, about a formal background check involving some outside agency. Rather, I'm talking about the basics: What's their grade point average? With whom have they worked before? Why do they want to work with you? You can ask easy-to-answer questions of that sort. Talk with former mentors. In some cases, you may save yourself headaches that were easily avoidable. Of course, there are students who fail to succeed with one adviser who then work well with another. You will have to be the judge of whether something that went wrong with a former adviser will go wrong with you. But at least you should know about the history and be able to judge your probability of success in working with a student by doing a little advance checking before you newly commit yourself to mentor a student.

DON'T EXPLOIT STUDENTS

Probably very few, if any, faculty members view themselves as exploiters. Yet most of us, during the course of our careers, have come to know faculty members with reputations in their department as exploiters. Perhaps they are the only ones who don't know who they are. But others do.

What, exactly, is an exploiter? It varies from one case to another, but the common characteristic seems to be a kind of professional narcissism—concern with one's own professional advancement and seeing students merely as a vehicle for that advancement. Students are treated as tools for enhancing the exploiter's own career success. Then, like tools that eventually have outlived their usefulness, the students are discarded when they no longer are needed.

Exploiters end up paying a stiff price in the end because students figure out who they are and then eschew working with them. In an ideal world, chairs of departments would call faculty members on such games. In the real world, they often don't because they don't want the confrontation or feel they could not prove their case even if they did risk a confrontation. The best way to avoid the situation is to create a win–win rather than zero-sum game with your students.

BE GENEROUS, BUT NOT PROFLIGATE, WITH CREDIT

Almost every scientist has a credit nightmare from somewhere back in his or her career—and I'm not talking about credit cards or credit bureaus! One collaborates with someone and then things go crazy. My own crazy story was a collaboration I did when I was an assistant professor. When the student and I got to the point where we were getting ready to write up our study, the student informed me that another professor—with whom she was widely known to be having an affair—should really be first author. As far as I knew, that professor had had nothing to do with the studies at all.

The best way to avoid credit nightmares is to make the rules for credit clear and explicit right from the start. You are the faculty member, so you should be the one to set the rules. But you also should be the one to make sure you, as well as the student, obey those rules. The American Psychological Association (2010) has given quite explicit guidelines for assigning credit. Those guidelines are about as good as you will get.

The worst cases, of course, are those who hog credit. But there are also cases where faculty members go so out of their way to give credit that they lose sight of what a true professional collaboration is. Collaborators should get coauthorship only if they contribute ideas to a project—they should not get coauthorship merely for scheduling or testing subjects. If you have a bunch of coauthors who did not contribute professionally to a project, you dilute credit away from those who did contribute professionally, and you teach students an unfortunate lesson—that coauthorship is cheap and to be had for the asking without a serious investment of work.

DON'T BE POSSESSIVE

At one point, I had a member of my undergraduate lab group quit. I asked her why she was quitting. The reason was that she was also in another lab group, and the professor who directed that lab group refused to allow students in her group also to be in anyone else's lab group. I inquired whether this was permissible within the rules of the department or the university and was told that there was no rule against it—which seemed like a punt to me.

I've seen this kind of behavior in other instances: Faculty members come to believe that they "own" students and don't want to share. So who loses? The students, because they are deprived of an opportunity to have multiple mentors, something almost every successful scientist has. Students don't "belong" to you: Don't imagine they do. And most of all, don't be selfish and possessive. If you have to be this way, save it for your romantic relationships and live with the consequences there.

WHEN RELATIONSHIPS WITH STUDENTS GO WRONG, SEEK HELP

Most relationships with students go fairly well. I've had more than 50 graduate students and postdoc advisees during my career, and more undergraduate advisees than I could count. Most of the relationships have gone well. But a handful of such adviser–advisee relationships haven't gone well. In most cases, the students simply moved on to another adviser. I have not had any blowups to the point that things got out of control.

As a dean and as a provost, however, I have witnessed instances in which things did spin out of control and complaints reached my office. In a few cases, they resulted in lawsuits. The problem was that by the time the faculty member realized he or she had lost control of the relationship, it often was too late. If things are not going well with a student, try to work them out without any ugly confrontations. If you can't, seek the help of a director of undergraduate or graduate studies, a chair, or a dean. Don't let things keep getting worse and worse. You may feel you are in the right, but the student may feel the same way. It's better to defuse conflicts before they ignite and cause damage to both your career and the career of the student.

One of the not-so-great cases I observed was when a professor felt that his student was failing manifestly to meet his expectations and the student felt that the professor's expectations were totally unrealistic. Neither was willing to give an inch. The professor became punitive; the student became hostile. After several rounds of going back and forth, the professor worked successfully to get the student terminated from the program. A lawsuit quickly followed. Like most lawsuits, it ended up getting settled for an undisclosed sum of money. Who really won, though? No one. The professor should have sought help in handling the situation before it got totally out of hand.

The worst cases were almost always ones in which sexual harassment was claimed. What made these cases difficult was that it usually was impossible to tell what actually had happened. The cases then ended up riding on the respective credibility levels of the involved parties. You never, ever want to get involved in a sexual harassment case. So don't ever risk behavior that could be construed as sexual harassment. If you slip, apologize immediately and quickly seek outside help. These situations get out of hand very quickly, and you don't want to be spending all your time defending yourself, whether to a tribunal or a courtroom.

CREATE OPPORTUNITIES FOR STUDENTS TO NETWORK AND PUBLICIZE THEIR WORK

My graduate adviser has helped me—throughout my career—to form a network of colleagues, despite the fact that I did not work in the same area of research he did. My wife Karin's graduate adviser did not really do much to help her to establish as widespread a network. Part of your responsibility as a mentor is to be like my adviser was—not only to advise students but also to help them get their work out through publications, talks, posters, and contacts with other psychologists.

As you know, such networks are crucial to success at any level. Although we often don't like to admit it, networks are one of the main ways people advance through a field. In any field, it is not only what you know but also whom you know. And you get to know people through introductions. Take every opportunity you can to provide students with the introductions and the opportunities to publicize their work that will help them succeed, regardless of the career they choose to pursue.

ENCOURAGE STUDENTS TO TAKE SENSIBLE RISKS

In many domains of our society, students learn that risk taking is, well, risky. They often learn what to say on tests, how to say it, and also what not to say. They figure out how to teach in ways that are safe—that won't offend anyone. They learn to do safe, paradigmatic research that will result in a publication—somewhere.

It is understandable why we would teach students to be careful about risks—we don't want them to blow their careers with ill-considered mistakes. At the same time, if students don't make mistakes, they won't learn from those mistakes, and most teachers and researchers find that their best learning is from their own mistakes. So you need to teach students not to be risk averse, but rather to make mistakes and learn from them. We need, culturally, to allow students to make mistakes so long as they can learn from them. If you look at the great researchers (see, e.g., Sternberg, Fiske, & Foss, 2016), they almost all have made mistakes in their careers, sometimes major ones. What distinguishes them, in part, from the not-so-great researchers is that they took their risks, made their mistakes, and learned from them so that they could do better facing their next challenge.

In my own career, I've taken many risks. Some have worked out great; some have worked out so-so; some have not worked out at all. Standing up against conventional theories of intelligence has been a risk that I feel worked out (Sternberg, 2003). I never expected everyone to accept my theory, but at least some people have, and it has woken up at least some people to the limitations of conventional ways of seeing intelligence. At the other extreme, taking on the presidency of a particular university was a mistake: I was not a good fit to the institution, and that became obvious pretty quickly. I got out. But in careers, nothing ventured, nothing gained, and if you want to experience successes, you also have to be prepared for failures.

TEACH STUDENTS HOW TO THINK, NOT WHAT TO THINK

Your job is to teach students how to think, not what to think. Of course, you need to teach them the basic content of psychology or your area of specialization within psychology. But if your goal is to create junior versions of you, then you are misperceiving your role as a mentor. In my career, I really never had any student who became a junior version of me; I had one student who tried to, but of course it didn't work.

My goal for students is that they combine how I think with how other faculty members think and how other experts in the field think and then come up with their own unique synthesis. They will succeed if they figure out who they are, not if they figure out who you are. That means you have to allow students to soar on their own wings, realizing, of course, that they then may crash or have accidents along the way.

A colleague of mine who is quite well known is very proud of all the junior versions of himself he has turned out. He views himself, I believe, as a creative genius and sees his role as producing clones who can profit from his creative genius. The problem is that he then does not allow his students the same creativity he has developed himself. The students end up doing variants of his work, and none of them has truly soared professionally. How could they? He taught them what to think, so they never learned to think for themselves.

TEACH STUDENTS THE IMPORTANCE OF EFFECTIVE SELF-PRESENTATION

In our field, it is important to not only have good ideas but also to know how to present them. I have taught courses in a half-dozen universities over the course of a career. I have been astonished at times at how poorly my students write. The question I've asked is how this could happen—how did these students get to college with such poor writing skills? I don't really know the answer, but I do know that teachers who pass such students through the system do these students an incredible disservice. In almost any job they hold, sooner or later, they will have to write—articles, reports, memos, books, whatever—and the students will not be served if their writing presents them as only semiliterate in a society that expects and values full literacy.

In some cases, of course, the students were nonnative speakers of English. But in many other cases, English was the student's native language. It may be that teachers have thought that what matters is the ideas the students express, not how the students express them. But in the real world, people often judge us not only by what we write but also by how we write it. And these students will not fare well in such judgments.

There are books to help students learn to express themselves better (e.g., Sternberg & Sternberg, 2016). But these books will not compensate for teachers who do not want to take the time or put in the effort or even see it as their job to help students learn better to express themselves. Moreover, oral expression is just as important as, or more important than, written expression. Job interviews, for example, demand effective oral self-expression.

We may wish that students' English teachers, many years ago, did the job we now find ourselves confronting. But if those teachers didn't do the job, we owe it to our students to put them on a track where they will not fail to get or keep jobs or to succeed at the level at which they are capable because they do not express themselves well.

BUILD SELF-EFFICACY IN STUDENTS

Almost all students go through periods of self-doubt, often intense ones. Counseling centers of colleges and universities are kept super busy by students wondering how they got into the college or university of their choice and how they are going to succeed there. Part of your job should be to help students through these periods of self-doubt—to help them achieve a sense of self-efficacy (Bandura, 1997).

I went to college planning to major in psychology. I had done poorly on IQ tests as a child and wanted to understand why. I took my first psychology test as a freshman and got an impressive 3 out of 10 points. My professor, handing back the test paper, commented that there was "a famous Sternberg in psychology and it looks like there won't be another one." When I ultimately got a C in the course, he told me it was a gift. So much for helping me through my period of self-doubt. I decided to switch to majoring in math, and when I took a course that was an introduction to real analysis, I failed the midterm. The professor suggested I drop the course, which I did. So I returned to psychology, because a C looked a whole lot better than an F. But I had developed fairly severe insecurity. Insecurity up to a point can be useful, but I was well beyond that point.

If you believe a student has what it takes to succeed, you want to support the student as much as you can and help him or her through the inevitable periods of self-doubt so that the student can succeed to the fullest extent of which he or she is capable. If you do not believe a student has what it takes to succeed, you may need to try a different tack. You may want to talk to the student about the future and whether he or she has the best future plans. But remember, you never want to have that conversation unless you are absolutely convinced that the student is on the wrong path.

BUILD RESILIENCE IN STUDENTS

Arguably the most important characteristic for any professional in psychology to master, the earlier the better, is resilience—the ability to forge ahead in the face of severe difficulties. Because the one sure thing about a career in academia is that one is going to have severe difficulties.

When I was in graduate school, I wondered what it took to have a successful career such as my advisor was having. Later, I wondered who among the graduate students in my class would become successful and who would not. Would I be one of the professionally successful ones? When I first started as an assistant professor, I heard about the work of many of my classmates and saw them fairly often at conventions. But as the years went by, more and more of them started to disappear into the woodwork. I wondered what had gone wrong. And even as I have grown much older, I have come to realize that only a small handful have really made it anywhere close to the top of the field.

What distinguished the ones who succeeded? Was it IQ points? Motivation? Luck? No doubt there are multiple factors that can contribute to success (or failure). But the conclusion I came to was that the most important factor was resilience in the face of extremely challenging obstacles—multiple rejections of papers or grant proposals, failure to get hired, divorce, ill health, loss of a parent or child or spouse, financial failure, or whatever. Over the years, almost everyone experiences some great loss. Some people experience multiple such losses. And in many cases, people just give up. They decide that they just cannot go on. And that, I believe, is what happened to many of my classmates.

My life has been pretty good, but it has had its severe challenges—failed intimate relationships, losses of grant funding, a job that totally did not work out, projects that seemed promising but failed, loss of children at birth. My life is probably no worse than many people's and better than most. There have been multiple times when I have felt like giving up. Sometimes I still do. But I keep going. I've never reached the top of the field, for sure, but I've reached as high as I could because I kept going even when at times I felt ready to call it quits.

TEACH STUDENTS THE IMPORTANCE OF DELAYING GRATIFICATION

Mischel (2015) showed the importance of delay of gratification to lifelong success. Academia is a field in which delay of gratification is more important than perhaps in many professions. It takes many years to establish a strong reputation. And there are many obstacles along the way. Even the first major promotion—tenure—usually takes 6 to 7 or more years to achieve. If one counts time in graduate school, postdoctoral training, and sometimes multiple jobs, it can be quite a bit more than 6 or 7 years. Academia is not a career for those who cannot wait.

Moreover, each step along the way also can be a long haul. One submits an article; more often than not, it is not accepted on the first pass. There may be multiple revisions, and it still may be rejected. Grant proposals also can be enormously time consuming to write, with only a very small probability of success. One may have to teach a course three or four times to get it right. Students need to learn the importance of delay of gratification because throughout their whole career, they will have a choice of either delaying gratification—or finding something else to do!

EMPHASIZE TO STUDENTS THE IMPORTANCE OF HAVING AN ETHICAL CODE

Why would an eminent Harvard professor distort his data to the point where he had to resign? If you are already at the top of the heap academically, isn't that enough? Why would an eminent professor at Tilburg University in the Netherlands fake data to the point of writing about experiments he never even conducted? Clearly, even academic socialization at top schools does not guarantee that students will develop a viable ethical code. But most examples of ethical failure are smaller than these. They are examples rather of professors exploiting students, of professors sabotaging grant proposals that might fund research that would compete with their own, of professors giving negative reviews to articles because their own work is cited less than favorably, and so forth.

In my own graduate training, I do not remember any specific instruction on the ethics of my future profession. There was a lot of implicit training, but nothing explicit. Moreover, I taught this past semester a course on professional ethics, and although I had a good enrollment (25 undergraduate and graduate students), I was more impressed by how many students and especially graduate students failed to enroll than by the number who did. There was nothing so special about my course. But we are living in a time in which there is a lot of skepticism among the general public and in the halls of Congress about the integrity of scientific research, in general, and of research in the behavioral sciences, in particular. We need to explicitly, not just implicitly, teach students how to think ethically in their work. Whatever we are doing, we need to be doing much more.

BE A POSITIVE ROLE MODEL

Perhaps most important, be a positive role model. Most of what students learn about being a professional is not from what you explicitly teach them but from their watching you and then modeling themselves after you. As with parents, it matters much more how you act than what you say. So be your best, and your students are likely to follow.

III
RESEARCH

5

FORMING IDEAS FOR AND IMPLEMENTING YOUR RESEARCH

Many institutions expect tenure track faculty to have a research program. Sometimes, although less frequently, adjuncts and lecturers also have research programs. This chapter is intended to help get you started on your research as a faculty member. Chances are you have done research before. But doing research as a faculty member is a bit of a different "animal," as we shall see.

GENERAL TIPS

Whatever You Do, Make Sure It Is Cleared by the Institutional Research Board First, Even If It Is Pilot Testing

Getting institutional research board (IRB) clearance may seem obvious, but there is a lot of pressure on researchers, especially in the beginning stages of their careers, to get material into publication. So there can be a temptation

---

http://dx.doi.org/10.1037/0000013-006
Starting Your Career in Academic Psychology, by R. J. Sternberg
Copyright © 2017 by the American Psychological Association. All rights reserved.

to get one's research started without going through all of what can seem, at times, to be bureaucratic hoops. Moreover, IRBs sometimes take a long time to act, and moreover, some of them are really quite picky and can keep one going with revisions for longer than any investigator would want.

Nevertheless, do not even think about starting any form of data collection without IRB approval (or an explicit exemption from the IRB), even if you find such approval bureaucratic and perhaps annoying. There are several reasons to wait. First, the rule is clear: You need IRB approval (or a statement from the IRB that your research is exempt) before you start any data collection. Second, if you start collecting data without IRB approval, you risk severe sanctions, including having your right to conduct research revoked. Third, if you are grant funded, you risk sanctions from the granting agency. Fourth, if you are untenured or not yet a full professor, you have just seriously compromised your future promotion; even if you are a full professor, you risk other sanctions besides having your right to conduct research revoked. Finally, you will have a black mark on your career, no matter what stage of career you are at.

Don't Change Your Protocol Without Notifying the IRB

Sometimes, right after starting to run your study, you realize that your materials or some other aspect of the method is not quite right. You need to make a change, perhaps a minor one, and then continue, probably discounting the data from the early participants. The change may be so minor that you are tempted just to go ahead and not inform the IRB. For better or worse, that is not permissible. You need IRB permission to change your protocol, even for small changes. You usually can get some form of expedited review for small changes. But you still need for the new protocol to be approved.

If Something Goes Wrong, Notify the IRB at Once

Hopefully, once you start collecting data, everything will go just according to plan. But sometimes it doesn't. For example, when I was in graduate school, I ran a study that I would have expected to be totally smooth sailing. It really was a piece of cake. But then something extraordinary happened. The study used a foot pedal. One of my participants was a hemophiliac. For some reason, the foot pedal did not work well for him, and he had an adverse reaction. I never could have predicted this. There are other things that can happen that one could not predict. If things go wrong, let the IRB know. It is far better, if there is a problem, that they hear from you first than that they hear first from someone who was adversely affected. No one can predict every possible adverse outcome; anyone, however, can immediately report an adverse outcome when it occurs.

Look to Various Sources to Get Ideas for Research

Like everyone else, you will go through stages of your career in which things do not go as you would have hoped. Maybe you have been pursuing a research paradigm and you (and perhaps everyone else) are tired of it. Or maybe you have found something new you want to study. Or maybe new opportunities are being presented to you. If you need new ideas, there are a number of sources to which you can look.

Your Life Experiences

Almost all my research has come out of my life experiences. I studied intelligence because I did poorly on IQ tests as a child. I studied creativity because I ran out of ideas at one point. I studied wisdom because I remembered a time when I gave a student really bad advice. I studied love because I was in a failing relationship. Well, you get the idea. Ask yourself what in your life has made a real impression on you or changed things, for better or worse. Is there something there to study?

Other People's Life Experiences

You don't need to limit yourself to your own experiences in generating new ideas for research. Sometimes the experiences of others can motivate you just as much as your own. You can draw on other people's life experiences as well. For example, my research on hate was generated in part by stories my mother told me of her and her family's experiences in, and trying to leave, Austria during the time of the Nazi regime. I know a distinguished researcher who started studying autism because he has a child with autism.

Talks

Talks can be a source of inspiration for research. Sometimes one goes into a talk just to listen and comes out with ideas about new problems to study or how better to study the problem one is currently pursuing.

The example I remember best in my own career happened in graduate school. I went to a debate between famous scholars on the subject of race. One of the debaters was a Nobel Prize winner for his work in a totally different field. His remarks at the debate were, I thought, outrageous. I became interested in the question of racial differences in intelligence and later wrote several papers on the topic.

Henry Roediger III gained great fame for his work on associative errors in free recall (Roediger & McDermott, 1995). He got the idea from an almost offhand remark that a psychologist, Endel Tulving, made while giving a colloquium. So you can get ideas from talks, even when you least expect to.

Do not limit yourself to talks only in your own field. Sometimes the most productive ideas come from outside your own field. For example, Herbert Simon, a Nobel Prize–winning psychologist and economist, got his ideas from far-flung fields by no means limited to psychology.

Articles and Books

When we read articles or books, we often do so to be informed of what others have done. But of course, what others have done can be the springboard for what we do. You never know when some scholarly article or book you read may give you an inspiration for your own future research.

Coincidentally, perhaps, just as Roediger got an idea for his research from listening to Endel Tulving, I got an idea in graduate school from reading Tulving's work. (Disclosure: Tulving was my undergraduate adviser at Yale.) Tulving showed that learning a list of words to be recalled could actually interfere with later recall when the same list was part of a larger list. That is, if you learn List A, learning that list can interfere with your learning List AB, half of which consists of the list you already learned. I thought that Tulving's interpretation of the phenomenon was not correct. My first major project in graduate school was trying (successfully, I think) to show an alternate interpretation to his (Sternberg & Bower, 1974).

The scholarly work does not have to be in your field of inquiry. It may be work from another field entirely. In my own case, several of my empirical studies resulted from reading I had done in philosophy. I was interested, for example, in how people make predictions about the future, and I relied heavily on the work of philosopher Nelson Goodman (1983) for the design of a series of studies. Later, when I did work on love, I drew heavily on literary work, especially by García Márquez (2007), to develop my theory of love as a story (Sternberg, 1998b). The point is that you can get ideas from other fields, sometimes ones you never would have gotten if you read only psychology books.

Beyond articles and books, another way to express yourself in writing is through book chapters. The advantage of book chapters is that you usually have more freedom to express yourself as you want to express yourself. The disadvantage is that they are usually not as carefully refereed as are journal articles, and they usually count less in tenure and promotion considerations.

Various Nonprofessional Media

You can get ideas from nonscholarly as well as scholarly sources. Sometimes newspapers, television, radio, or whatever can be a source of inspiration. I became interested in conflict resolution in part because, at the time, there were a lot of international negotiations going on, the results of which were being reported in the media on a daily basis. I wondered, at the time, how experienced negotiators could be doing such a bad job of resolving conflicts that could have been resolved more easily had the negotiators been willing to step down rather than step up the conflicts (Sternberg & Soriano, 1984).

Conversations

Random conversations sometimes can be a productive source of ideas. That's just one of many reasons to network with people outside your field. For example, I once was having a more or less random conversation with a parasitologist who was then at Oxford University. I never imagined myself doing work on parasites. I have no training in parasitology, nor, I would have said, any interest. But she mentioned that there are children in rural Kenya who know the names of a hundred or more natural herbal medicines that can be used to combat parasitic illnesses. I pointed out to her that, for them, this was practical intelligence and that it was quite different from what might be considered practical intelligence in a typical U.S. or other setting in the so-called developed world. The conversation led to a collaborative study showing that children in rural Kenya often had practical intelligence that our tests in the United States never would measure, and that scores on these tests are actually negatively correlated with scores on conventional tests of intelligence (Sternberg et al., 2001).

Beware of Collaborations With Previous Advisers and Colleagues

When you start out in your new career, it often is necessary to finish up collaborations that you started during your student days. It also may be tempting to start up new collaborations with your advisers and colleagues from graduate school or from your days as a postdoc. Indeed, some great research can come from such collaborations, because if you had success with these collaborators in the past, chances are you will have success with them as well in the future.

There is a risk in sustaining old collaborations, however. The risk is that when you are considered for reappointment or for tenure, colleagues at your present institution may worry about your independence in research. Seeing old collaborations that have been sustained over a period of time, they may wonder how much of the collaborative work is yours and how much is your former advisers'. Such a consideration should weigh on you. If you have productive collaborations with former collaborators, by all means keep them up, but make sure that you have enough new research, even with other but new collaborators, so that when you are considered for promotion, your independence will not be questioned.

Check Your Budget

One really bad way to start a new job is to overspend the budget on a start-up grant, if you got one. Some institutions will not allow this to happen. They have spending controls so that when you are about to overspend, your purchases are rejected. But other institutions do not have this higher level of surveillance. So you want to make sure that your spending is within your limits.

In some institutions, start-up funds are limited (or even nonexistent). As a starting faculty member, you often need a plan for low-budget research. During my first year as an assistant professor, I did not do the research I ideally would have liked to do, because I just didn't have the money. Indeed, I spent most of the year writing up my dissertation for publication. And regardless of your budget, time your spending. Don't use it up so quickly that you find after a year or two that you have nothing with which to work.

You may wonder what actually happens if you overspend your budget. Because it is an institutional grant, the institution is liable. However, they will be within their rights to require you to reimburse the institution for the overage. So you are likely to end up paying for the overage out of your personal money, and to get a black mark with your institution at the same time. This is definitely not a good bargain.

Pace Your Spending

Not only do you want to stay within your budget, you also want to pace your spending. Academics always have a lot to do, and their first priority usually is not watching their spending on a continual basis. But you must do so or have someone else do it for you.

You would think that granting agencies, whether internal or external, would be happy if you underspend your budget. Actually, they usually aren't happy at all, especially external agencies. In some agencies, programs are cut in the next fiscal year by the amount grants were underspent in the current fiscal year. In other words, if you underspend by $50,000, the program may have its budget cut by $50,000. A reason for this is that, typically, multiple programs compete for money from some central allocation authority. If money is unspent, that is money that might have gone to another program that very well might have spent the money. So the money went to a program that did not need it. Moreover, sometimes programs lose unspent money. In other words, they do not get the money to spend on another project; the money goes back to some central authority.

So you want to keep track of your spending to ensure that you are not overspending but also not underspending. It never looks good when, in the last months of a grant, you suddenly start spending large sums just to use the money up. Better to monitor your spending and make sure you are spending money as you need it.

Ask Yourself Whether You Are Really Excited About the Research Project

In the end, there may be nothing more important in getting into research than ensuring that you are excited and passionate about the research you are about to do. Research on creativity shows that people do their most creative and their best work when they are enthusiastic about what they are studying (Kaufman & Sternberg, 2010). There are lots of things you can study, but you will study best if you really get into whatever you are studying. Don't settle for something that you find merely somewhat interesting or minimally intellectually engaging. Go for the best you can do.

PLANNING

Ask Yourself What the Best, Worst, and Expected Outcomes Are for the Research You Plan to Do

When you do research, there always is an opportunity cost. That is, the time, money, and energy you put into one project suck away resources that you might put into another project. So you want to assure yourself that your investment in research is an appropriate one. In this regard, I have found it useful to ask three questions before undertaking a research project.

The first question is, What is the best possible set of outcomes that could emanate from this research? If the best possible outcomes are not particularly good, then you probably don't want to bother with the research. That is, the best possible outcomes should be pretty darn good for you to put the effort into doing the research.

The second question is, What is the worst possible set of outcomes that could emanate from the research? If the worst possible outcomes are too awful, then you probably don't want to do the research. Usually, the worst outcomes are simply that nothing comes of the research—for example, all your results are null. But if there are other possible perverse consequences, any of which might actually result in a loss to your reputation, you don't want to do the research. An example would be that people wonder how you could have been foolish enough ever to do the work in the first place.

The third question is, What is the most likely set of outcomes that could emanate from the research? If the most likely outcomes are only so-so, or not particularly alluring, then you may want to reconsider.

Of course, some research is high risk, and you do it even though the research is unlikely to pay off. But if you are doing high-risk research, it makes sense also to have another line of research that is lower risk so that if your high-risk bet does not pay off, you at least have something else you can publish.

Ask Yourself What the Big Question Is Behind Your Research

I have edited or associate edited half a dozen journals. The first thing I look for when I get a submission is, What is the big question? What will I know after reading about this research that I did not know before? When you formulate a research project, you ought to have a big question in mind and be able to say what someone would know when you are done that they previously did not know. Any study worth doing has a big question. If you cannot find one, you may want to ask yourself why you are doing the research in the first place.

Some of us may not look at ourselves as big-picture thinkers. That's fine; not everyone is. But that does not mean that your research cannot have a big question. It always needs one, however much or little you see yourself as a big-picture thinker.

Prepare an Elevator Speech

One way to think about your research is in terms of an elevator speech (a speech that would last no longer than the duration of an elevator ride). The elevator speech is most often discussed as an aid for finding a job, because when you apply for a job, you need an elevator speech. It is the speech you give to people who might want to hire you but who don't have time to read your papers, attend your talks, or really try to understand in any depth what you do. Even for the people who do pay serious attention to your work, the elevator speech helps them understand how you perceive what you do and what you think is important about it.

Similarly, an elevator speech can help you promote your research. Even before you start the research, think about what you would like others to know about your research and why you have done it. What do you expect and why? How is the research important to others beside yourself? How will it make some kind of a difference? In your career, you often will be asked briefly to tell about what you are doing. You should not make up a speech on the spot. You should be ready with an elevator speech, about any particular study and about your research in general.

Look Into Quick Internal Sources of Research Funding

Even if you have start-up funding, the college or university often provides internal grants that can help supplement your funding for your research. Such grants tend more often to be for entry-level faculty members. Typically, they are small. But they may well be enough to pay participants and even to hire part-time help. So if you need some supplementary funding, talk with your department chair or dean, or even your departmental business officer, about possible sources of funding in your institution.

Realize You Can't Please Everyone With Your Research

When I was starting out in my career, I thought that if I did good research, everyone in the field, or at least in my department, would be pleased. How wrong I was! There is almost no research you can do that will please everyone. Some people will think the question you are asking is not worth asking. Or they won't like the way you go about answering the question. Or they won't like the results you got. I quickly learned that trying to please everyone was hopeless.

This became especially clear to me when I was coming up for tenure. I had always known that there were some members of my department who were not thrilled with the kind of research I did. So I thought that what I better do is figure out a way to modify what I was doing so that I would please them. I figured I would need their votes when the tenure vote was taken. Well, I learned that, really, there probably was nothing I could do to please some of these people and still be true to myself. Maybe there are others who can please more people, but I was not one of those others. And I came to realize that the most important person to please was myself. If I could not believe in what I was doing, it really didn't matter what others thought. So do your best work, work hard at it, and don't expect to make everyone happy. Most important, make yourself happy.

Don't Be Limited by Your Past Instruction

Although my graduate diploma did not state on it "cognitive psychology," that was the field in which I received my PhD. I entered my assistant professorship as a "cognitive psychologist." Initially, I was teaching courses that could be, for the most part, classified as either "cognitive psychology" or "general psychology" (such as the introduction to psychology course). But then I became interested in other topics, such as love and conflict resolution, even though my initial training was in cognitive psychology. I learned on the job. Graduate school does not teach you everything you need to know. What it does do is to prepare you for lifelong learning.

Don't Be Limited by Labels You or Others Assign to You

Earlier in my career, around the time I was starting to study love, a famous cognitive psychologist came to my office. I pointed with pride to a book I had just authored called *Cognitive Psychology*. The psychologist then said to me that, the book notwithstanding, I was not a cognitive psychologist anymore. His point was that with my recent foray into the study of love, I had forfeited my claim to the title of "cognitive psychologist."

At first, I was very upset by his remark. I always had considered myself to be a cognitive psychologist. But then I realized that his remark liberated me. I did not have to be any particular kind of psychologist. What did I need the label for? I could and should study what interested me, and forget about the labels. In our society, we are very quick to label people—smart, stupid, beautiful, ugly, personable, unfriendly. Often we would do better without the labels. I didn't need a label other than that I was a psychologist who studied whatever happened to interest him. To this day, I still study whatever interests me, and the heck with the labels. That said, you often need the label to get hired, and you may need it to be tenured or promoted as well. So make sure that others have some sense of your professional identity, even if you view yourself as eclectic.

EXECUTION

Make Sure You Have Backup for All Data Files

I know, I know. You already know this. Everyone knows he or she should have backup files. What's amazing is how many people just never get around to doing it. They mean to . . . but they don't. In the days of yesteryear, you actually had to remember to physically back up your data on a regular basis. Today there are remote online services that do it for you. They are well worth the cost. You can't afford to lose everything in the computer crash that will come, sooner or later.

If you are teaching and have your grades and student information stored online (as I do), you need a double backup. You simply cannot afford to lose these data. Last year, I took a course as a professor, so I was not taking the course for a grade. One day the instructor (a graduate student) came in and said he had lost his record of grades. He wanted the students to bring in their old tests so he could rerecord the grades. I can't speak for the other students, but I lost much of my respect for him. If a teacher doesn't keep careful records of grades, what does it say about how seriously he takes his teaching? So I keep one backup in the cloud with a backup service and one on a flash drive I have conveniently available to me separate from my computer.

Make Sure, If You Are Not Running the Research, That You Observe Some Research Sessions

When I was a graduate student, I tested all my own participants, sometimes with the help of an undergraduate research assistant. Sometimes it was grueling work. As I moved to become a faculty member, I started finding the money (or the credit to offer) so that I was able to have assistants test participants for me. For the most part, it was far better having others do the testing than having to do the testing myself. But there actually was one distinct advantage to having to do my own testing. When things in testing sessions were not going as they should have been, I could pick up on it right away.

Things do go wrong. One summer, when I was much younger and worked at a testing organization in a summer job, I proctored a testing session for entry-level workers. The instructions for the test were given by tape recording. The session was being held in New York. The individual reading the instructions spoke with a thick Texas accent. All one had to do was look at the faces of many of the New Yorkers in the room to see that they were having trouble understanding the voice on the tape recording. I was having trouble understanding it, too, at that point in my life having never traveled beyond the New York metropolitan area. A lot of the examinees were going to do poorly on the test because they could not understand the voice. But if you only looked at their test data, without having been in the testing room, you never would have known that the problem was that they could not understand the voice on the tape. You would think that the examinees just were not very bright.

Start Looking at the Raw Data Before You Get Too Far Into the Study

It is often hard to know what to make of raw data that have not been analyzed in any way. So it can be tempting not to look at the raw data before the data all have been collected and then analyzed. At that point, hopefully, they will make some kind of sense. There is a serious problem with this strategy, however. The problem is that if something is going wrong with the data, you will have no way of finding it out before it is too late.

What kinds of things can go wrong? Actually, there are quite a few. One is a result of participants not having enough time to finish all the test items, survey questions, or whatever. In this case, you may want immediately to increase the time, decrease the number of items, and then start over. But if you wait until all the data are collected, you won't know about the problem before it is too late. A second potential problem is an item or survey question that just is not working—people are omitting it or giving nonsensical answers or giving answers that contradict the results—or that produces results that do not correlate with those for other supposedly similar items. Problems with individual items can be picked up early, but only if you look at the raw data.

A third potential problem is when you have people who misunderstand the instructions and simply are giving the wrong kinds of responses. You don't want to wait until the end to figure this out. A fourth potential problem is when people are filling out forms at random, or close to it. The list goes on. The moral of the story is that you want to look at your raw data early to ensure that your project is on track.

Make Sure the Conditions in Which the Study Is Being Conducted Are Suitable

You need to check out the testing conditions. Of course, you may rely on research assistants to check out the conditions, but if you do so, make sure that you trust the assistants implicitly. Is the lighting adequate? Is the noise level sufficiently low so that participants can concentrate? Is there enough space for participants to function comfortably? Does the layout of seats discourage copying? Is there any odd odor in the room? Again, any number of things potentially can go wrong. It is your responsibility to make sure they don't.

Make Sure the Data Analyses Are Appropriate for the Data

In my experience as a journal editor, I have been surprised at the number of times investigators submit manuscripts based on data that are clearly analyzed incorrectly. Sometimes the errors are really obvious, like using a one-tailed test for an analysis that requires a two-tailed test, doing analysis of variance for independent groups even though the groups obviously are not independent, or using correlation coefficients for data that obviously have an underlying nonlinear relationship. Sometimes the errors are more subtle, such as having data analyzed by analysis of variance when there are gross violations of homogeneity of variance among groups.

None of us is likely to know every trick there is for doing optimal data analysis. But you need to make sure that you are not making mistakes that not only are embarrassing but also will lead reviewers to question whether they can trust your data.

I have found it useful always to look at raw data as well as inferential statistics. If what I see in the data does not match what I see in the data analysis, I try to figure out whether something went wrong—a miscoded variable, treatment of missing data as having a zero value, improper scoring of data, or whatever. Better to discover any such errors before you submit your article for publication, not after.

Have a Plan for Missing and Bad Data

It would be nice to do a study in which you had no missing or bad data. It's pretty rare that that happens. You need to plan in advance for what you are going to do about missing or bad data. At what point do you pronounce a case hopeless? How aberrant do data have to be for you to declare them outliers and either trim them or set them to some other value? You need to plan for this in advance, and you need to make sure that the plan you have will meet the standards of the journal to which you submit. Moreover, you have to treat all missing and bad data the same. You don't get to pick and choose what you want to do with each exemplar.

WRITING PAPERS

Start With an Elevator Speech

I talked about an elevator speech earlier in this chapter. One you have a paper ready to write up, it helps to have an elevator speech. It may not be a speech you ever will give to anyone. But it is a speech about what your big question was, why you thought the question was important, what you did to answer the question, how you did it, and what you found. The elevator speech should serve as the frame on which you build your article. Too often readers get lost in the details of an article. They may even forget why the research was done or what it was supposed to find. An elevator speech helps you make sure you know what you most want to convey, and it helps you write a paper with the critical points in mind. As you write, never lose sight of the elevator speech, and don't let your readers lose sight of it, either. It's that speech that will keep you going—and your readers going—when the going gets tough.

When You Write Up Research, Ask Yourself for Whom You Are Writing

Often we write an article and then decide what journal we want to submit it to. I encourage researchers to decide on a journal—and an audience—first. Or at least decide on two or three possible journals. Why?

First, you need to write with an audience in mind. What kinds of articles does the journal take? Empirical? Theoretical? Literature review? How many pages will you be allowed? Who is the modal reader, and what kinds of questions and answers interest them? How much background in your field of specialization does that audience have? That is, how much can you take for granted, and how much do you need to make explicit to ensure the audience understands what you are writing? What is the expected format for references? APA Style? University of Chicago? Modern Language Association? Something else? The answers to all these questions and others like them depend on the audience and the journal. Answer the questions in advance so you won't write the article up and find that you have nowhere plausible to submit it or that you have a place to submit it but it is not a place with which you really are content.

When You Write Up Research, Make Sure You Tell a Story

Many of us associate stories with fiction. We think, say, that novels tell a story, but that professional articles are different—that they are largely statements of facts and ideas associated with them. In fact, though, a good article tells a story.

I have coedited many books with contributions by many distinguished psychologists. What always has impressed me is that the best writers—and often the most eminent psychologists—realize that a good article or book chapter or book, for that matter, tells a story. You don't want to put down what they write because, as when you read a novel, you want to know how the story develops and how it ends. The others may write a coherent piece, but it is hard to discern the story they have to tell. Emulate the best: Tell a story, with a beginning, middle, and end, something readers won't want to put down.

Tell the Story That the Data Tell, Which Is Not Necessarily the Story You Planned to Tell

Remember that elevator speech you prepared for your article? By the time you're done writing the article, the elevator speech is likely to be yesterday's news. It is relatively rare that data come out just the way we expect them to, or as simply as we expect them to. What you hoped would be a simple, clean story often turns out to be a more complex and slightly muddier story.

A trap in writing an article occurs when you are tempted to write the story you had hoped the data would tell rather than the story the data actually tell. You would like to think this never happens, but it happens more often than any of us would like to admit. You need to ensure that you are faithful to your data, even if it means admitting that your hypotheses were wrong or that your hopes for your work were not realized. That's what makes science special: It is capable of empirically disconfirming what we initially believed. Some philosophers of science (e.g., Popper, 2002) believe that it is through such disconfirmation that science moves forward.

When You Write Up Research, Don't Lose the Forest for the Trees

It's easy, when writing up a scientific article, to lose the forest for the trees. In an introduction to an article, you may feel a need to cite every study ever done that is relevant to the phenomenon you studied. In writing up the method section, you may feel obliged to make sure readers know every detail of what you did so that they easily can replicate your work. In the results section, you may feel a need to describe every analysis you did and what you think it means. And in the discussion section, you may be inclined to show the relation between your work and that of anyone else you can think of whose work is vaguely relevant to your own.

All of these temptations are understandable, but they all result in an overly long, dense, and often boring article. You need to keep your eye on the ball. So in writing the introduction, you instead can decide to include only work that has a direct bearing on what you did and found. In the method section, you can tell the important details and include a footnote that a detailed description of the method is available upon request. In the results section, if there are analyses that are peripheral but nevertheless even mildly interesting, you can include them in an appendix or post them online. In the discussion section, stick to communicating the meaning of your results, how they relate to key research by others, and what the flaws or sources of incompleteness are in your work. Readers will appreciate it and will be more likely to make it through your reports.

Proofread Papers Before You Submit Them

Editors generally are paid only modest stipends for their editorial work on journals. If one were to translate their stipends into an hourly wage, they probably would be making well below minimum wage. Reviewers typically are paid nothing at all. Because editors and reviewers work for little or no money, they expect, with good reason, that authors will be respectful of the editors' and reviewers' time. One way to be disrespectful is to submit a paper chock full of typographical and other obvious errors. Reviewers do not want to be proofreaders. They do not want to correct the errors you easily could have corrected had you spent the proper time reviewing what you wrote. So be sure to check your paper for obvious errors. If you don't, you are likely to antagonize those whom you expect to review your manuscript, with less than positive results. (I proofread this book manuscript before I submitted it!)

Have At Least One Colleague Read a Paper Before You Submit It

Have you ever noticed that people who live in messy houses stop noticing the mess in their house? Ditto for people with messy desks. They not only get used to the mess, they sometimes come to value it. By the time you submit a paper for publication, you are likely to no longer notice anything messy about it—weak arguments, missing but crucial methodological facts, misinterpretation of a particular data analysis. For this reason, it is always wise to have someone else read your paper before you submit it. Better yet: Have two people read your paper. And tell them that you want feedback that is the real deal, not just feedback that will make you feel good. In my experience, it's pretty rare that a paper won't benefit at least somewhat from comments from a peer or from your students before it goes out for submission.

Make Sure the Journal to Which You Plan to Submit the Paper Is Relevant to the Topic of the Paper

Earlier in this chapter, I talked about the importance of thinking about your target audience and journal before you submit an article for publication. Before you push the button that submits the article, make sure that the journal is a fit for your paper. Usually, editors write statements saying what they are looking for, and usually, papers recently published in the target journal can give you a pretty good idea of what the journal does and does not publish. You don't want to be in a position where you submit an article and lose a few days, a few weeks, or even a few months, only to find that your article is inappropriate for the journal. In that time, you might already have been able to start on a revision of the article on the way to publication in a journal that is appropriate for what you have written.

Write in a Way That Is Comprehensible and at a Lower Level Than You Planned

I have written a number of textbooks. I have learned to start writing with chapters in the areas with which I have the least familiarity. (Earlier in my career, I did the opposite.) Why do I start with areas of lesser familiarity? Because, ironically, the areas about which I know the least are the easiest to write about. When we know an area really well, we often assume our readers have more background that they actually have about what we are writing. We forget all the information we once did not know.

In my experience, authors almost always think they are writing in a clearer, more comprehensible manner than they really are. They also think they are writing at a lower level. I am editing a textbook series now for a publisher, and getting academics to write at a level students, especially freshmen and sophomores, can understand often is like pulling teeth. No one is going to be impressed by your throwing around complex terms that you leave undefined, fancy mathematical formulas that you do not explain, or concepts that are way above the heads of your readers. Write in a way that is clear and comprehensible, and when you are done, go over what you have written to try to find all of the concepts and terms you did not sufficiently explain to readers who probably have far less background in your area of research than you do.

Make Clear Why Readers Should Be Interested in Your Research

If you are doing research in a given area, hopefully you are interested in it. If not, you are making a huge mistake and ought to reconsider what you are doing. But just because you are interested does not mean all or even any of your readers will be. I see this in my own family. My wife loves to read books about karate; I could not care less. I love to read books about numismatics (coin collecting); she could not care less. It is the same with areas of research. Do not assume that because you find your work interesting, anyone else will. You need to show the reader why he or she should be interested. How does your research relate to the reader's research, or the reader's life, or her or his general well-being? The best writers recognize that they need to motivate their reader to keep going, and often they need to do so with the abstract and then again in the first paragraph they write. If you can't get the reader right away, you may never get a second chance. The reader may be gone before he or she ever will try again.

Realize That the Hardest Papers to Get Accepted Are the Exceptionally Uncreative Ones—and the Exceptionally Creative Ones

When I started out in my career, I figured that the trick to getting papers accepted and read was to do creative work. That was then. I remember one of my advisers in my early years as a faculty member, Wendell Garner, telling me that the hardest papers to get accepted were the really uncreative ones, because they were uncreative, but also the really creative ones, because they threatened the existing scientific order. No one wants to read a paper that tells him or her that everything he or she thought for years and years was, well, wrong. No one wants to see the research he or she did quickly cast on the dust heap of history. If you do creative work, it will threaten some people, maybe many people. And the problem is, it sometimes takes just one negative or even less than wholly positive review to get an article rejected. So if you do creative work, you need to persist, often in the face of failure to get your ideas accepted or even listened to. That's always been true for creative people, and it still is.

What you can do, if you do truly creative work, is to go out of your way to show how what you have found relates to what others have found. And you can make an effort to show how what you do draws upon what others have done. The more you can fit your work into some existing framework (even if you later topple that framework), the better your chances of getting your work accepted.

* * *

Now we have talked about doing your research. Let's consider what is involved in forming and maintaining the collaborations that can help keep the work coming.

6

SETTING UP A LAB

In most new positions, you will be judged largely, although not exclusively, by your research. It therefore is essential that you set up your lab as quickly and as expeditiously as possible. The purpose of this chapter is to give you some tips for setting it up.

GET YOUR BEST START-UP OFFER

If you are going to work in a research-based institution, you may get a start-up offer for your research. In some institutions, the amount is small and fixed. You can argue until you are blue in the face, and the offer will not change. But in many institutions, the start-up offer is flexible. Unless you are one of the very few fortunate faculty members who are coming in with a research grant already in place, you will need to inure yourself to the fact that it probably will take some years before you are funded. Of course, some junior faculty members receive government grants or contracts quickly; more typically, they have to wait 3 or 4 years or more. So what you get as a start-up offer is likely to be pretty much what you will have for research in the early years of your career.

Start-ups are really important, as discussed earlier. Start-up offers also vary widely. When I started my career as an assistant professor, many years ago, I was offered $5,000. There was no negotiation. But when I was offered jobs later in my career, the start-ups were substantially larger, going into low six figures. In general, start-ups today range from about $10,000 to close to $1 million. The larger start-ups are typically for researchers in the neurosciences, who often need very expensive equipment and who sometimes have to pay their participants substantial amounts of money. The question arises, of course, as to what you can do to get a strong start-up offer.

Know the Range of Funding Within Which You Can Ask

If the range of start-ups in your institution is from $10,000 to $25,000, you don't want to start off your career on the wrong foot by asking for $100,000. You will show that you don't understand the institution or how you are going to fit into it. The research you will be able to do, at least initially, will have to fit into the start-up budget. So you want to ask for as much money as you can without sounding like a greedy pig. However, if you are worried about the range of asks, from extremely frugal to lavish spender, it is often better to be on the lavish spender side of the continuum, simply because you then have the money to do the research you wish to do.

Have a Budget

If you appear to pull a number out of a hat, you probably will not impress the chair or dean or whomever you ask for funds. You want to have a detailed budget that shows you have good judgment in requests. The requests you make should be relevant to the research you want to do. The budget should be comprehensive and clear. Generally, you will not get a second chance to ask for money, so be sure that you have put into the budget request all that you want.

Have a Budget Justification

Budget justifications are sort of boring to prepare. Actually, they are very boring to prepare. Just thinking about preparing a budget justification makes me want to drink a cup of coffee—or a glass of wine. But it is just as important as the budget. The budget justification explains why you need the money. You don't want to be nickel-and-dimed on your budget. One way to prevent that from happening is to have a comprehensive budget justification, so that anyone reading the budget will see why you requested each item in the budget. For big-ticket items, explain in even more detail why you need the money. Don't be sparing in justifying your needs. If the chair or dean wants to cut your budget, he or she is likely to start with the items you have not fully justified. Generally, the chair or dean will care more about the big-ticket items, so pay attention especially to those.

Explain How You Will Seek Outside Funding

There are few things chairs and deans like more to hear than that you plan to apply for external funding. About the only thing they like more is to hear that you actually got the external funding you applied for. But when you ask for a start-up, you would do well to make it clear that you view the request as seed money for a larger request later on to one or more external funding agencies.

In general, chairs and deans view start-ups as seed money for bigger things. What they usually do not want to hear is that, down the road, you are planning to ask them for more money to supplement the money you got as a start-up. So you already should be thinking about a later phase in which you will be seeking external funding, and perhaps say something about how your initial start-up can be used to leverage larger external funding down the road. The important thing is to show that you are serious about external funding and do not plan to be coming back for more money from the chair or dean once the initial start-up is spent.

Have a Fallback Plan

I knew what kinds of research I wanted to do my first year as an assistant professor. My problem was that my start-up was insufficient to cover the cost of doing the research. So I ended up not doing it—until I got a grant later that year. Unfortunately for you (but fortunately for me), that was back in 1976, when there actually was a decent chance an assistant professor could get major funding in his or her first year out of graduate school.

The question then became, What am I going to do, given that I do not have the funding to do the research I really want to do? I had the fallback plan that I suspect a lot of early-career assistant professors do. I wrote up my dissertation for publication, and I started doing new research that was much less expensive to run than the research in which I was most interested. Regrettably, the research did not work out. But inevitably, in a research career, there will be garden paths and dead ends, and that was one of the latter.

Consider yourself lucky if you learn early that a path is leading nowhere, as was the case for my alternative path.

What constitutes the best fallback plan (sometimes called your "Plan B") is up to you. But I have found that, in my career, it is almost always important to have a fallback plan, almost without regard to what I am doing. There just is no way of knowing whether one will get funded as one hopes (or get the articles accepted one hopes for).

Ensure There Is No Overhead on the Start-Up

Start-ups are usually taken out of college or university budgets. Because they are drawn from internal funds, institutions usually charge no indirect costs or overhead—that is, a percentage taken out of grant funds to support institutional infrastructure. Overhead varies widely across institutions and grants, ranging from 0 to as high as 70% or 80% or more. You should check to ensure that overhead will not be taken out of the start-up money, simply because overhead cuts into the funds available for you to spend.

Check on the Benefits Rate

Although overhead is usually not taken out of internal funding, such as start-up grants, benefits almost always are. Benefits are money taken out of a grant for personnel costs such as retirement plans, health plans, life insurance plans, and so forth. Benefit rates generally have been on the upswing over the years as employees have come to expect more and more benefits as a concomitant of working for an institution. Benefit rates usually apply only to some kinds of employees but not others. For example, an employee might have to work at least 51% time, or perhaps more than 20 hours a week, to receive benefits.

Be Cognizant of When the Funds Run Out

When new faculty members receive start-ups, they often want to hold onto the money as long as possible so that they can continue to use it for research, just in case they fail to receive external funds. Before planning on how long you want the money to last, make sure you know whether there is a termination date to the funds, and if so, when it is. You do not want to discover late in the game that your funds are going to expire and then desperately try to spend the money just to use it up. Or worse, you do not want to try to draw on the funds, only to discover that they have expired already.

Be Cognizant of Limitations on How You Can Spend the Funds

Institutions differ widely in what they consider to be allowable expenses for start-up funds. You need to know up front what are considered allowable expenses. Can you use the money for travel, for research assistance, for equipment? Sometimes special purchases, such as expensive equipment, have a separate approval process.

Avoid Front-Loading or Back-Loading Spending

When I received my first start-up, as a beginning assistant professor, I front-loaded, spending a large proportion of my money immediately on what would quickly turn out to be an outdated piece of equipment. A better plan would have been to allocate my spending more smoothly across the duration of the start-up, allowing myself necessary expenses along the way until I received a grant. I was lucky—I received a grant at the end of my first year as an assistant professor. But that is much harder to do in today's world, so do not count on external funding coming anytime soon.

Have a Competitive Offer

Institutions typically cannot afford a start-up package at the level you ideally would like. It often helps, however, to have a competitive offer. An institution may offer you a certain figure as a start-up package, but if you have a competitive offer with a higher start-up, the institution may be willing to match or even exceed the competitive offer. When negotiating, never give an ultimatum unless you really mean it. If you say that you expect X, Y, and Z or you will go elsewhere, then be prepared to go elsewhere if you do not get X, Y, and Z. In my experience, ultimatums are generally a mistake unless you absolutely are ready to leave if your terms are not met. Sometimes ultimatums generate in university administrators what psychologists call *reactance*: The administrators tell you to go elsewhere because they don't like the way you are negotiating and thus would rather be rid of you.

Ask to See Your Lab Space Before You Accept the Offer

I cannot count how many times I have talked to new faculty who understood one thing about their lab space, only to find that the administrators with whom they negotiated understood something else, or at least later said they did. You want to see your lab space in advance of accepting your offer, if at all possible. Take a picture of it. You may wonder what could go wrong. Actually, a lot of things can go wrong. By the time you arrive, the lab space may have been assigned to another use, given to someone else, subdivided among multiple people, or under long-term construction, to name a few. So it is important to be completely clear about the space before you arrive. Sometimes new faculty members accept assurances of a certain amount of square footage. But a given amount of square footage can be prime space or junk space. The upshot is, you need to see it in advance and have a photo or other schematic to make sure that the space you get is the space you were promised.

Check for Issues With the Lab Space Before You Arrive, and Arrange for How the Issues Will Be Corrected

Here's what you don't want: to arrive at your new job and be told that the renovation of your lab space is almost complete, only to have to ask again and again as the term moves on. The problem is that if a renovation is needed, there is no guarantee as to how long it will take. Ask that, if possible, any renovations start well before you arrive, not after you arrive. If they start only after you arrive or only soon before, you may lose valuable time you could have spent using the lab waiting for it to be finished.

Realize That You Lose Most of Your Leverage Once You Accept an Offer

Earlier in this chapter, I mentioned that a competitive offer may help you get a better start-up for your lab and its equipment. What I did not mention, and what is equally important, is that the leverage available through a competitive offer disappears the moment you accept the offer from your chosen institution, or sometimes, the moment you reject the offer from the competitive institution. You probably would like to think that your incalculable value to your new institution will be sufficient that the institution will want to give you whatever you ask for, now or forever. But a more realistic appraisal is that the institution has many demands on its resources, and so it spends money most often where it absolutely needs to spend the money. If you have not yet agreed to accept the offer, the institution needs to spend money on you to ensure you sign on the dotted line. But once you have signed, the institution moves on to its next problem, not its last problem, namely, you. So make sure that any serious negotiations are completed before you sign. The institution may well tell you just to sign—the details all can be worked out later. But they are more likely to be worked out to your advantage if you have not yet signed.

ONCE YOU ARRIVE

Set Up a Calendar for Expending Money

Whether you are using a start-up grant or other financial resources for getting your research going, you want to set up a calendar for expending money. If you do not keep careful track of your expenditures—how much they are, when they occurred, what they were for—you may find, as have so many others, that the money just kind of dribbles away. You want to control your budget, not have it control you.

Check Your Accounts at Least Once a Month

Sometimes expenditures happen of which you are not aware. Some of them may be legitimate, but some may not be. For example, you may give your copying number for research to a student, only to find that the student has been copying his course papers or other materials using the number. Or an assistant may have needed supplies for other work that he or she charged to your account, accidentally or on purpose. Or salaries may be charged to the wrong account. Avoid having your funds depleted by illegitimate expenses: Check your accounts frequently, and at least once a month.

Get It in Writing

In my experience, the administrators with whom I have negotiated have almost always told me, with respect to one thing or another, not to worry about what is or is not in writing—it all will be taken care of. The problem is that people have really bad memories, sometimes deliberately. Not only do people have bad memories, but also, administrators come and go. The administrator with whom you deal once you arrive, or shortly after you arrive, may not be the one with whom you negotiated your terms for starting your lab. If you do not have something in writing, do not assume it will happen. If it's important to you, get it written down. You'd be surprised how many misunderstandings there are, later on, over just what was agreed to orally.

Consider How Equipment Depreciates

When you are deciding what equipment to buy, consider rate of depreciation. All equipment depreciates. The only question is how fast. You don't want to spend a lot of money (like I did when I started) on a piece of equipment that will be well on its way to obsolescence by the time it arrives. With less expensive equipment, it may matter less. For example, laptop computers can be bought so cheaply these days that if they depreciate in a few years, chances are you can find the money to buy new ones. But if you are talking about more serious equipment, then you must consider just how long-term an investment it is. If you have limited funds, as almost every researcher does, don't buy equipment that will have a short shelf life.

Find Out What You Can Borrow

A way to save yourself money, particularly on expensive equipment, is to look into what you can borrow or, at worst, rent from others. If you do fMRI research, for example, you are very unlikely to have the funds (or desire) to buy your own magnet. You will want—probably before you even accept an offer—to figure out what facilities are available for doing your research, and how much using them will cost. But even for less expensive equipment, there may be senior faculty members who have been around a while, have been able to buy the equipment you need, and are not fully using that equipment. Find out first whether you can borrow or rent from them before buying your own. But remember that your use then will be at someone else's pleasure, which can be a headache for facilities that get a lot of use or for which the individuals in control of use are not maximally cooperative.

Find Free Assistance From Students

When you start out, you are unlikely to have large sums of money to hire all the people you ideally might want to hire to help in your research. I found early in my career that it sometimes is easier than one might expect to get free help that, although free, benefits the helpers as well as you by giving them valuable research experience. Where is this free help? First, you can ask undergraduate or graduate students in courses you teach whether they would be interested in research experience. Preferably, have them sign up for a research seminar or listing so that they can gain credit for their participation in the research. Second, you can post advertisements in your department seeking research help. Third, new faculty members are sometimes invited to give seminars in the departments they join. Use this as an opportunity to advertise your research program. Fourth, there may be neighboring colleges or universities where faculty teach heavy loads and do not have time for research and where there are students who would be interested in doing research with you. These are just some of the methods you can use to recruit student assistants.

Warning: Do not just agree to work with whoever comes along. As a new faculty member, you may be desperate for help. But check references. Bad research assistants are worse than none at all. I find this out constantly, even in late career. I recently had a research assistant who lost the key to the lab, lost the key to the filing cabinet where the cash box was kept, presented receipts that did not fully match the payments that were made . . . well, you get the idea. Verify his or her credentials to the extent possible before agreeing to work with a student.

Write a Grant Proposal as Soon as Possible

During your initial time as a faculty member, you will have much too much to do. You most likely will have courses to prepare and teach, students to meet, committees on which to serve or other administrative obligations you agree to, a dissertation to write up, and any number of other things on your plate, including, most likely, moving into new quarters. A grant proposal always will be among the easier things to put off. Yet, to get your research truly going, chances are you will want a grant (unless your work is purely theoretical or historical or just super inexpensive). Try to put the grant proposal at high priority. Not only will it really kick-start your research; it most likely will count a lot when you come up for tenure and promotion. Institutions almost always prefer faculty members who bring in their own funding.

Allocate Your Research Between Risky and Safe Projects

If you want to make a splash in the field, you need to take some risks in your research. Safe research usually is not the research that changes the way scientists think about a field. At the same time, if you want to make sure you have the publications you need for tenure and promotion, you need to do some safe research that pretty much assures you that you will get some publishable work into print. The best way to run a research career is to have a portfolio of projects, some of which are safer and some of which are more risky. This is essentially what good investors do when they invest their money: They put some of it into safe assets, like money market funds, and some of it into more risky investments, like small-cap stocks. By balancing the risk levels of your portfolio of projects, you ensure that you will have at least some publications at the same time that you allow yourself the opportunity to make a splash, should one of the riskier projects pay off.

Collaborate With Other Labs

Especially early on, collaborating with researchers in other labs can give you a head start in producing publishable work. It may also lead to collaborative opportunities for grant proposals. Moreover, it may provide an opportunity for you to work with, and learn from, more senior investigators. As always, there are some caveats. First, investigate potential collaborators, even senior ones, to ensure that they are people you can smoothly work with. For example, you don't want to collaborate with someone who is a credit hog. Second, beware of acquiring the role of "junior collaborator" to so-and-so. When you come up for promotion and tenure, committee members will be examining whether you have established yourself as an independent researcher. You don't want to seem to be someone's junior assistant, especially if that person is someone, such as an adviser, from your graduate or postdoctoral institution.

Treat Lab Members With Respect

Junior faculty members are almost always under great pressure to publish. Moreover, they know that not only publications count, but also order of authorship. For promotion and tenure committees, it usually matters whether you are a senior or junior author on a given publication. Inevitably, there will be junior faculty members who make the mistake of putting their careers well ahead of the careers of their students. The faculty members may take on senior authorships they really don't deserve, or demand their students work overly long hours, or have students do menial tasks, or even worse (and less commonly), steal ideas from students. These tactics represent a foolish game because it gets around who exploits students and who, in contrast, seeks only the best for them. If you become known as an exploiter, future students are less likely to want to work with you, and your department may be less likely to want to keep you because of the reputation you have acquired for looking out for yourself before anyone else.

Be Especially Nice to and Respectful of the Business Manager and Office Staff

Academic institutions are notorious for the salience of their hierarchies. In many institutions, full professors are at the top of the hierarchy, followed by associate and then assistant professors, then postdocs, then graduate students, then undergraduate students. Academic staff members do not quite fit into the hierarchy and often are viewed as there to serve everyone else. But these staff members can make your life either very easy or incredibly difficult. Almost all junior faculty rely on the staff for various things, and if you treat the staff nicely and with respect, you may find that they treat you ever so much better than if you act like the staff are your personal servants.

Make Requests for Resources a Plea for a Common Good, Not Just Your Own

When requesting resources from your department, see whether you can make the request not just about your personal good but also about the good of others—students, other faculty, the department, the institution, or whatever. Department members have no difficulty recognizing faculty members who are selfish, and they generally try to stay away from them. At worst, they may try to thwart their requests because they believe the requests represent only an individual good, not a common good. So ask yourself how any request or even statement you make may look to others. Do you come across as a team player or as someone looking out only for himself or herself?

Be Careful With Students Who Come to You From Other Advisers

When you start as a new faculty member, chances are you will have no students. The first students who approach you may end up being students who have been unsuccessful with one or more other advisers and are seeking someone new with whom to work. Such students can be valuable assets to your lab if there simply was a mismatch of personality or interests between the student and the former adviser. But at least some of these students may be ones who will get along with absolutely no one, because they are not motivated, or lack initiative, or lack independence, or in the worst case lack integrity. Be especially careful, therefore, in accepting students into your lab from other advisers. This does not mean you should reject them. Rather, it means you should first talk to their former adviser and maybe to some other faculty members who know them to ensure you are not getting students with whom you will have no more success than did the previous adviser or advisers.

Think About the Bang You Can Get for the Buck, Focusing on Value Rather Than Cost

When you spend money, ask yourself how much bang you can get for the buck. You need to think not only of the cost of a particular employee or item but also of how much benefit the person or item will bring to your research endeavor. Some things may be cheap but not even worth their low cost. Others may be expensive and worth something, but not what you have to pay for them. So concentrate on value rather than cost.

Promptly Report Irregularities of Any Kind to the Proper Authorities

When things go wrong or seem to go wrong, report them to the proper authorities. If a student accuses you of something, consider talking to your chair at once. Don't wait for the student to get there first. If you feel you have to accuse a student of inappropriate behavior, seek guidance from your chair or dean. In my days as an administrator, I found that when things went seriously amiss, it was usually because a faculty member thought he or she "could handle it." These days, one never knows what will lead to disciplinary actions or even lawsuits. Students have different and higher expectations than in the past, and sometimes these expectations clash with what faculty members believe is realistic. When things start to go wrong, don't just hope for the best. Report them to the appropriate authority and seek help. For example, if a student questions whether you are acting appropriately toward him or her, you don't want to wait to see whether the student reports you to the chair or dean. Get there first.

What You Can Do If an Institution Reneges

Sometimes institutions renege on promises, even written ones. What can you do? Unfortunately, the answer is sometimes "not much." You can report to the next higher authority than the one who reneged, or you may be able to complain to an ombudsman, or you may in extreme cases end up in arbitration or even in court. But in any job, some things will not go according to plan. If an institution reneges on a promise, you have to decide how important the promise is. If it is important, you may choose to do something. Or you may choose to wait. But if it becomes a pattern, your best bet is not to lodge one complaint after another. It is to start looking for your next job!

* * *

Now that we've talked about setting up a lab; let's move on to forming collaborations, another aspect of your success.

7

FORMING COLLABORATIONS

Collaborations are a great way of getting research done and also can be highly effective in teaching. The emphasis in this chapter is on research collaborations, although much of the chapter applies to teaching collaborations as well. In my own case, the large majority of my empirical publications have been collaborative, and I think my career would have been much diminished had I not had the opportunity to collaborate over the years with a broad range of individuals.

At the same time, collaborations involve risks that are not present in individual endeavors. This chapter discusses some of those risks and also ways of minimizing and, in some cases, coping with them.

---

http://dx.doi.org/10.1037/0000013-008
Starting Your Career in Academic Psychology, by R. J. Sternberg
Copyright © 2017 by the American Psychological Association. All rights reserved.

EMPHASIZE NEW COLLABORATIONS

If you are early in your career, as mentioned in Chapter 5, you are better off emphasizing new rather than old collaborations. That is not to say that you should never work with collaborators from graduate school and any possible postdoctoral years, but rather to say that tenure committees get nervous when they see new faculty continuing to collaborate extensively with former collaborators and mentors. You need to find new collaborators and emphasize those collaborations. Once you get tenure, you can do pretty much as you please.

There is another reason to seek new collaborations, namely, that you are starting out in a new phase of your career. Once you (hopefully) publish your dissertation, you and others are going to expect new things to come from you, not just extensions of the dissertation. New collaborators will likely open your eyes to new problems and new ways of seeing old ones. If some of those new collaborations are with colleagues in your present institution, the collaborations also will provide a way for you to get to know your new colleagues and learn to work with them.

SEEK OUT PEOPLE WHO DO WELL WHAT YOU DO POORLY OR NOT AT ALL

If there is a fundamental principle of interpersonal attraction, it is that we tend to be attracted to people who are similar to ourselves. For example, cognitive psychologists tend to seek out cognitive psychologists, members of a political party tend to seek out others of the same party, people interested in collecting stamps reach out to other stamp collectors, people who are from urban backgrounds often seek out others from urban backgrounds. Effective research (and teaching) collaborations, however, typically play by another set of rules.

Research, particularly complex research, always requires an abundance of diverse skills—synthesizing past literature, designing studies, running studies, interpreting data, writing up data, and much more. Almost no one excels in every possible skill that research requires. Moreover, many research projects require far-flung knowledge. The upshot is that you are best off seeking out collaborators who are good at what you are not good at. Find people who complement you, not just people like you. Such collaborations often are more challenging, because the more different people in a group are, the more they are likely to see things in different ways and potentially to argue about them. But in the long run, projects with mild amounts of conflict often end up better off because issues are discussed and resolved that otherwise might be neglected and come out only when it is too late—after the research is published.

LOOK TO OTHER DEPARTMENTS AND SCHOOLS

When we do research, we sometimes ask who in our department, perhaps among the students or other faculty, would be able to collaborate with us on a particular project. But sometimes the best collaborators are somewhat farther away. They may be in other departments, other schools, or even other countries.

My collaborators and I have done research on five continents. Some of my best collaborations have been not only with psychologists but also with anthropologists, economists, educators, parasitologists, medical doctors, and others whose expertise and talents are very different from my own. As a team, we have been able to do research that I never would have been able to do individually or even in a team comprising just psychologists.

ACTIVELY SEEK OUT STUDENT COLLABORATORS

When I started out as an assistant professor, I eagerly awaited the opportunity to work with students, both graduate and undergraduate. And I waited and I waited, until I realized that, for students, I was an unknown quantity. They knew virtually nothing about me. I realized that if I was going to get students to work with me, I would have to seek them out. So I started talking with students about my research where it was relevant—in my classes, in talks sponsored by student organizations, in internal colloquia. Eventually, I acquired a team. But it would have been a very slow process had I been merely reactive and not also proactive.

That said, it's important to be discriminating in forming collaborations. You don't want to collaborate with whoever just happens to come your way. A problem early-career faculty face is that the first students who come to them may be students who have failed to work successfully with other faculty members. In some cases, such failures are because the faculty members truly were difficult to work with. But in other cases, inevitably, there are students who cannot work successfully with any faculty member—who are essentially tossed around from one faculty member to another. Such students often take up a lot of time that, in the long run, proves not to be time that is productively spent. So you want to ensure that the time you spend is spent wisely, working with students with whom a collaboration will prove to be mutually beneficial.

MAKE PROCEDURAL AGREEMENTS IN ADVANCE

Procedural agreements define who is going to do what, how. You definitely want to figure out who is going to do what, how, before you start a collaborative project. You may not be able to assign work in all its details, but you need general understandings of who will do what and how they will do it. The reason is that what is not explicitly assigned will be implicitly assigned. That is, collaborators will make assumptions about who is responsible for what aspects of the project. It may seem obvious who is going to do what—until it's not and there is a dispute.

Sometimes collaborators fail to make explicit procedural agreements because they find it uncomfortable or even embarrassing. There may be a sense that the details can be worked out later. The problem is that later may never come, or may come only when there is a dispute and there is no basis for resolving the dispute because agreements were not worked out in advance.

Sometimes things may seem obvious that later turn out not to be so obvious. For example, in one instance I was involved in a collaboration with a student, and I thought we had worked out the details. I later discovered, to my chagrin, that the student assumed I would be testing the participants. Well, that sure had never happened before! But it would have been very easy to make clear in advance who would be doing what, including collecting the data.

HAVE AN ADVANCE SYSTEM FOR SHARING CREDIT

The American Psychological Association (2016) provides general guidelines for determining authorship. The basic idea is that authorship represents a professional and scientific contribution to work and that one takes credit only for work actually performed. Moreover, the status of an individual should have no impact on his or her authorship. That is, one does not get extra credit, say, for being a full professor rather than assistant professor or being an assistant professor rather than a graduate student. In theory, then, one would hope that authorship disputes would never arise.

Of course, authorship disputes, or at least disagreements, do arise. How do you trade off, for example, the value of writing up a report versus designing a study? Moreover, when groups come up with an idea, each member may give himself or herself more credit than do others. An analogy is housework. When couples are asked what percentage of the housework each of them does, the total percentage inevitably ends up exceeding 100, with each individual viewing himself or herself as having done more than half the work.

Most scientists do not find it enjoyable or even comfortable talking about how credit for a collaboration will be assigned. But it is far better to have the conversation before the work occurs than after. The conversation can take a variety of forms.

One form the conversation can take is for credit to be allocated after the work is done on the basis of who did what. In that case, collaborators should have at least a general agreement as to how much various aspects of the project count. For example, how much does it count to come up with the idea, design the research, analyze the data, write up the report, and so forth? Sometimes collaborators are not sure who will do what, but they should have a general understanding of how much each activity counts.

A second form such a conversation can take is that it is agreed in advance that one member of the team will be first author (or second, or last, or whatever). For example, sometimes with invited chapters, the invitee is instructed that he or she may take on coauthors but that he or she must be first author. In these cases, collaborators need to agree to be willing to take the remaining authorship slots. If they are not, they should not enter into the project.

A third form is to agree on a system for allocating credit that is unrelated to contribution, such as alphabetical order of authors' last names. When this system is used, it is common to include a footnote indicating that the order of names is alphabetical. The advantage of this system is that it precludes arguments about who did what. The disadvantage, of course, is that it does not specify who did what. A supplement to this system is to indicate in a footnote exactly who did what so that it is clear from the footnote what the respective contributions of the authors were.

FOR MULTI-INSTITUTION COLLABORATIONS, MAKE SURE ALL REGULATIONS OF ALL INSTITUTIONS ARE FOLLOWED

Multi-institution collaborations are essential in certain large projects, such as multisite tests of the cognitive or personality effects of a new therapy or drug. Such collaborations are also complex and sometimes messy. Different institutions inevitably have somewhat different rules that need to be followed. Typically, there is a primary institution—such as the one where the principal investigator is housed—and the rules of that institution are especially important. But no institution will give up its own rules in favor of those of another institution. For example, if an institution has an ethical code for research, it is not going to forgo that code and use that of another institution, especially in an area that potentially might give rise later to litigation. Nothing gets an institution into hot water faster than when it does not follow its own rules. So all coinvestigators or collaborators need to make sure that they are within the parameters of the rules of their home institution and those of the institution of the principal investigator, and they may need also to be sure not to run afoul of any other institution where a violation could mean a team in the project being forced to drop out.

SEEK A COMMON GOOD

In my experience, academics are socialized to seek one good above all others—their own. It's not that anyone ever says to be self-focused or selfish or even narcissistic, but tenure and promotion and most salary increases are awarded for individual work, and the lesson is not lost on most academics. The result is that the academic always has to keep his or her own interests in mind, lest the academic be a victim of baseball player and manager Leo Durocher's saying that "Nice guys finish last."

When you get one or more individuals in a collaboration who are always looking out for Number 1, the collaboration quickly goes sour. It becomes obvious to both, and to everyone else, that the collaboration is a sham effort on the part of the individuals merely to advance their own interests. Such collaborations usually are not successful because they are not "collaborations" in any real sense of the word.

I have engaged in many collaborative ventures over the years and have found that the best results are virtually always when each collaborator seeks the common good of the collaboration and the collaborators. This is a case of a rising tide raising all ships. Some people may find it odd that subordinating your own interests can actually serve your self-interests. But all you have to do is engage in one collaboration in which an individual is primarily self-concerned to see how much time and energy are absorbed catering to the individual instead of doing what is best for the project as a whole.

FROM TIME TO TIME, BE WILLING TO TAKE ONE FOR THE TEAM

Collaborations, especially ones with multiple teams, sometimes involve shared resources. For example, five teams working in different institutions may need money to pay participants, money for salaries, and equipment to make the joint study viable. Often there is a zero-sum aspect to such collaborations when some teams get resources that other teams believe that they need and may feel that they deserve more than the teams that in fact got the resources. I have been in this position multiple times. On one joint project, I felt that the main team was keeping more of the funds than would have been ideal. But I realized that if I started arguing about distribution of resources, it would harm the collaboration and divert our efforts from getting the research done. And we did get the research done. I took one for the team, and I still believe I did the right thing.

DON'T MAKE IT A HABIT TO TAKE ONE FOR THE TEAM

On the one hand, you need to be willing to take one for the team. On the other hand, you don't want to put yourself in a position in which you are doing this regularly and without a break. At a certain point, your collaborators may start to take advantage of you because you make it so easy to do so. They even may come to feel that because you are not speaking up, you are happy with the allocation of resources, or at least that you are getting what you believe you deserve. So, you need to know when it is time to speak up. You may feel it is disgraceful that people would want to take advantage of you. At the same time, if you create a situation in which it is easy for them to do, they soon may start believing that you are getting your fair share and that you feel that you are.

UNDERSTAND CULTURAL DIFFERENCES

When we think about cultural differences, we often think about people who live far away, maybe in France, or even in Egypt or Kenya. But cultural differences are not merely or even primarily about place of residence, but rather about different accepted practices for adapting to, shaping, and selecting environments.

There really are major differences among cultures in the world. In my African collaborations, the layers of red tape sometimes seemed insurmountable. Moreover, my collaborators were often used to working at a slower pace than my team was used to. They probably thought we were rushing the project and perhaps introducing errors because we were in such a hurry.

I remember a project in Venezuela where a small difference in cultural customs was a source of consternation to me: I was talking to a collaborator, and he kept moving closer to me. I then moved away because his closeness—his "social distance"—made me uncomfortable. We ended up doing an uncomfortable and unexpected dance. At that point in time, I just did not realize that acceptable social distances in Venezuela, at least then, were considerably closer than they were in the United States at that time.

Such differences often exist between institutions. One institution may emphasize teaching, another research. One institution may be willing, another not, to give buyouts for courses or to lower teaching loads in the face of other major responsibilities, such as editing a journal or engaging in a major grant-funded project.

The greatest differences, however, I have found to be between disciplines. In work with economists, for example, I often felt frustrated by what I felt was the emphasis of my collaborators on seeing so much of human behavior as motivated by maximizing economic outcomes. In some cases in which they were seeing a problem that way, I did not think the participants saw any particular monetary gain from what they were doing. No doubt, the economists were equally frustrated by my emphasis on behavioral principles. Similarly, working with educators was sometimes a challenge. They were very concerned about making sure that children all learned as much as possible, sometimes to the extent that they were willing to contaminate a treatment for a control group to ensure that the control group got the same (hopefully) great instruction as did the experimental group. Likely, those educators saw me as cold-blooded for withholding from control students a program that might be helpful to them. And then there were the cultural anthropologists with whom I collaborated, who, I thought, sometimes emphasized cultural differences so much that they failed to see the similarities. I'm sure they thought that I was trying to homogenize cultural differences.

My point is not that my culture, as a psychological scientist, was better than the other cultures, but rather that the cultures were different in sometimes frustrating ways. Moreover, I learned a heck of a lot from observing the cultural differences. I would not give up the experiences for anything, but at the times the differences occurred, none of them led me immediately to wish for more.

Sometimes cultural differences are temporal rather than spatial. A challenge in teaching and research is dealing with students who have grown up in an era very different from the one in which I grew up. Is it OK today to be having a conversation with someone who is constantly staring at his or her cell phone? Is it OK for students to be shopping on the Internet while I am teaching a class? I don't know. I actually have talked to my classes about these issues—asked them not to use cell phones and not to shop or use social media during class. Was I doing the right thing? Or were they thinking that I'm a relic of the past? Beats me. But I'm still asking them not to do e-mail or shop during class!

BEWARE OF SOCIAL LOAFING

Some of my research projects have involved many different and diverse collaborators. Like others involved in such collaborations, I have had to confront the problem of social loafing. *Social loafing* occurs when some people in a multiperson effort do less than their share because they can, or think they can, get away with it. A group sing-along is an example. Inevitably, the volume of the singing reflects some voices much more than others, and not just because some of the voices are better than others.

If I had an optimal solution to the problem of social loafing, I probably would not be writing this book as I would be ensconced on my personal island in the Caribbean drinking rum punches and taking in the rays of the sun. But a decent solution is to have conversations with social loafers to understand how they believe they are contributing. Such conversations are important to help smooth over resentments and, at times, exploitation that may arise when some collaborators want credit for doing less than their share of the work.

The results of such conversations are variable. Sometimes the loafers drop out. Sometimes the hard workers drop out. And in some cases, the loafers start putting in their full share of work, or something closer to it.

KEEP IN MIND THAT TOO MANY COOKS SPOIL THE BROTH

Academics are rightfully taught to think for themselves. In a collaboration, you always can think for yourself, but you can't always act for yourself. As mentioned above, you need to achieve a common good. Sometimes that means you need to be the cook's assistant, even if you are the leader of a project. If you insist on having your own way in every group decision, you will encourage a defensive reaction on the part of other collaborators and probably will find that people don't want to collaborate with you the next time around, with the possible exception of some undergraduates who just want to be told what to do. Even in their case, however, always telling them what to do and how to do it is no favor: You can't teach people to think independently by controlling their every move.

PUT IN PLACE AN ESCAPE CLAUSE FOR YOURSELF AND OTHER COLLABORATORS

Most collaborations, no matter how challenging, work out well in the end. Of course, the key word in the previous sentence is *most*. In the course of a career, some collaborations will go better than others. And possibly some will be downright awful.

There are different degrees of awfulness. Pretty close to the top of the awfulness scale was a collaboration by a professor at an Ivy League university with a junior colleague from the West Coast. The junior person convinced the professor to put his name on a paper that eventually was accepted by a highly prestigious journal. Before long, it turned out that the junior collaborator had falsified data. A national scandal ensued, causing great embarrassment for the professor and his institution. Suffice it to say, the professor will not be collaborating with that individual again.

But collaborations can go bad for many reasons. Certainly unethical behavior is one. Another is a collaborator who does not come through with his or her share of the work, or a collaborator who may be just impossible to work with, or a collaborator who makes demands you cannot meet. The bottom line is that you need to have an escape clause—a way of extricating yourself from truly disastrous collaborations. You do not want to exit from collaborations on anything close to a regular basis. But if things are going seriously wrong and your efforts to repair them are failing, consider parting ways.

How do you leave a bad collaboration? The best way, I have found, is simply to tell your collaborator that the collaboration is not working as you had hoped and that you need to move on. Don't go into detail about all the things that have gone wrong—once it's over, it's over, and explanations often just make things worse. By the time you get to this point, you already should have had all the conversations about saving the project, and if you reach the final point, you should be past soul-searching conversations.

Why don't people regularly leave bad collaborations? There may be many reasons, but almost certainly one is the sunk cost fallacy. You feel that you have invested so much in the collaboration that you just don't want to throw away the investment. But when an investment is going bad, what may have happened in the past is a sunk cost: You never can recover it, no matter what you do in the future. In the case of truly awful collaborations, you may spare your mental and perhaps physical health by getting out while you still can. There always are other things to do in, and with, your life.

KEEP IN MIND THE POTENTIAL PERILS OF COMMITTEE DECISIONS

With large-scale collaborations, there sometimes is a committee, or even several committees, charged with making decisions for the entire group. Such is life: Committees do much of the work of a university. The risk with any committee is that it starts to indulge in what Janis (1972) called *groupthink*. Groupthink involves people coming to a uniform decision not because it is a good decision but rather because they feel pressure to conform to a group norm. Groups may enforce a harsh standard of intellectual conformity: Individuals who dissent are chided, reprimanded, punished, or even removed from the group. If you are in such a group, you want to ask yourself whether the decisions being made are optimal ones or rather are ones that represent some kind of imposed group consensus. Or, if you are affected by such decisions, you might want to ask whether the decisions are in your best interest, or anyone's.

MAKE SURE YOU KNOW WHOM YOU ARE WORKING WITH

The Ivy League professor mentioned earlier in this chapter obviously did not engage in due diligence in his choice of a collaborator. You should. Ask for references. You don't have to do it in an overt way. You merely need to inquire regarding who the potential collaborator or collaborators have worked with in the past, what (if anything) they have published from those collaborations, and who funded the collaborations. If you have an informal network, use it. Performing due diligence can be worth its weight in gold in preventing collaborations that are likely to go wrong.

CHECK THE DATA

No matter whom you are working with, it is a good idea to check the data you receive from them. Do the same for your own data! When we have research assistants collect or enter data, we spot-check the data. Although it is not a particularly enjoyable task, it can prevent major embarrassments later on. Anyone, including you, can make mistakes. Better to catch them soon after you receive the data than after the data are published.

Anyone who has done research knows that there are many points in the research process at which errors can be made. The best way to avoid their becoming permanent is to find them as soon as possible after they are made.

SET DEADLINES

No one likes deadlines. Everyone needs deadlines. Faculty members, in a way, are strange creatures: They often are quite strict in setting deadlines for their students but are reluctant to set or at least enforce deadlines for themselves. I have edited a lot of books—more than 100—and it is the rare book in which all the contributors have their chapters in by the deadline. Offhand, I cannot think of even one case, although there may well have been one.

When it is just one individual working for himself or herself, deadlines may matter less. After all, if you are late, you have only yourself to blame, and only you experience the consequences. But if there are multiple collaborators involved in a project, one person's being late holds up everyone else. Be on time in meeting deadlines.

IF GRANT FUNDING IS INVOLVED, BE AWARE OF THE GRANTOR'S AND PRINCIPAL INVESTIGATOR'S EXPECTATIONS

When you receive money through a grant or contract, there typically are many restrictions on the ways you can spend money and also in the activities that are permissible or not permissible. When I was starting out in my career, things were much looser. That was then. Today there can be severe penalties for violating procedures, such as spending money for one grant on activities for another grant or for unfunded activities. You therefore need to know the rules and make sure you follow them scrupulously. The risk of not doing so is losing all the money and facing disciplinary action as well.

BE TRANSPARENT

In a collaboration, there are few things more important than transparency. People don't want to be guessing about what you are doing, how you are doing it, and why you are doing it the way you are doing it. When collaborators are nontransparent, they tend to arouse the suspicions of others, even if they are doing nothing wrong. Don't encourage suspicions: Keep your operation totally transparent and available for inspection to anyone authorized to inspect it.

* * *

Now that we have talked about collaborations, let's talk about one area of academic work that almost always involves collaboration—getting a grant.

8

GETTING A GRANT

I started as an assistant professor in 1975. My department gave me $5,000 in seed money as a start-up for my research. At that point, I had no extramural (outside) funding at all. A quarter century later, I had over $6 million in extramural grants. But there was nothing smooth about going from having no grant money to having a lot of it. There were some years that I seemed to have the golden in touch in getting grants, and other years in which everything I touched seem to turn to lead. Oddly, I never could predict which grant proposals would get funded, even after years of experience writing proposals.

That is the first lesson you need to learn about securing research grants. The grant-getting process is uncertain: One never knows which grant proposals

---

Portions of this chapter are from (a) *The Compleat Academic: A Career Guide, Second Edition* (pp. 169–184), by J. M. Darley, M. P. Zanna, and H. L. Roediger (Eds.), 2004, Washington, DC: American Psychological Association, and (b) *Writing Successful Grant Proposals From the Top Down and the Bottom Up* (pp. 3–24), by R. J. Sternberg (Ed.), 2013, Newbury Park, CA: Sage. Adapted with permission.

http://dx.doi.org/10.1037/0000013-009
Starting Your Career in Academic Psychology, by R. J. Sternberg
Copyright © 2017 by the American Psychological Association. All rights reserved.

will be funded, or even how long one's funding will last. It is not uncommon for budgets to be cut in midstream, leaving the principal investigator with expenses and commitments that were made in good faith but that no longer can be met. Worse, those multiyear projects can disappear at the drop of a hat if Congress decides, for one reason or another, not to budget certain funds or if a foundation decides that its interests have changed and your work is no longer of interest to them.

Although the funding landscape is fraught with booby traps, there are steps you can take to maximize your chances of avoiding those traps—of securing and maintaining your funding, at least to the extent possible. This chapter discusses some of those steps (Gorsevski, 2015; Sternberg, 2004a, 2013a, 2013b).

Before making suggestions, I should add that my comments are based on experiences (a) I have had seeking funding, (b) my colleagues have had seeking funding, (c) I have had reviewing grants, and (d) I have had serving on a panel that funded research (sponsored by the Air Force Office of Scientific Research [AFOSR]). I hope my experiences are helpful. But do not limit yourself to learning from my experience! Talk with others in your department or unit who are experienced in getting grants, and ask them for tips. You might even ask to see their old grant proposals, just to get a concrete sense of what successful proposals look like.

In the granting enterprise, to some extent, you make your own luck. First, let's consider why you should apply for a grant. Next, let's discuss the kinds of organizations that fund research and the difference between a grand and a contract. Then let's talk about the actual process of getting funded, including techniques to maximize the chances of your getting funded.

There are many different kinds of grants. Some grants fund research, but others instead fund travel, teaching, or development of particular commercial products. This chapter focuses on research grants.

WHY APPLY FOR A RESEARCH GRANT?

Why should you apply for a research grant? There are several reasons.

Money for Research

First, a grant will provide you with funds to do your research. Even relatively inexpensive research costs something, and having a research grant helps ensure that you can get done the research you would like to do. Even if you do relatively inexpensive research, having a grant means you will no longer have to rely on departmental funds or perhaps your own.

Money to Support Students

Second, research grants help support students. Many graduate students and postdoctoral fellows are supported partly or exclusively by research grants, and without such grants, some members of the next generation of researchers might never have the opportunity to be trained. Moreover, you are helping your department by investing your grant funds in students so that the department (or university) can invest in other things.

Reallocation of Responsibilities

Third, a research grant can free you from responsibilities you may wish to delegate to others. For example, you may use the research grant to pay someone other than yourself to test participants or to prepare stimulus materials under your direction. Although there are fun parts of research, copying documents, coding data, and preparing each and every piece of research material are probably not among those fun activities but rather are ones you would rather delegate to others who are paid through grants.

Summer Salary

Fourth, research grants can provide you with summer salary if your institution pays you for less than 12 months. Many universities do, in fact, pay salaries for less than 12 months. A research grant can provide 1, 2, or sometimes even 3 months of summer support, thus supplementing the researcher's income. Of course, when you take summer salary, you are expected to work on the research during the time you are drawing the salary. Many investigators find that, as a result of teaching obligations, it is hard to devote the time they would wish to research during the 9 or so months in which they are teaching. So having summer support can greatly accelerate one's research enterprise while providing needed funds for living expenses.

Scholarly Reputation

Finally, obtaining a research grant marks you as a serious (and fundable!) scholar and can help you when it comes time for promotion and tenure decisions. At a major research institution, getting a grant may be a sine qua non for promotion or tenure. Even at an institution that emphasizes teaching, having a research grant can set you apart from your colleagues.

Thus, it makes sense to apply for a research grant as soon as you possibly can once you begin your career. Some scholars even apply during their postdoctoral years in order to get a head start on their research.

WHO FUNDS RESEARCH, AND HOW DO THEY FUND IT?

There are many different kinds of funding organizations. Some of these organizations are very specific in the kinds of research they fund, whereas others are more general. The main types of organizations that fund university research are universities themselves, government organizations, nongovernmental organizations, foundations, and corporations.

Intramural (Internal) Grants

Universities often have limited funds to support the research of their own students and faculty members. These funds may be available to anyone who applies or may be available only to certain individuals, such as new faculty members, junior faculty members, or faculty members who have not succeeded in gaining external support. The funds are typically awarded on a competitive basis. Universities are often willing and eager to provide first small seed grants to new faculty, so be sure to check on the availability of funding from your own institution.

In my experience, universities are more likely to provide funds to early-career researchers than to later-career researchers, on the view that those in their early career need some initial funding to kick-start their careers. However, there are various kinds of exceptions. For example, at Tufts, a university where I was a dean, my colleagues and I in the office of the dean of arts and sciences initiated a program to help senior faculty who had gotten off track in their research to get back on track again. At a subsequent university where I was a provost, Oklahoma State, my colleagues and I in the office of the provost initiated a program of funding for planning grants to support creative interdisciplinary research that helps to support the land-grant mission of the university. In sum, it always pays to check whether there are special intramural programs in your institution that will fund your research, no matter where you are in your career.

Extramural (External) Grants

Government Organizations

Government funding organizations are sponsored by national, state, and local governments. Examples of government organizations in the United States are the National Science Foundation (NSF), the National Institutes of Health (NIH), the military (e.g., Army Research Institute, Office of Naval Research), and the U.S. Department of Education (e.g., Institute for Educational Science). National organizations such as these have regular grant competitions, and you can find out about these competitions either through your grants and contracts office or through the agencies' websites. State and local government organizations may have research funds but not have regular competitions for them. Many agencies, especially NSF and NIH, have special grant opportunities available only for early-career investigators. The exact programs change. Find out what programs are especially tailored to your early stage of career.

Government grants are typically for 3 years, although they may be for less time (e.g., 1 year) or for more time (typically up to 5 years). It is important to realize that a commitment by the government to fund your research for a specified period of years does not guarantee you will actually get the funding you were promised. Many variables can intervene. The agency's budget may be cut, resulting in your budget's being reduced or sometimes even eliminated. The agency may be dissatisfied with your progress and terminate your funding (which is relatively rare but does happen). Or the agency may change its priorities and decide your project no longer fits its goals. You should thus be optimistic that commitments to you will be met, but you should by no means feel certain of it.

Most grants require progress reports at least once a year, and it behooves you to do such reports with the utmost care and to put your research in the most positive light possible. Some agencies also conduct site visits: Members of a team come to the site of the research in order to evaluate the quality of the work. These visits also should be taken very seriously.

As you will learn in later chapters, government organizations have diverse programs. Some fund only research of a particular kind or in a particular area. Others are more wide ranging. Grants.gov is a source of information about a wide variety of government grants. Typically, there are many steps in submitting grant proposals to government agencies, so it behooves you to start the process of preparing the proposal early. The best way to start is to look on the appropriate website to see what is available and to determine what might be a good match to your own research. It is also an excellent idea to talk with a relevant program officer before you start writing to ascertain his or her views on the appropriateness of your ideas for the particular program he or she heads.

My best experience with a government grant was my first: I was funded by NSF my first year as an assistant professor, despite the fact that the grant proposal I wrote was anything but exemplary. I learned then that granting agencies often go out of their way to fund new investigators if they possibly can. My worst experience was with the Department of Education: We got all excellent ratings from outside reviewers, something that had never happened to me before. But the program director turned down the grant because she thought it too similar to another proposal we had submitted that they had funded. We pointed out that the other grant proposal had not, in fact, been funded. After further investigation, she conceded this fact, but unwilling to admit she had made a mistake—an event not uncommon in life—she refused to reconsider.

Nongovernmental Organizations

Nongovernmental organizations are entities that are not tied to any one government or that are tied to multiple governments but are run somewhat independently of these governments. Examples of nongovernmental organizations are the World Bank, the North Atlantic Treaty Organization, and the World Health Organization. These organizations are less likely to have regular funding competitions, and you need to consult their websites or, if you have contacts, individuals within the organizations to find out about funding opportunities.

My best experience with a nongovernmental organization was funding that created a program for enhancing the intelligence of Venezuelan college students. The proposal was a real shot in the dark, and this grant gave me an opportunity to visit Venezuela several times in the early 1980s, to learn Spanish, and to write a book that I otherwise never would have written. My worst experience was with the same organization. When the political party in power was thrown out, I learned that the nongovernmental organization was not as nongovernmental as I had thought. The new president had campaigned on the silliness of programs to increase intelligence and indicated he would not support them if elected. When he was elected, the "nongovernmental" organization proved to be more "governmental" than we had thought, and that was the end of the funding.

Foundations

Foundations are privately owned and operated and typically are more targeted and mission oriented than governments in the particular kinds of research they will fund. Examples of foundations are the Spencer Foundation, the W. T. Grant Foundation, the John Templeton Foundation, the James S. McDonnell Foundation, and the MacArthur Foundation. There are hundreds of foundations that fund research, but the chances are that only a small number, if any, will fund the particular kind of research you want to do.

Foundations generally run with small staffs. This means that you need to rely heavily on website and other documents because their staff members often are already hard pressed to meet all the demands on their time. Nevertheless, there are occasionally foundation officers who will be willing to talk with you about your grant proposal. The foundation website will probably indicate the level of assistance that is available.

My best experience with foundation funding was with a grant from the James S. McDonnell Foundation through the Partnership for Child Development, then at Oxford University. It enabled us to collaborate with other psychologists as well as epidemiologists, parasitologists, anthropologists, and economists on a project investigating the effects of parasitic illnesses on children's cognitive abilities. The project enabled us to do research in parts of the world in which we never had imagined we would work—Jamaica, Kenya, Tanzania, Zambia, and other locations—collaborating with individuals who taught us lessons we never would have learned from our typical research. My worst experience with foundation funding was submitting a proposal and hearing—nothing. I just never got a response, despite my having cleared the proposal through the foundation office.

Corporations

Corporations are private entities. They may be for-profit or nonprofit. Corporations tend to be the most selective in the kinds of research they fund. Typically they are interested in research that will improve sales of their products or services. You need to be especially careful in selecting corporations to apply to for funding.

Sometimes corporations have rules regarding publication of data that render problematic the receipt of funding from them. For example, they may insist on reviewing potential publications before they are submitted, or they may have a nondisclosure policy that forbids publication at all. If the research does not go the way they hoped, they may lose interest in continuing funding of the research and may even hamper the research enterprise. It is therefore important carefully to check the terms to which you agree to make sure that the terms suit you as well as the corporation. Universities sometimes will not approve corporate-funded research if the corporation places too many constraints on publication of the data—for example, requiring approval of the corporation before any documents based on the research are published.

My best experience with corporate funding was when a large testing organization agreed to fund what was, to that time, what I considered to be the most important research project I had ever done—one that showed that tests of creative and practical thinking could double prediction of college freshman grade point average over standardized test scores taken the senior year of high school. That experience became my worst, however, when the corporation cut off our funding immediately upon learning that supplementing their test with our test resulted in much better prediction (and also reduction in ethnic group differences) relative to the use of their test alone.

GRANTS VERSUS CONTRACTS

Most funding takes the form of either a grant or a contract, although there are hybrids as well. A grant is basically a sum of money that you are given with minimal restrictions in order to accomplish the research you have proposed. Although major changes in what you plan to do may require approval, generally granting agencies are somewhat flexible, realizing that plans change as time goes on. Contracts are agreements for prespecified and generally fixed deliverables—in other words, products that you agree in advance to provide. You are expected to do pretty much what you said you would do and then turn over the products to the contracting agency. There is typically somewhat less flexibility in contracts than in grants. Nevertheless, there often can be some flexibility if you negotiate with whoever awarded the contract. Should you wish to change the terms of the contract, however, it is important that you get permission rather than doing so unilaterally without such permission from the funder.

In much earlier times, when I started my career in the mid-1970s, granting agencies did not closely monitor whether funds from a grant were being spent on the activities specific to that grant. For example, my graduate advisor generously and selflessly devoted some of the funds from his grants to support some of my research on human intelligence, and without that support I doubt my career ever would have jump-started. Today, however, granting agencies monitor such expenses extremely carefully. You must make sure that expenses from a grant are for research under that grant only. Transferring money between grants or across programs of research without permission can land one in serious trouble.

BEFORE WRITING YOUR PROPOSAL

The process of getting funded starts before you write the proposal.

Think Up an Idea

The first step to getting funded is having an idea. The idea does not have to be the greatest one since sliced bread, and as I will say later, it's often better if it isn't the "greatest" idea. You just need a good idea or, at least, one you can sell to a granting agency. People come up with ideas in different ways. Some do it on the basis of reading articles and deciding what needs to be done next; others do it by observing problems in the world around them; still others combine these and perhaps other techniques. Everyone has to find his or her own preferred ways of generating ideas.

It usually helps you to get funded if the idea is theory based—that is, if it derives from some kind of existing theory or theory you are newly proposing. Innovative methodologies can also be of interest to many funding agencies.

In thinking about what to propose, keep in mind that many grant proposals represent collaborations. You might want to collaborate with people either in your own institution or in other institutions. Within your institution, you may choose to work with people in your own department or in another. Some of the best proposals are collaborative. And some programs even require that proposals be collaborative.

Operationalize the Idea

Next, you need to put the idea into terms that represent a program of research or development or both. In other words, you need to do something with the idea.

Find Out Who Might Be Interested in Your Idea

There are thousands of sources of funding, although most psychologists stick to a much smaller number of sources. Find out what funding organizations might be interested in what you have to offer. You can get tips from colleagues, your department chair, the grants and contracts office of your college or university, or books and the Internet. Electronic bulletin boards also can be helpful. You can list relevant key words, and then when calls for proposals come out that use the key words you provided, you will be notified of the funding opportunities. These days, an Internet search is usually a great source of ideas for finding funding agencies, but there is no substitute for knowledgeable individuals who have worked before with the agencies in which you are potentially interested.

When searching for a potential funder, it helps to have an entrepreneurial spirit. In the past, researchers could apply to the major funding organizations such as NSF and NIH and expect that if they had a reasonably good proposal, they would be funded. This was the case when I started my career. Moreover, my graduate adviser, Gordon Bower, told me that when he started his career, anything that was even reasonably good had a substantial probability of being funded. But with the increase in the number of researchers in the field and the decreases in research budgets, many good or even excellent proposals fail to get funded. It therefore behooves you to think about places where your colleagues are less likely to apply and hence where you may have a better chance of obtaining funding. Organizations like NSF and NIH receive huge numbers of proposals because their funding priorities meet the needs of so many researchers and because these organizations are so visible. Ask yourself whether there might be organizations interested in your research that are not as widely sought after.

Another issue you may have to face is that the areas of heaviest funding may not correspond to what you most want to investigate. This is an issue that has faced me many times in my own career. You therefore may find yourself facing a choice of writing a proposal that is your dream research project, but without much hope of funding, or writing one for research that is not quite as high on your priority list but that is higher on the list of priorities for agencies that are providing funding.

Also find out whether an organization requires a preproposal. A *preproposal* is a brief document, often of as little as three to five pages, that describes the concept of the proposed research, how the research would be executed, and the rough budget for the research. Preproposals are commonly required by foundations and corporations, and by some government organizations as well (e.g., the military ones). Preproposals require a little extra work initially but often can end up saving you a lot of time later on. If the organization does not accept your preproposal, at least you have saved yourself the bother of having to write a full proposal, a process that typically is quite time consuming.

Even if an organization does not request a preproposal, often a program officer will be willing to chat with you or communicate in writing regarding ideas you have. The program officer often can give you an idea of whether your idea sounds appropriate for the program he or she administers. Thus, it often makes sense to talk with the program officer to make sure you are targeting your proposal to the right agency or group within that agency.

The granting agency is not the only source of help you can get. Many colleges and universities have grants officers who specialize in helping faculty write and especially prepare budgets for grant proposals. Find out if there is someone at your institution who may be willing to help you, and take advantage of his or her services.

WRITING YOUR PROPOSAL

Next, you write the proposal that presents your idea. Different organizations have different specific requirements as to the format and content of a proposal. But typically you will need to state (a) what your big idea is, (b) why the idea is important, (c) what the theory is behind the idea, (d) what research previously has been done on the idea, (e) what research you propose to do, (f) how you plan to analyze the data from the research, (g) how you plan to manage and share the data with others, (h) how much money you will need to do the research and how you will allocate the funds, (i) how you will handle human participant issues (e.g., informed consent, debriefing), (j) why you are the person (or team) to do the research (i.e., your qualifications), and (k) what resources are available that will enable you to get the research done (e.g., space, available equipment, time available to do the research).

When you write your proposal, there are steps you can take to increase the chances of your proposal succeeding.

Tell Your Story

You may think science is somehow the opposite of storytelling, but this is not the case. As noted earlier, good science tells a story. The story begins with a problem. It typically continues with people who, in the past, have tried to solve the problem (or who may not have correctly identified just what the problem is). And it continues with how you plan to solve the problem or at least contribute to its solution. So a good grant proposal has a narrative quality to it that holds the whole thing together. It has a big idea, like the plot of a story, and it develops the idea in a way that gives the whole proposal coherence, just like a story. If you cannot figure out the story behind your grant proposal, do not expect your reviewers to do so.

Justify the Scientific Importance and Interest of the Research

Because you have probably thought a lot about the research you are proposing, it may be totally obvious to you why the research is important. But do not expect it to be obvious to the reviewers of your proposal. You have to justify to them the importance of the research. Do not assume that others will see this importance without your stating it. If you really do not know why the research is important, do not expect the reviewers to.

An ineffective argument for the importance of research is to point out that X, Y, and Z have been done, but A, B, and C have not yet been done, and your goal is to do A, B, and C. The fact that something has not been done does not, in itself, make that thing important. There are an infinite number of studies that could be done that have not been done and never will be done because no one will care about the results. You need to show why your particular set of studies is worth doing.

Be Clear, and Then Try to Be Clearer

If you are writing a proposal about a specific area, chances are you have at least some expertise in that area. You therefore may assume that reviewers have the same kind and level of background you have. They may not. You must therefore be extremely clear in your presentation of ideas. Moreover, because you have thought about your ideas many times, it is easy, in writing, to leave gaps. After all, it should be obvious what you meant. But it rarely is obvious to anyone but yourself. Be as clear as you possibly can be, and after you have done that, try to be clearer yet. When you write, write for someone who is generally knowledgeable in your broad area of research (e.g., cognitive psychology, social psychology, developmental psychology), but who is not necessarily specialized in the particular problem within the area or areas you are studying. (For tips on how to write clearly, you may wish to consult Sternberg & Sternberg, 2016.)

Organize the Hell Out of Your Proposal

Actually, I think this is a statement made to me years ago by my graduate advisor, Gordon Bower. Proposals tend to be technical. They also tend to be complex. It's easy for a reviewer to get lost in the thicket. You therefore want to make sure your writing is as organized as possible.

Organize your proposal in a hierarchical way. Make sure that the major points stand out and that the minor points are properly subordinated. No reviewer possibly can remember everything you have written. By writing hierarchically, you ensure that the reviewer will remember the most important things—the things you really want him or her to remember.

Sell Your Ideas

After you have paid attention to how you present your ideas, you need to think about how you are going to sell your ideas. Good ideas typically do not sell themselves (Sternberg & Lubart, 1995). You have to sell them. No matter how good you may think your ideas are, do not expect it to be obvious to reviewers why your ideas are so great. You have to convince them. It therefore is important to write the proposal in a way that is not only descriptive but persuasive as well. You are not just saying what you want to do. You are telling the reader why anyone in his or her right mind would want to fund you to do it.

Be Comprehensive but Selective in Your Literature Review

Usually, you are writing under the constraint of being allowed only a certain number of pages in your proposal. Thus, although it might be possible to devote the whole proposal to the literature review, you need to be selective. Cite as much as possible of the research that is directly relevant to your proposal, but skip the stuff that, although peripherally relevant, does not bear directly on what you propose.

When people in my group at Yale wrote proposals, we tried to keep in mind likely reviewers of these proposals. Most reviewers consider their work in the area to be important. After all, they may feel that they would not have been asked to review the proposal if their work were not important. So they will not be thrilled to see their classic book or article roundly ignored. The lesson is to try to cite likely reviewers, whenever possible.

Although you cannot be certain of who will review your proposal, you can make reasonable guesses. People who are central to the field, people who have reviewed your articles (should you know who any of them are), people you run into in professional meetings and symposia on topics of interest to you—these are among the likely reviewers. Write with them in mind, as you would wish they would do for you. Have you ever gotten an article or proposal to review and turned first to the references to see if you were cited? Others may well do the same!

Be Respectful in Your Literature Review

Sometimes the research one proposes is designed to set the record straight—perhaps to correct the errors the researcher sees in past work. But even if you believe past work has led to wrong conclusions, which you are going to correct, it is important to be respectful of this work. First, disagree though you may with those who came before you, these very scientists are the ones who created the methods or results that are serving as the basis for your work. Hence you owe them a debt because you are building or rebuilding on their work. Second, it is unprofessional and, arguably, immature to be disrespectful. Third, and pragmatically, the people who did this past work are those most likely to review your proposal, and if you are disrespectful toward them, you endanger the viability of your own proposal.

Have a Strong Theoretical Basis for Your Proposal

One of the main reasons I have seen for rejections of proposals is that there is no theory, or the theory is only sketchily portrayed, or the theory is only marginally relevant to the research that is proposed. It is therefore important for you to pay close attention to the theory section of your proposal. Explain the theory clearly, and also the hypotheses that derive from it that are relevant to your research. Be sure you show how the hypotheses derive from the theory. Don't expect reviewers to see the derivation of the hypotheses on their own. Then, when you are describing the research, make sure it is clear how the research tests the hypotheses that you generated from the underlying theory.

Follow Directions

Funding agencies, especially government ones, have many rules to follow in the preparation of a proposal. Just following all these rules and doing all of the required paperwork can become enormously time consuming and, at times, can be frustrating. Yet it is imperative that you follow all of these nitty-gritty rules lest your proposal be returned or even rejected because you disobeyed the rules. I once had a proposal sent back and then had to wait for the next granting deadline because a few questions on a form inadvertently had not been answered.

Today, college and university grant and contract offices generally check for these mechanical kinds of errors, but ultimately, it is your responsibility, not theirs, to make sure that the guidelines are followed. You do not want your proposal to be rejected because it did not follow the guidelines. If it must be rejected, it should be because of the science. Therefore, do not make yourself vulnerable by ignoring or flouting the rules. Be creative in your science, not in the mechanics of writing the proposal.

Make Sure Your Budget Is Reasonable and Matches the Proposed Research

Reviewers of grants are typically experienced and can recognize rather quickly when a project is underbudgeted or overbudgeted. If you underbudget, you are showing that you do not understand the full cost of the research, and your underbudgeting calls into question whether you really understand the resources your research requires. If you overbudget, you may give the impression of being more concerned about the money than about the research or even of being greedy. It therefore is important that your budget be reasonable.

Some organizations state that evaluation of budgets is separate from evaluation of the merits of the work. My own experience, though, is that unrealistic budgeting can sour the way reviewers perceive the work you propose. You typically will be asked to provide a justification for your budget, and this justification should make totally explicit why you are requesting the level of funding and allocation of funds you have requested. Unfortunately, budgets are often cut before funding is awarded.

In budgeting, keep in mind that most institutions charge overhead. *Overhead* is a portion of the grant or contract that the university takes out for its own use. In theory, overhead pays for things such as space, library use, heating, electricity, costs to the university of administering the grant, and so forth. Rates of overhead vary widely among universities and can reach 65% or more. The overhead may be computed on the whole grant, or only on salaries and wages. For example, if the overhead rate is 50%, then the university will take 50 cents out of your grant for every dollar you spend. Rates of overhead are negotiated between the university and the funding organization.

Universities differ in their flexibility regarding overhead. Generally, though, they are willing to do some negotiation. For example, my own institution typically charges a fairly high rate of overhead but is willing to accept less if the funding institution writes a letter saying it is their policy to pay less. You thus may have some leverage in negotiating rates, although probably not much.

Universities also may charge benefits on salaries and wages. This is money taken out of the grant to pay for employee benefits such as health care, retirement plans, life insurance, disability insurance, and so forth. Benefit rates vary widely across universities. From the researcher's standpoint, the important thing to realize is that you do not get to spend the entire amount of money that a funding agency allocates to you.

It is important also to realize that universities have policies regarding grant spending, and it is wise to check these policies. For example, when a grant is used to pay for a professional trip, the university may have a maximum daily amount that it will reimburse for lodging or food expenses.

Foundations often are unwilling to pay overhead or are willing to pay only a small percentage (e.g., 10%). Sometimes the overhead is called by another name, such as "administrative costs." If you are thinking of applying to an agency that does not pay overhead or that pays only a minimal amount, make sure your university will support the proposal. Hard to believe though it may be, universities often lose money even on grants that pay full overhead. So they may be reluctant to accept grants with little or no overhead, especially if you have not also been funded with grants that pay overhead at the full rate.

AFTER WRITING YOUR PROPOSAL

Your work isn't over once you've finished writing your proposal. What you do with it afterward is critical for getting funded.

Be Sure to Proofread and Check Over Your Proposal

Reviewers typically donate their time to evaluating proposals. They do not want to see and may have little patience with typographical or word-processing errors in what they read.

When you proofread, be sure to proofread with the agency guidelines in mind. I once submitted a proposal with margins that were not according to the prescribed guidelines. The proposal was immediately declined because of the margins! This is not a mistake I ever made again. You can do better: Don't make it the first time. Make sure margins, fonts, and all aspects of the proposal meet the guidelines.

Moreover, I always read over a proposal as though I were a reviewer, and try to ask myself the questions I would ask were I reading the proposal for the purpose of reviewing it. Reading over your proposal with a critical eye can often resolve problems in advance so that reviewers do not have to bring them up.

Solicit Feedback on Your Proposal

You may find, as I often have, that others readily can see flaws in your proposal that are invisible to you. Therefore, ask colleagues for feedback before you finalize your proposal. Also, read over your proposal from the standpoint of a reviewer.

I once wrote, with colleagues, a proposal for the military that I thought was really compelling. We even went to great lengths to line up military participants at several bases. I solicited feedback from the program officer and found out, to my horror, that for the basic research program to which I was applying (called "6-1" in military parlance), military participants were neither required nor even wanted. Had I submitted the proposal without getting that feedback, it would have been rejected summarily.

Get the Proposal Approved by Your Institution

Almost all institutions have a formal approval process that a grant proposal needs to go through before the proposal can be submitted. This is so because the grant actually goes to the institution rather than to you. You may be the principal investigator or a coinvestigator, but the actual allocation of funds goes to the institution, not to you.

Part of the approval process may be human participants approval if, in fact, you are using human participants. Such approval can take time, and so you should be sure to submit your human participants forms to your institutional review board well in advance. Monitoring of the rights of human participants has been tightening up over the years, and you may find that getting approval is nontrivial, even if the research seems to be benign. NIH has started requiring potential principal investigators to get training in human participants protection, and at the time this chapter is being written, other government organizations are expected to follow suit.

Do not submit proposals to the university for approval the day the proposal is due or without sufficient lead time for administration to process the proposal. Your proposal may not go out, either because there was no time to read it or because it had a minor error.

Send Out the Proposal on Time

Most funding agencies have deadlines. Therefore, you need to pay attention to the time frame in which you are allowed to send out your proposal. Deadlines tend to be strict. If you miss a deadline, you probably will have to wait until the next round of funding takes place.

Don't Try to Fund the Same Research With Multiple Grants

You cannot send out minor variants of the same proposal to different agencies and, if more than one version is funded, accept funding for all of them. In order to meet the ethical requirements for submitting proposals, you must ensure that the research you propose to the different agencies is substantively and substantially different.

Wait for the Proposal to Be Evaluated

Each funding organization has its own criteria for evaluating proposals and its own timeline for doing evaluations. Evaluations may take just a few weeks, but they typically require 4 to 6 months or even more.

Evaluations may be internal, external, or both. *Internal evaluation* means that employees of the funding organization evaluate the proposal. Such evaluations are common with foundations and corporations. *External evaluation* means that reviewers outside the funding organization—often people like you—evaluate the proposal and provide their evaluations to the funding organization. In writing your proposal, you need to keep in mind the reviewers who are likely to evaluate your proposal and write with these potential evaluators in mind.

When proposals are sent out for review, they are sent out with the explicit understanding that the proposal is a privileged document. This means that a reviewer is not permitted to show or even discuss the proposal with others, and certainly is not permitted to use any of the ideas in the proposal for his or her own research. Usually, reviewers are asked to destroy the proposals after they are done reviewing them. In my experience, reviewers are basically honest in adhering to these guidelines. After all, they do not want people stealing their ideas! Of course, there can be a bad apple in any basket, and there is no guarantee that things will go as they should. But in my experience, reviewers generally take their ethical responsibilities seriously.

Different organizations use different criteria in evaluating proposals, but certain criteria tend to be common across many different funding organizations. A first criterion most organizations use for evaluating proposals is whether the proposal even fits the kinds of research the organization sees itself as funding. A second criterion is likely to be the scientific (or educational or commercial) value of the research. Organizations typically look for some degree of originality in a proposal, as well as quality of the way in which the research is designed and is to be executed. A third criterion is whether the data analysis is appropriate for the research that has been proposed. A fourth criterion often is the appropriateness of the budget. And a fifth criterion is the level of qualifications of the proposer and the facilities available to the proposer. This criterion is important because it helps ensure that the research will get done, and get done well.

Revise the Proposal, if Necessary; Otherwise, Abandon It for Now

Relatively few proposals are accepted the first time they are submitted. Typically, they need to be revised. Therefore, expect to have to do a revision if your proposal is turned down. If you receive really awful reviews or simply can't see how to revise the proposal into an acceptable form, stuff the proposal into a file drawer and wait. You may never see how to revise the proposal, but more likely, incubation will enable you to see things in a more positive light after some time has passed.

There is one thing I cannot emphasize enough: Grant writing is not for the faint of heart. One of the most important determinants of whether you get a grant is your persistence. Getting a grant usually is very difficult. It may require multiple revisions and resubmissions, and even submissions to multiple agencies. Getting a grant is often a long, difficult, and even painful process. Nothing pays off like persistence.

Agencies have different policies on revisions. At NIH, you now are allowed only one revision. At NSF, you can do multiple revisions. But whatever you do, make sure each revision counts. You cannot afford to do a sloppy revision because at worst, you lose the ability to submit a third time, and at best, you lose another funding cycle and lead reviewers to believe that you are not really serious about revising the proposal.

Sometimes you really are best off abandoning the proposal for the time being. For example, at NIH, if you are not judged to be in the top half of submitters, you will not get a priority score. Such proposals may be funded on the second round but typically aren't. So ask yourself whether you truly are ready to do a fundable revision, and if not, consider filing the proposal away for a while until you either have other proposal ideas or can review your proposal and see what you need to do to make it fundable.

If you wait, don't wait too long, because ideas have a limited shelf life. I once did a proposal on concept naturalness and received back reviews suggesting that the concept of concept naturalness is itself unnatural. The reviewers just weren't interested. I shelved the proposal, only to find a few years later that the topic had become hot, and it seemed like everyone was studying concept naturalness! Indeed, the topic had peaked by the time I became interested in it again. I was too early the first time around, and then I waited too long and was too late for a second try.

Resubmit and Explain What You Have Changed

If you do resubmit, you typically will be expected to indicate how you have responded to the earlier reviews. You should follow all or most of the suggestions of the reviewers. If you have chosen not to follow a suggestion of a reviewer or a panel of reviewers, explain why.

You can afford to pass on a few suggestions and explain why, but if you find yourself passing on more than a few reviewer suggestions, then you probably are not ready to do a resubmission. Wait a while until you get over the feeling that the reviewers have dissed you unforgivably!

Get Funded, or if Not, Start Over

You may get funded, in which case, congratulations. Enjoy your funding. But whether or not you get funded, you soon will be back to writing proposals. For most of us, writing proposals is not a one-time thing. It is a regular part of a research career. Sometimes you will succeed, other times not. But whatever happens, soon you will be back to proposal writing again.

YOUR FRAME OF MIND

This chapter describes the bare bones of the proposal-writing process. But of course, some proposals get funded and others do not. What can you do to maximize the chances of your proposal's getting funded? One thing is to have the right frame of mind.

Believe in Yourself

Proposal writing is a time-consuming process. At times, you may draw a blank. Or you may become dissatisfied or even disgusted with what you have written. Moreover, when you get reviews back, you may feel even worse about yourself. It's easy to give up. If you still believe in your idea, don't give up! Believe in your ability to get funded. Reverses are the rule, not the exception. The people who succeed in getting funded and staying funded are those who believe in themselves. They do not believe that every idea they ever have is a good idea. No one has only good ideas. Rather, they believe that, over the course of time, they will be able to produce research ideas that are worthy of funding and that, ultimately, will get funded.

That said, sometimes we start writing and find that an idea we thought we had worked out is not in fact ready for prime time. The details we thought we had straight in our mind now elude us. If you feel the proposal getting away from you, there is nothing wrong with shelving it for a few weeks or even a funding cycle and trying again when you feel your head is clearer.

Go For It

For several years, I thought it was not worth applying for a grant to pursue my interests in the psychology of wisdom because granting agencies would find the topic just too flaky. In fact, our first proposal was rejected. We then wrote a different proposal, sent it to three foundations, and one foundation funded it for 3 years. I was shocked! But the lesson is one I should have learned earlier. If you tell yourself you can't get funded, you won't get funded, because you will never try. You have to go for it. You may or may not succeed, but the only way to know is to try.

Don't Worry About Having the Greatest Idea

What is the correlation between the quality of ideas in a proposal and its getting funded? If I had to venture a guess for my own career, it's probably about 0. Really bad ideas generally don't get funded. But sometimes really good ideas don't get funded, either. There are a number of reasons for this.

Sometimes really creative ideas do not fit into existing zeitgeists, and reviewers may not understand them, know what to make of them, or see the value of them (Sternberg, Kaufman, & Pretz, 2002). Other times, really creative ideas threaten those who read about them. Reviewers may have a vested interest in another point of view and may not be thrilled to read that what they have been thinking all along has been wrong. Still other times, really creative ideas just seem crazy.

So if you have an idea that you think is pretty good, but not world shattering, don't worry about it. And if you think you have an idea that is world shattering, be sure to express it in a way that makes as much contact as possible with the frames of mind of the reviewers. I have sometimes soft-pedaled ideas that I thought might antagonize reviewers in the hope that they then would react more positively. I do not sell out on the ideas, but I do soften the way I present them. Often, this technique has worked.

Sometimes ideas can be ahead of their time, as with the concept naturalness idea about which I wrote a proposal too early. Many of us have had the experience of applying for a grant, being turned down because the reviewers did not see the relevance of the problem or the research on the problem, and then reading some years later about funded research that does essentially what we proposed. If your ideas are particularly novel, then you have to make even greater efforts to convince potential reviewers of the importance of the work.

Persist!

During the 30 years I was at Yale, my group was fairly successful in obtaining grant funding. Some colleagues assumed we must have had a wonderful track record in getting grants. False! We probably had more grant proposals turned down than any other individual or group of which I knew at the time. We just wrote more grant proposals. I found that the rate at which my proposals got funded held more or less steady during my career before I entered administration, with minor fluctuations from time to time. The principal key to getting your research funded, therefore, is to write a lot of proposals.

Many people give up after being turned down once or twice. They conclude that their research—or they—are just never going to be funded. They're right. Their lack of persistence has guaranteed that they will not get funded because they have stopped writing proposals. When we get turned down, a frequent event, we just keep trying, and eventually something works out.

Thicken Your Skin

One reason many grant writers do not persist is that they are dismayed by the negativity and often even what seem like the personal insults contained in reviews. No one enjoys being flayed alive—metaphorically speaking—so it is easy to give up. A key lesson is never to take reviews personally and to ignore the tone if a review is sarcastic or insulting. Simply concentrate on what is constructive in the reviews, and if you think you can respond to the reviews, do so without responding to their tone. Just take the substance of what is said, and respond to that.

I went through a period of my career in which I thought several agencies just had it in for me. But then I realized that these agencies were funding only about 10% of the proposals that were submitted, so that even good to excellent proposals were being rejected. I realized I was making a mistake in taking the rejections personally. And I persisted, despite the large number of proposals being turned down. When I was a dean at Tufts, our faculty member in arts and sciences with the greatest success in getting funded—in the biology department—told me that only roughly one in 10 of his proposals was being funded. He just kept sending out proposals.

Focus—Don't Be Distracted

There are almost always many things you would rather do than write a grant proposal. Few people delight in writing proposals; most proposal writers would rather be doing something else. Moreover, there are always many other things to do. Your course preparations need to get done. You may have scholarly articles begging you to write them up. Your committee work may be falling behind. Personal commitments may be on hold and need to be given more attention. Truly, anyone can find excuses not to write a proposal. But if you wish to do research, chances are good you will need at least some funding. So you need to focus on proposal writing and find a way to make sure that your proposals get done, regardless of all the other things that genuinely need attention as well. You have to make the time.

Many institutions give most credit—for tenure and promotion—for your getting funded. But many will look at whether you have at least tried. They are more likely to look favorably on someone who has tried and not yet succeeded than on someone who never even gave it a shot.

Find Your Right Audience

You can end up wasting a lot of time by submitting a proposal to a funding organization that simply does not fund the kind of work you are proposing. Before you write your proposal, make sure that the agency or agencies to which you are applying actually fund the kind of work you are proposing. Some funding agencies release the names of the individuals who serve on and head various grant panels, so that you can know in advance who is likely to evaluate your proposal. Even if you obtain such a list, though, you still will not know what external referees the proposal will be sent to for outside evaluation.

IN SUMMARY

Would you like to get a grant? Chances are, you can and even will. Of course, you need an idea, but chances are you have that idea, or even more than one. So the main thing you need to do is organize yourself and your time to write a grant. You want to give it your best shot, but don't wait until you get every thought and every sentence perfect. Wait too long, and the time for doing the research may well be past! Find out the organizations that fund the kind of research you would like to do, and go for it. Most of all, remember the importance of persistence. Some lucky people are funded the first time around. Probably, many more are not. You may have to revise the proposal once or even twice. Or you may have to submit the proposal elsewhere. Or you may have to write a new proposal. But if there is one key to getting funded, it is persistence. Keep trying, and sooner or later, you will be funded.

IV
SERVICE

9

SERVICE TO YOUR DEPARTMENT AND UNIVERSITY

When you come up for reappointment, tenure, or promotion, usually you will be expected to have done some service to the department and to your college or university. Institutions vary widely in their service expectations. Although probably few, if any, people get promoted just for service, some probably are denied promotion if they are seen as unengaged in their department.

When you look to do service, find the kinds of service opportunities that best match your skills and interests. Some kinds of service may seem deadly to you (as they do to me), but others may be really exciting. I took on the job of director of graduate studies with some dread, finding instead that it was a terrific opportunity to serve the department and get to know better the graduate students, their needs, and their wants.

On the one hand, then, you do not want to get so involved in service that you have little or no time for anything else. On the other hand, you want

---

http://dx.doi.org/10.1037/0000013-010
Starting Your Career in Academic Psychology, by R. J. Sternberg
Copyright © 2017 by the American Psychological Association. All rights reserved.

to have enough service on your record so that you are not denied advancement because of a lack of service.

The options for service differ from one institution to another. A higher order goal of service is to establish a visible presence on your campus—for people to know who you are, how you work with others, and what you can do for the college or university. In a sense, then, the particular committees you are on matter less than how you perform on them. Service also will enable you to get to know other members of the university community and allow them to get to know you. Good will matters and especially can make a difference when you come up for promotion and tenure. So look at service as accomplishing multiple goals while at the same time taking care not to become so involved in it that you cannot get other work done.

Although most of your service will probably be to your department or institution, do not hesitate to seek out opportunities for community service as well. Relations between colleges and universities and the communities in which they are embedded are sometimes strained because the communities do not view the institutions as giving back sufficiently. Helping your community will also help your institution show that it cares about those outside its campus.

This chapter describes some of the typical kinds of service that may be offered in your institution, along with some comments on each.

DIRECTOR OF UNDERGRADUATE STUDIES

The director of undergraduate studies (DUS) is responsible for the undergraduate program in the department and often for the success of the students in the program. The DUS is frequently the first person to whom undergraduates turn when they have questions about requirements or how to fulfill them. Questions also may be about research opportunities, summer job opportunities, poor performance in one or more courses, poor relations with an adviser, harassment of one kind or another, and postbaccalaureate opportunities, among other things.

The DUS job typically is a demanding one. The demands of the position tend to be greatest at the beginning and at the end of each academic term. In colleges or universities with very large undergraduate major pools, there may even be one or more assistant DUS positions.

If you are asked to take on the role, there are probably some questions you want to ask before accepting the position. First, and most important, will you get help in the form of administrative or other assistance? This is an extremely difficult job to do without some form of staff assistance, and you probably want to have someone in place who knows the ropes and can help you out. Second, you want to ask whether you will get any form of teaching reduction or other reduction in departmental responsibilities. Departments often give the DUS a one-course teaching reduction, recognizing that the duties are beyond those of just a normal administrative assignment. If you are not given a reduction, you should ask yourself whether you can find the time to do the DUS job, teach your courses, and also get enough research done. Third, you may want to ask whether there is any stipend or even raise associated with the job. In my experience, stipends are rare, but it never hurts to ask. Fourth, you may want to ask what your role will be in disciplinary issues. If you are the person who will handle disciplinary problems of undergraduates, then you may want to ask yourself whether you have the stomach for such a role.

The upside of the DUS job is the ability to help undergraduates and even shape the undergraduate educational program. The main downside is that the job is very time consuming, and if you are the person handling discipline, it can be emotionally draining as well. The DUS position is a good entry-level position for those who might be interested in a career with administrative responsibilities. For example, having been DUS will help you obtain and satisfactorily execute the responsibilities of a chair's role, as you will know the undergraduate program very well.

The greatest risk of the DUS job is that disciplinary matters begin to take over your life. The problem with such matters is that, in advance of your taking the job, you have no idea of how many there will be and how much time and energy they will take up. A single disciplinary matter can go through multiple levels of university administration, from a department to a college or school to a university body. Moreover, on some (rare) occasions, students pursue legal remedies, which can be extremely time consuming as well as resource draining. The chances are that you will have to deal with few or even none of the issues that lead to litigation. The problem is that you never know for sure in advance.

In general, I would give a thumbs-up to this position. It is a good one, and you'll learn a lot doing it. But don't take it unless you have sufficient administrative or other support.

DIRECTOR OF GRADUATE STUDIES

The position of director of graduate studies (DGS) typically is available only in university settings, where there are graduate students to supervise. The pluses and minuses are similar to those for the DUS position. The greatest difference, obviously, is that you will be working with graduate instead of undergraduate students.

The DGS position is usually somewhat less time consuming than the DUS position, just because there are usually fewer graduate students than undergraduate students in a department. As with the DUS position, the greatest demands often are at the beginning and end of the academic term.

I served as a DGS for 4 years early in my career. I enjoyed the job. The most challenging part of the job, in my experience, was the aftermath of the annual student evaluation meeting. Inevitably, there are graduate students who are floundering through the program. These are students who, for one reason or another, are falling behind in meeting milestones or who meet them but only in the most minimal fashion.

The greatest challenge I faced was convincing faculty that, in some cases, the kindest thing we could do for the students would be to separate those students from the program. These were students whose careers were going nowhere. For one reason or another, they had chosen the wrong career path. They actually might have considerable aptitude or motivation, but not for the field they had chosen. So I believed, and believe today, that although separation might have been traumatic for them, it actually would have been a favor to them, allowing them to find a career that was a better match to their talents or motivations. The problem always seemed to be that if there was at least one person willing to supervise them, the department was unwilling to terminate their studies. And there seems to be in most departments at least one faculty member who is willing to give students a second, third, fourth, or fifth chance. I believed that, as DGS, my role was to help them find their optimal career path, not to find more and more ways for them to stay in a program that was an ill-fitting match. I can say two things with confidence: First, the students who were highly problematic in the beginning tended to stay that way throughout their careers; second, none of these students who actually managed one way or another to get a degree has had a distinguished level of professional success. But maybe that was not their goal.

DEPARTMENTAL DIRECTOR OF TRANSFER STUDENTS

Some colleges and universities accept enough transfer students that integrating the students into the life of the institution becomes a serious and sometimes time-consuming job. The job is an important one because the demands of life in the first institution may be very different from the demands in the new one.

There is a large bureaucratic component to dealing with transfer students. Typically, a college or university has articulation agreements with community colleges (or other institutions from which they receive transfers) specifying what courses count, how much, toward what. You probably do not want to be the person who pores over transcripts, deciding whom to credit how much for what. But you may well want to be the person who counsels transfer students and helps them succeed in a new environment.

CHAIR

If you are asked to be a chair early in your career, you know one of two things. Either none of the senior faculty was willing or able to do the job, or you are viewed as potentially a super academic leader (or both). Unless you plan to transition into academic administration—perhaps become a dean in the not-too-distant future—you do not want to be a chair as a junior faculty member.

The reasons are straightforward. First, you will not have the positional clout to effectively enforce your decisions, or anyone else's. Put another way, senior faculty have trouble taking orders from junior faculty. Second, you likely will not have the time for the research and teaching that generally lead to academic advancement. Third, you probably will not have enough of the tacit knowledge—hidden agendas within the department—that you would need to know in order to be able to lead effectively. Fourth, as a chair, you will almost inevitably antagonize some people, no matter how well you do the job. If you are going to have to antagonize people, this is not the time to do it, before you need their votes for tenure and promotion. The last thing you need is to antagonize people who later will be voting on your advancement. This is a job much better left to later in career, definitely after one has tenure and preferably after one is a full professor.

ASSOCIATE CHAIR

Your department or a dean may try to prevail on you to become an associate chair, on the view that although the chair position is beyond the easy reach of a junior faculty member, the associate chair position is eminently doable. But many of the problems associated with being chair also are associated with being associate chair. Moreover, if your department has an associate chair position, it most likely is a very large department. The associate chair tends to get a disproportionate share of the administrative grunt work. That is not the kind of work you should be doing while trying to burnish your academic record to rise to the next rank.

MEMBER OF THE DEPARTMENT EXECUTIVE COMMITTEE

Many departments have an executive committee. The executive committee, together with the department chair (or head), makes important decisions about the department and its direction, or at least makes proposals to the department faculty for their consideration.

Because an executive committee has multiple members, you are less likely directly to antagonize people if members of the department do not like the decisions the executive committee makes. Often, department members are only vaguely, or not at all, aware of who is on the executive committee. Nevertheless, the job comes with a lot of responsibility, and you should think carefully whether you want to be held accountable in any major degree, early in your career, for decisions the executive committee makes on behalf of the department.

A particularly useful role you can play, if you are allowed to, is to represent junior faculty on the executive committee. A problem in some departments is that senior faculty members run them, sometimes seemingly for the senior faculty. Membership of a junior faculty member on the executive committee can provide junior faculty with a voice in governance that they otherwise might not have.

MEMBER OF THE GRADUATE ADMISSIONS COMMITTEE

Although, in the United States, undergraduate admissions usually are done by some centralized authority, decisions on graduate admissions usually are made by an individual department. Typically, a few faculty members are collectively designated as the graduate admissions committee, and they are charged by the department with admitting graduate students, subject to approval of a dean. Normally, the committee seeks input from the faculty as they make their decisions.

Depending on the number of members in the committee and the number of applicants, membership on the graduate admissions committee can be a fair amount of work or practically none at all. Typically, most of the work is in the early spring, when most universities make their admissions decisions.

This is a very good committee assignment. If you are offered it, or are asked to run for election to it, I suggest you agree. First, in my experience, members of the graduate admissions committee somehow manage to get more graduate students working with them than nonmembers. Although these committees are supposed to be fair, nevertheless, human nature being what it is, people are more likely to overlook flaws in an applicant if the applicant is applying to work with them than if the applicant is looking to work with someone else. This is not as things should be, obviously, but it seems to be the way they are. Second, serving on the committee gives you a good idea of who the graduate students are and what their various interests, strengths, and weaknesses are. Finally, whereas it is difficult to see much impact of some committee assignments on the actual life of the department—reports may be written, read, and forgotten—service on the graduate admissions committee immediately affects who is in the department and how it functions. So this is a committee where you really can make a difference.

MEMBER OF THE EDUCATIONAL CURRICULUM COMMITTEE

The educational curriculum committee is another committee on which you can make a real difference. Curriculum committees have varied roles. They may set minimum standards for newly proposed courses. They may decide which courses to approve or disapprove. They may monitor students' compliance with curriculum requirements. Although occasionally they may recommend which courses are required and which are optional, more often they would make recommendations to a department, which then would put this issue to a vote.

Faculty members sometimes complain about course requirements, or about course offerings, or about how the course offerings are structured (e.g., requiring so many from such-and-such a group and so many from another). Serving on a curriculum committee is a good opportunity to have a voice in these matters.

UNION REPRESENTATIVE OR STEWARD

If your college or university is unionized, it may have a representative in each academic unit. If only staff members are unionized, the representative will be a staff member. But if faculty members are unionized as well, they typically have a representative, likely elected but possibly appointed.

I do not recommend this position for a junior faculty member. First, you are placing yourself in a potentially antagonistic position with an administration in whose hands your fate partially may rest. If you are going to do so, you are better off if you have tenure. Second, if you have any aspirations for an administrative career, placing yourself as a union representative likely will diminish the chances of those aspirations being fulfilled. Third, if you have aspirations of rising in the union, you can wait until you have tenure. You do not want to spend a lot of time as a junior faculty member on union matters—better after you have tenure.

REPRESENTATIVE TO THE AMERICAN ASSOCIATION OF UNIVERSITY PROFESSORS CHAPTER

The American Association of University Professors (AAUP) is an organization that in some ways resembles a typical union but is different in other ways. For one thing, it is composed solely of academics (in contrast to unions that may represent academics but other kinds of workers as well). Furthermore, it has three different parts. One part is a union and functions as a regular union, but another part is a professional association. (The third part is a foundation.)

If you are at an institution in which the AAUP functions as a union, the same cautions apply here as with the union representative or steward. If you are at an institution in which the AAUP functions as a professional association, serving with the AAUP is an opportunity to look out for faculty interests (free speech, collegial governance, due process) that you might not otherwise find. The one thing you always need to remember is that faculty are only one interest group among many in a university, and administrators constantly need to be balancing the interests of the multiple constituencies wanting to be heard, including but not limited to faculty.

REPRESENTATIVE TO THE FACULTY SENATE OR COUNCIL

Many colleges and universities have a faculty senate or council. This body represents the faculty to the administration. Although such bodies sometimes are in opposition to the administration, more often they work with the administration to achieve common goals. Serving on such a body is a good opportunity to learn more about what's going on in the college or university beyond your own department. Typically, such service is not hugely time consuming, and it also gives you an opportunity to meet faculty members in departments other than your own. I would recommend, if you are interested, that you put yourself up for election to such a role. However, the role is likely to be enjoyable only to those who are interested in governance. For those who are not, sitting through meetings can be boring and even grueling. Many of the issues discussed in such meetings are fairly mundane and can seem pointless to those who are not attracted to issues of governance.

NEW-FACULTY SEARCH COMMITTEE MEMBER

Search committees typically recommend candidates to the faculty for new faculty positions. They usually formulate the advertisements, decide in what media to advertise the position, vet applications as they come in, form a long short list of applicants, arrange for job interviews (either on campus or via telephone or teleconferencing), and then form the final short list. Almost always, the entire faculty, rather than just the search committee, votes on the final slate of applicants to make an offer. However, the job of the search committee member is not necessarily over once an offer is made. Search committee members often are involved in trying to recruit the selected individual actually to accept the offer. The search committee does not decide on the terms of the offer; terms are typically decided in consultation by the chair and relevant dean.

This is another terrific committee assignment for a junior faculty member. It gives you a say in who joins you, it gives you a chance to see from the inside how a search process works, it gives you an opportunity to peruse the credentials of various candidates, and often it gives you an opportunity to meet with several of the candidates. There always is a chance that, sooner or later, you will be in the job market again yourself, and serving on a search committee gives you an excellent opportunity to reflect on the kinds of actions that are more or less likely to lead to a job offer. I found, in my early years, that I had very little sense of what I could do that would enhance my chances of being hired in a future job search. After serving on a few search committees, I had a much better idea, and I did eventually move on to a different institution.

DEPARTMENTAL COLLOQUIUM COMMITTEE

If your department has a colloquium committee, offer to serve on it. You will not only interact with your colleagues but also give yourself an opportunity to meet the distinguished speakers from other departments or universities.

DEPARTMENT INFORMATION TECHNOLOGY CONSULTANT OR LIAISON

If you are information technology (IT) oriented, serving as an IT consultant or liaison is a good way to indulge an interest and get service credit for it. What you do want to do is consult with the college or university about its IT needs. What you do not want to do is end up solving various faculty members' IT problems for them. Even if this is an activity that interests you, it can be enormously time consuming, and your college or university should have people for whom this is a dedicated role. Therefore, make sure of the responsibilities you will be given before accepting a position that may or may not be your dream committee assignment.

LIBRARY LIAISON

Library liaison is a good and usually not overly taxing assignment. It means either that you, individually, are a liaison to the institutional library or that you serve on a college or university committee that makes decisions about the library.

The importance of this position in many ways has increased in recent years. As institutional budgets have become more strained, and as the number of scholarly journals has increased, it has become more challenging for institutions to find the funds to pay for all the journals psychologists or anyone else might want. So libraries, more and more, have had to make tough decisions as to which journals to purchase and which to forgo. Many arrangements with publishers these days are in the form of licenses for electronic versions of journals. Thus, decisions often are made about electronic licenses that can affect multiple journals, not just one.

Another important issue for libraries today is how much to invest in print books and how much in electronic media. Obviously, libraries are moving more and more toward electronic media. It might seem like a nonissue: Why not invest everything in electronic media rather than print? But the issue is more complex than it seems. Formats of electronic media change. Have you tried reading any 5¼-inch electronic disks lately, or even 3½-inch ones? How about Sony Betamax tapes? Have you ever seen a book hacked? Electronic formats pose problems, just as do books, so the choice is not always entirely straightforward.

Yet another issue for libraries is which databases to buy. Databases can provide invaluable information to scholars in a given field, but they are often expensive. In general, then, as you can see, library issues are probably more complex than ever before, and serving as a library liaison or on a library committee can be a challenging and rewarding task.

DISCIPLINARY/JUDICIAL COMMITTEE

Disciplinary/judicial committees are generally of two kinds: permanent or ad hoc. The two do somewhat different kinds of work.

The permanent committees are ones that handle disciplinary cases on a regular basis. You need a bit of a strong stomach for this kind of committee. You get routine cases, for example, academic cheating or plagiarism, and some of them are difficult to adjudicate. But you also may get cases involving student-on-student violence, and those are even tougher to handle and to adjudicate. Junior faculty members (and many senior faculty members) may lack the experience and knowledge of procedure to perform optimally on such a committee. Take this responsibility on only if you like involving yourself in very challenging behavioral issues for which the evidence is often confusing and sometimes less than compelling.

Ad hoc committees deal with cases of misconduct, usually by faculty members. Most often they are staffed only by senior faculty members. They handle cases of alleged plagiarism, failure to fulfill responsibilities such as attending all classes, harassment, or whatever. They are created on an ad hoc basis to deal with individual cases. Chances are you will not be asked, as a junior faculty member, to serve on such a committee, and if you are, it would be better to wait until you are senior to agree to serve, especially because the accused faculty member may stay around and remember being judged by you.

ACADEMIC STANDARDS COMMITTEE

Academic standards committees sometimes set, but more often enforce, academic standards. For example, they may be asked to deal with a case of a student whose academic average has fallen below the minimum allowable but who has extenuating circumstances, such as a health problem or some other personal crisis.

Many committees, although important, do not directly influence the remaining course of people's lives. The decisions of academic standards committees do potentially have serious long-term impact. These are high-stakes decisions for the students involved. A student who is suspended possibly may never return; a student who is expelled will have difficulty gaining admittance to any other college or university and will almost certainly lose some years before any other institution will consider admission. Therefore, you should accept service on such a committee only if you are willing to take a high degree of responsibility for very high stakes decisions about other people's lives.

REPRESENTATIVE TO THE UNIVERSITY ATHLETICS COMMITTEE

If you are interested in college or university athletics, this is the committee for you. The athletics committee usually deals with the interface between the academic community and the athletics department. You will be representing the academic community, so at times you may find yourself in conflict with the athletics department. Such a committee may deal with such issues as athletic scholarships, special academic assistance for athletes, policies regarding students participating in games away from home, and awards. In an institution with a Division I athletic program, service on this committee actually can become stressful because the financial and other stakes of the athletics are so high.

DEPARTMENT REPRESENTATIVE TO THE DIVERSITY COMMITTEE

The diversity committee deals with ways of promoting diversity on campus. In recent times, service on such a committee has become more important but also more stressful because of demands of some students and faculty for diversity-related initiatives or concessions that the university may not be willing to meet. Nevertheless, because diversity is so important to the academic mission of all institutions, service on such a committee can be valuable to the institution and to you personally.

If you are a faculty member who is also a member of an underrepresented group, you are more likely to be asked to serve on this committee—but also on many other committees. A skill that you will have to cultivate to preserve your ability to accomplish your career goals, and also to preserve your sanity, is how to say no. You are likely to be asked to do much more than you possibly could have time for, and unless you learn how to say no, you may find yourself frittering your time away with a multitude of responsibilities that will not get you over the tenure and promotion bar.

DEPARTMENT REPRESENTATIVE TO THE FACULTY COMPENSATION COMMITTEE

Compensation committees generally study compensation across units of a university, across different colleges and universities, across genders or other groups, and historically over time. Their goal is to ensure that compensation is fair and distributed in an equitable manner. For example, such a committee might find that one ethnic group appears to be underpaid, holding constant various other factors that might confound the analysis, or that the institution shows salary compression—that is, individuals who have served a long time tending to show salaries that are squeezed together, so that although starting salary may be adequate, raises may not be.

For a compensation committee to do its job adequately, it needs some members with advanced statistical expertise. This is important because simple comparisons often are deceiving. For example, one group may be paid less than another, but the difference in pay may be attributable to the average number of years of service or to levels of professional advancement. It is important, therefore, if you serve on such a committee, that you carefully document any claims that are made so that they are not later found to be confounded and the credibility of your committee thereby reduced.

DEPARTMENT REPRESENTATIVE TO THE COMMUNITY RELATIONS COMMITTEE

Relations between academic institutions and the towns or cities in which they are located are usually less than completely smooth. There are a number of reasons for this. First, the culture of the townspeople and the college or university personnel may be somewhat different. Second, nonprofit academic institutions are tax-exempt, and townspeople may feel that they bear an unfair tax burden as a result of the fact that the academic institution is not paying taxes. The institution may make voluntary payments in place of taxes, but towns rarely feel that these payments are sufficient to compensate for the lost taxes. Universities claim they bring many benefits to town, but it is incumbent on the universities to show these benefits.

Some colleges and universities have committees that serve to enhance relations between the college or university and the community. This is an excellent committee on which to serve. At one point, I was at a university whose relationship with the community went up and down over the years. One thing that was clear to me is that the fortunes of the university were tied much more closely to those of the community than it was willing to admit. The relationship matters in terms of recruitment of faculty members, staff morale, and even attitudes of store personnel in town business establishments when serving you as a customer.

DEPARTMENT HONORS ADVISER

If you like to work with students who are academically advanced, serving as a departmental honors adviser may be the service position for you. The honors adviser makes sure that honors students meet the requirements to graduate with department honors and also advise students individually. Sometimes they do so in addition to a regular academic adviser, but other times they serve as the sole academic adviser. This is a great job because it will bring you in touch with the very best students in the department. It also may result in some of these students deciding they want to work with you in one capacity or another.

DEPARTMENT REPRESENTATIVE TO THE INSTITUTIONAL REVIEW BOARD

The department representative to the institutional review board (IRB) carefully reads IRB submissions from researchers and helps decide whether each submission meets the ethical requirements of the institution (and funding agencies). This is not an easy job because ethical lapses are not highlighted in the submissions; the committee members have to ferret them out. Often there are ambiguities in the submissions that need to be resolved with a revision of the original submission. One thing to realize is that many researchers resent having to submit to an IRB or else believe that their submissions have been unfairly tied up with the committee, lost in trivial detail. So you may find yourself having to justify the efforts of the board to faculty members who are skeptical about the work you are doing in vetting submissions.

DEPARTMENT REPRESENTATIVE TO THE HONORARY DEGREES COMMITTEE

Some colleges and universities award honorary doctorates to distinguished individuals who may or may not have attended the institution. These individuals are usually chosen from the ranks of the extremely accomplished. The job of the committee is to vet nominations for honorary doctorates. Often the final decisions are made not by the committee but by a high administrative official, such as the president or chancellor (or his or her representative).

Generally, work on such a committee is gratifying because it is a chance to review the credentials of outstanding individuals. But not infrequently, names are slipped in that are those of prominent benefactors of the institution, who may or may not have shown outstanding accomplishments beyond contributing to the institution. Or the names may be of people who are not benefactors but nevertheless have strong political connections. It is then a responsibility of the committee to decide whether these individuals truly deserve honorary degrees.

DEPARTMENT REPRESENTATIVE TO THE UNIVERSITY CAPITAL CONSTRUCTION COMMITTEE

The university capital construction committee makes recommendations on capital construction projects, such as new libraries, research facilities, classrooms, or athletic stadiums. These decisions are typically very complex, involving issues of funding, location, naming, and competing demands from multiple constituencies. The committee almost never will make the final decision on a capital construction project, but administrators who do make the decisions usually take committee recommendations seriously.

DEPARTMENT REPRESENTATIVE TO THE UNIVERSITY TECHNOLOGY TRANSFER COMMITTEE

A university technology transfer committee is concerned with how technology devised by university personnel can be transferred into active commercial use. It deals with issues such as which projects to support, how to allocate revenue, and what directions in technology transfer the university should pursue. In current times, many millions of dollars can be involved in the decisions that are made, so if you are interested in technology transfer, this is a worthwhile committee on which to serve.

DEPARTMENT REPRESENTATIVE TO THE WORK–LIFE BALANCE COMMITTEE

The work–life balance committee may look into issues such as leave time for impending births, leave time after a birth occurs, sabbatical leave policies, vacation policies, and the like. It is a worthwhile committee for those concerned that the institution put in place policies that recognize family life, and not just work, as important to an individual's life development.

AD HOC COMMITTEE MEMBER

Departments form many ad hoc committees to deal with various matters as they come up. You need to decide on the value of each of these to yourself and to your career as you are offered opportunities to be on them. If you are asked by a chair to serve, consider doing so unless you really do not want to be on the ad hoc committee. This is a chance to show that you care about others beside yourself.

* * *

This list is likely to be highly incomplete for any given institution. As a junior faculty member, you will not have time to do a lot of service work. So choose carefully what you do so that it not only checks off a service box but also gives you professional and personal satisfaction.

Here we have talked about service to your institution. Next, let's talk about service to your academic discipline.

10
SERVICE TO YOUR ACADEMIC FIELD

All academics are expected to contribute some service to their academic field. Such service may or may not be an explicit consideration in a promotion or tenure decision, but it is nevertheless expected. For example, the system of academic peer review would break down if academics only wanted their articles reviewed but were unwilling to review the articles of others. Professional organizations, such as the American Psychological Association (APA) or Association for Psychological Science (APS), could not exist if their members were unwilling to serve. There are a number of options, ranging in responsibility from quite minor to very major.

JOURNAL REVIEWER

The most basic form of service is probably as a reviewer for a professional journal. An article is sent to you, these days usually electronically, and you are expected to comment within a given period of time, typically 3 to 4 weeks.

Journal editors usually ask for your comments, perhaps for ratings of the article on a Likert scale, and for a final recommendation (usually, "accept," "accept with revisions," "revise and resubmit," or "reject"). All but the last option enable the scholar to resubmit the article to the journal in a revised form.

Most reviews of articles for journals are not particularly arduous and can be done expeditiously. But then there are articles that are hard to slog through, such as ones with many mathematical equations or ones with many experiments.

I strongly recommend that you review when you can, because you will want others to review your work. Also, you will get a sense of what works well in articles and what does not work so well. As a three-time journal editor, I also would suggest that you agree to review only if (a) you plan to take the job seriously and read the submission carefully and (b) you can get the review back to the action editor on time. I would venture to guess that you do not like it when journal editors take seemingly forever to get back to you. Neither does anyone else.

Before you review an article, you need to ascertain that you have no conflict of interest. Do not review articles from colleagues at your own institution, former mentors, friends, relatives, and so forth. You also should be careful about reviewing an article that you might see as competing with an article you have submitted or plan to submit. When you come up for promotion, institutions typically are interested in how much reviewing you have done and for what journals, because being selected as a reviewer shows you are getting name recognition in your field.

REVIEWER FOR A PROFESSIONAL CONFERENCE

Professional conferences, such as those of APA and APS, are always looking for reviewers of submitted proposals. You can help your field—and yourself—by agreeing to serve as a reviewer for conference proposals, which may take the form of posters, single talks, or symposia.

JOURNAL CONSULTING EDITOR

A consulting editor is typically a scientist who has reviewed multiple times for a journal and whose reviews have proved to be particularly valuable to the journal editor. If you accept an appointment as a consulting editor, you should expect to receive articles to review from the designated journal on a fairly regular basis. Again, accept only if you have time: Being a consulting editor means you are planning to do a substantial amount of reviewing. In general, a consulting editor should turn down a reviewing assignment for the relevant journal only if he or she really feels he or she is an inappropriate choice to review the article or is facing a serious time crunch.

When you are a consulting editor, you usually will get articles further outside your main areas of expertise than is the case if you are a regular reviewer. Being a consulting editor as a junior faculty member is one way of showing that you have "arrived," at least to some meaningful extent—that you are being recognized by one or more key people in your field as someone to reckon with.

JOURNAL ASSOCIATE EDITOR

An associate editor is a step above a consulting editor. The associate editor is assigned articles by the editor-in-chief, and he or she then seeks reviewers for the assigned articles. Typically, the associate editor is authorized to make decisions on submitted articles, usually subject to approval by the editor-in-chief. Being an associate editor is quite a bit of work, and I recommend you defer taking on this position until you are a senior faculty member. Associate editors generally receive some financial compensation for their work, although it usually is not very large. If you agree to be an associate editor, you should be familiar with the editor for whom you will work. You do not want to spend your time resolving frictions with the editor!

JOURNAL EDITOR

If you are a junior faculty member, in two words, *forget it*. As a junior faculty member, you generally should not accept a journal editorship. An editorship easily can take up 20 hours a week or more, and this is not the way you should be spending your time as a junior faculty member. It's a great job, but for later in your career. Journal editors almost always receive financial compensation for their work. The amount depends on the publisher.

PREPUBLICATION BOOK OR PROPOSAL REVIEWER FOR A BOOK PUBLISHER

When book publishers are thinking of publishing a book, they often seek reviewers at two stages of the process. The first stage is a book proposal. A book proposal basically tells the reader what the author plans to write, why he or she plans to write it, and how he or she plans to get it done. Book proposals usually range from about 10 to 25 pages of text. Reading book proposals is a good way of learning about what is happening in your field. As usual, be careful to avoid any conflict of interest or even the appearance of a conflict of interest.

The second stage is a prepublication book. Reviewing a prepublication book for a publisher is a much more time consuming process. It involves your reading an entire manuscript and, typically, providing detailed comments and recommendations, which the author will consider during the revision stage. Because the job is more work than reviewing a proposal, it almost always is better compensated. I recommend that you do this job only if you are seriously interested in the contents of the book.

Reviewers of books for publishers are typically compensated either with free books from the publisher or money, or sometimes both. Sometimes you get to choose which you want. The value of the free books is typically substantially greater than the financial compensation you will be offered, but at the same time, you may be able to get the books more cheaply than the publisher normally would sell them for.

COMMITTEE MEMBER OF A PROFESSIONAL ASSOCIATION

Most professional associations have various committees. Examples are a publications committee, a membership committee, an awards committee, a fellows committee, and so forth. The larger the professional association, the greater the number of committees it is likely to have. Serving on a committee is an excellent way to meet other people with interests related to yours and also to make a difference to the association. These days, much committee work is done over the Internet and through a single in-person meeting tied in with the (usually) annual meeting of the association. Occasionally, other meetings will be scheduled as well, especially for very large associations such as APA. Committee work generally is not onerous and is a way of showing to the world that you are involved in and care about your profession.

COUNCIL MEMBER OF A PROFESSIONAL ASSOCIATION

Some professional associations, such as APA and the Federation of Associations in Behavioral and Brain Sciences, have a council. The council often is charged with making important decisions for the association. Council meetings may be once a year in conjunction with an annual meeting of the association or, as in the case of APA, more often. Serving on a council is another way of learning a lot about what's going on in your field and of meeting people. However, service on a council is probably optimal for those with some kind of political bent. Especially when an organization is in a time of crisis, council membership can be demanding. And some of the demands are in terms of political skills rather than the substantive research skills that tend to be valued more in academic work.

BOARD MEMBER OF A PROFESSIONAL ASSOCIATION

Generally, junior faculty members are not asked to serve on boards, but their service is not unheard of. The board is the executive arm of the association. It is charged with the well-being of the organization and its membership. It often makes recommendations to the council, and may make decisions itself about governance if an emergency presents itself. Board membership is usually demanding in terms of time and energy requirements and, in my opinion, is better left until after one achieves senior status in one's institution.

SECRETARY OF A PROFESSIONAL ASSOCIATION

The secretary of an organization is typically a recording secretary who keeps minutes of meetings and then circulates them to relevant members. Often the minutes are voted on. They may be modified if someone on a council or board has a different recollection of what transpired in a meeting from what the secretary recorded. Sometimes secretaries also serve in a corresponding secretary role and handle some of the correspondence of the organization.

TREASURER OF A PROFESSIONAL ASSOCIATION

Being the treasurer of a professional organization is a lot of work and usually requires knowledge of spreadsheets as well as of conservation and investment of funds. It is an extremely responsible position. You probably want to wait until you are a senior faculty member before you take on this role. Large organizations have an internal person who handles the books (e.g., a chief financial officer) and thus makes the treasurer's job easier—at least in theory.

PRESIDENT OR VICE PRESIDENT OF A DIVISION OF A PROFESSIONAL ASSOCIATION

Some professional associations, such as APA and the American Educational Research Association, are so large that they have divisions representing different interest groups. Being president (or vice president) of a division is far less work than being president or vice president of an entire association. Such a job will give you a taste of the kinds of responsibilities a top officer has without the level of responsibility of the top job. I did four of these division presidencies for APA and learned a lot from them. However, I did them after I had acquired tenure, which is probably the best time to do them because they are a fair amount of work and can sometimes lead to one's making enemies in unexpected places. Not every policy decision pleases every member, and as a junior faculty member, you may not want to risk a weaker promotion letter because of a political grudge over association business.

PRESIDENT OR VICE PRESIDENT OF A PROFESSIONAL ASSOCIATION

President or vice president is usually a highly responsible job that puts you in charge of an entire professional association. As a junior faculty member, don't even consider it. You will have too many other things you need to get done in order to advance to tenure.

BLOGGER OR TWEETER

Blogging is a relatively new way of serving a field. It typically is at the interface between service and outreach, teaching, and research. Most institutions do not fully count blogging as scholarly work, especially because blogs are not typically refereed, but some may consider it as countable toward research. Don't bank on it unless you confirm that it will count as research. Blogs more often are viewed as service in informing the field of developments, either in your own thinking or in the thinking of others. Because blogs generally count less than refereed scholarly work, I suggest you look at blogging as something you do in your free time rather than as something you do as part of your job seriously to advance your career. The same can be said for tweeting. Do it in your free time.

FORENSIC WORK

Forensic work involves working in one way or another on court cases, perhaps as an expert witness or as a consultant to an attorney or a court. Forensic work is time consuming, although it also can be quite remunerative. You should check with your department chair regarding any concerns your department might have about your getting involved in forensic work.

Forensic work can be a good way to bring your psychological work into practice. But if you are an expert witness, prepare to deal with attorneys whose ways of thinking and acting are very different from your own and who may view shaming you as simply part and parcel of their job.

CONSULTANT TO A COMMERCIAL OR NONPROFIT ORGANIZATION IN YOUR FIELD

I mentioned earlier in this chapter that publishers may call on you to review prepublication books or book proposals. But other kinds of commercial or nonprofit organizations may call on you as well. For example, a school may ask you to consult, or a software company. Such consulting is usually limited by your contract with your college or university, and you need to make sure you do not fall afoul of any institutional regulations, such as ones limiting external consulting to 1 day a week. I have done quite a bit of consulting for publishers, schools, and educational organizations of various kinds, and have found the work to be very rewarding and modestly lucrative. Colleges and universities generally do not count such work toward tenure and promotion, although some might.

FOUNDER OR OFFICER OF A COMMERCIAL VENTURE IN YOUR FIELD

Founding or serving as an officer of a commercial venture typically will require the approval of your institution and in all likelihood will be vetted for conflict of interest. Such ventures can make a lot of money and also can lead some scholars to leave academia when they realize they can make more money through their commercial work. In my opinion, such work is better done after tenure, especially if your institution is concerned that your time with the commercial venture will take time away from the teaching and research for which they believe they are paying you.

* * *

Doing service to your field is a way of networking. Let's consider networking in more detail.

V
PROFESSIONAL ADVANCEMENT

11

NETWORKING

When I thought about writing this book, the one chapter I dreaded writing was . . . this one. The reason is that I do not fancy myself to be much of a networker. I tend to be introverted; given the choice between going to a party and staying home and reading a book, I'd always pick the book. So I asked myself how I possibly could write a chapter on networking when, at best, I'm mediocre at it.

Then I thought about something else. I recently coedited a book of 100 chapters written by some of the most eminent senior psychological scientists in the field. When it came time to write to them to ask them to write a chapter for the book, I realized I knew almost all of them, at least at some level. So I asked myself: How could I know almost all of these famous psychologists if I am such a lousy networker? I'm still not sure, but I think I have a better idea than when I first thought about writing the chapter.

http://dx.doi.org/10.1037/0000013-012
Starting Your Career in Academic Psychology, by R. J. Sternberg
Copyright © 2017 by the American Psychological Association. All rights reserved.

The key word is *know*. I came to realize there are many different levels of the word *know*. There is "know of," which means that you know someone exists. Then there is "know about," which suggests that you know not only that someone exists but also something about who that person is and what he or she does. Then there is "know the work of," meaning that you know someone's work but not necessarily the individual personally. And then still further there is "know personally," meaning that you have met the person and know the person at some level. And then, of course, there is "know well."

I certainly did not know almost all of the eminent psychological scientists either well or personally. Rather, I had had enough contact during the course of my career that I felt I could address them by their first name (my criterion for feeling like I "knew" them). So maybe I am not much of a networker when it comes to knowing people well personally, but I guess I am a better networker than I thought, at least at a level at which I feel comfortable addressing many colleagues around the country (and the globe) by their first name.

How did I come to know so many people? How can you? In this chapter, I discuss the many ways you can get to know colleagues at least somewhat well—well enough possibly to call them by their first name.

GIVING TALKS AT PROFESSIONAL MEETINGS

When you give a talk at a professional meeting, people not only hear what you are working on but also get a sense of you both as a presenter and as a person. If possible, after your talk, don't rush to the next session. Hang around long enough so that people who want to talk to you after the presentation (just in case there are any!) can get to meet you and know you better than they can just by listening to a talk.

ATTENDING PROFESSIONAL MEETINGS AND ASSERTIVELY MEETING PEOPLE

Attending professional meetings is one of the best ways to meet people in your field, especially if the meetings are ones with colleagues from other institutions who have interests related to your own. But it is not enough to show up at the meeting. You need to make a serious effort to meet people. Don't stay in your room or just in talks. Hang around hallways, book exhibits, conversation groups, and so forth. The networking is not in the attendance but rather in the actual meetings you have with people.

SERVING ON COMMITTEES OF YOUR COLLEGE OR INSTITUTION

Serving on committees in your home institution is an excellent way to meet people from departments other than your own. It is worth meeting others at your institution just to establish a social network. But there is also a more serious professional reason: Promotion and tenure committees at the college or university level often comprise people from departments other than your own. It's generally advantageous for you to know some of the people on these committees before your case comes in front of them.

GOING TO BOOK EXHIBITS AT CONVENTIONS

Book exhibits are a place where you bump into all kinds of people. Some people go to the book exhibits just to bump into others—accidentally, on purpose. Book exhibits also offer an opportunity for you to meet editors and salespeople from the various publishers. If you ever submit a book proposal, it will help grease the wheels if you know in advance the acquisitions editor with whom you are dealing. (An acquisitions editor is the editor at a publishing house who is charged with acquiring new books for the publisher. There also are other kinds of editors at publishing houses. A developmental editor helps transform your book from the product you submit to one that is publishable and salable. A production editor takes the book from final manuscript to published book format. A copyeditor reads the text carefully and corrects errors as well as suggesting more felicitous ways of saying what you want to say.) And if you know the salespeople, they may be more likely to want to sell your book. Even if you do not plan to write a book, you are more likely to be asked to review book proposals or books if you have a personal relationship with the acquisitions editor at the publishing house.

SERVING ON COMMITTEES OF A PROFESSIONAL ASSOCIATION

Serving on committees of professional associations is a great way to meet people. Usually you meet not only the people on the committee but also other people in the professional association with whom the committee interacts. For example, members of a publications committee may work not only with each other but also with journal editors, journal staff, and higher-ups in the publishing operation of the association that publishes the journal.

SERVING AS A CONSULTING EDITOR OR ASSOCIATE EDITOR

I have met hundreds of people, at some level, through being an editor of three journals, an associate editor of four journals and a book series, and a consulting editor of more journals than I can count. As you work more and more with the submitters, you get to know them better. You also get to know other associate or consulting editors as well as reviewers. There is one important constraint: You must be fair, constructive, and honest. This is especially important because chances are that you will be rejecting more submissions than you accept. If you gain a positive reputation through your editorial work, you will get to know many diverse people with relatively little effort. I even have had people write to me to thank me for constructive rejection letters. Treat submitters constructively and fairly, and it will alleviate much of the pain of the rejection.

SERVING ON A GRANTS PANEL

Grants panels make recommendations on funding for grant proposals. There are many such panels. The best-known ones are probably at the National Institutes of Health and the National Science Foundation, but some of the military agencies (e.g., the Air Force Office of Scientific Research) and some foundations have grants panels as well. You not only get to know the other members of the grants panel, you also meet foundation or institute staff personnel and get a better sense of what you personally will need to do to get your grants funded. Serving on a grants panel is time consuming, so you may want to wait until you have tenure. Indeed, you may not be asked until you have tenure. But if you have the opportunity before tenure, consider taking it. You will be networking at the same time that you learn valuable lessons about how to write a fundable grant proposal.

SERVING AS AN OFFICER OF A PROFESSIONAL ASSOCIATION

Chances are that you will not be asked to serve as president of a professional association while you are still a junior faculty member. But you may be asked to serve as an officer at some lower level. If you do, you will meet a lot of people who will be useful to you in your future. Some of them may even become friends.

WRITING A BLOG

A blog is a way for people to quickly get to know what you think about various issues in your line of work. If you write a blog, make sure people have an easy way to contact you. Some of your readers likely will contact you, and some of them may even be people you want to communicate with. Even if they are not, you never know what the future holds. The advantage of a blog is that it gets your ideas out quickly and in a way that usually is more accessible than a journal article. The downside, of course, is that it probably will not count toward promotion equally with refereed journal articles.

There is one other downside of a blog: You must be very careful of what you say. Once something is on the Internet, it's there forever. Even if you delete it, it's somewhere, and others may already have copied it and passed it on to others. You hit the button, and you own it. So be careful that you don't say anything that you will come to regret later.

SEEKING A FOLLOWING ON TWITTER

Twitter is a bit of a wild card. Some people tweet endlessly and find few people to pay attention to them. Others do a few tweets, the tweets get passed around, and all of a sudden they are famous among Twitter users—or infamous. Some psychologists are almost as famous for their tweets as for their other work.

The great risk with Twitter is that you say something, perhaps in jest, perhaps without thinking, and your reputation is destroyed in moments. This is what happened to Justine Sacco, a public relations executive who made an ill-considered tweet just before boarding a flight from London, England, to Capetown, South Africa. By the time she arrived in Capetown, her tweet had been retweeted more than 2,000 times and to her great detriment. She lost her job and much of her personal reputation. In the age of the Internet, it takes only one tweet to cause a great deal of damage. So above all, be careful of what you say!

HAVING A FACEBOOK ACCOUNT THAT IS AT LEAST PARTIALLY OPEN TO COLLEAGUES

Facebook has many of the same advantages and disadvantages as Twitter. An advantage is that you can section off some material as private. But given how successful hacking has become, are you sure that you trust any privacy setting anymore?

If you are using Facebook (or Twitter, or any other form of social media) for professional purposes, please be very careful about including any personal content or any professional content that might later come back to haunt you. Statements that at the time may seem innocent or off-color jokes later can be very costly to a career, because they never disappear.

SENDING ARTICLES TO COLLEAGUES IN YOUR OWN INSTITUTION OR OTHERS

When I was starting out in my career, I was funded by an agency that encouraged its grantees to produce technical reports and then distribute them, prepublication. I put out a number of technical reports and distributed them to colleagues at other institutions who I thought might be interested in reading them. I don't know how many of the colleagues actually read the tech reports, but they certainly got to see that I was producing serious research. There is nothing wrong with sending articles with a note, as long as you realize that many people will not have time to read what you send. Even if they don't, however, they may learn what you are working on and even read the material later if they remember it and it seems relevant to them.

ATTENDING MEETINGS OF GRANT HOLDERS OR GRANT SEEKERS

Some granting organizations have occasional meetings of their grantees. I have attended a number of such meetings during the course of my career. Although the meetings are not necessarily the best way of obtaining information directly relevant to your interests, they can be an excellent way to meet other people in your field or fields related to yours. If you have a chance to attend such meetings, go to them.

WRITING ARTICLES FOR NEWSLETTERS OR NEWSPAPERS

I have found that when I publish an article in a journal, I rarely get much feedback, or at least not right away. But if I publish a less technical piece in a newsletter or newspaper (especially one like *The Chronicle of Higher Education* or, more generally, *The New York Times*, *The Wall Street Journal*, *The Washington Post*, or even regional or local newspapers), I am much more likely to get feedback. Do not hesitate to write for more general audiences.

It's a way to get your name and your views out. Realize, of course, that such publications are not a substitute for scholarly articles or books.

PRESENTING COLLOQUIA

If your career goes reasonably well, you may begin to get invitations to present departmental colloquia. If at all possible, accept such invitations. They are a great way to present your work and meet people in departments other than your own. There are important techniques you need to learn to make your colloquia effective (see Sternberg & Sternberg, 2016). Be sure to learn what these techniques are so that the colloquia enhance rather than diminish your reputation.

I learned these techniques the hard way. I remember one of the earliest colloquia I gave. Even I knew it was a bust. I was 40 minutes into a 1-hour talk, and I was still going over a flow chart from the theory section of the talk, which was worth at most 15 minutes. At 40 minutes, a fire alarm rang in the building in which I was speaking. The moderator asked everyone to leave and then come back after the fire alarm was over. You can guess how many people came back after the fire alarm. Looking back, I wonder whether someone set off the fire alarm just to relieve themselves from the pain of hearing me talk and talk and talk.

ATTENDING COLLOQUIA

Obviously, when you attend other people's colloquia, you are not, or at least should not be, the center of attention. Never use someone else's colloquium to call attention to yourself, such as by asking a series of offensive questions. If you must call attention to yourself, ask one thoughtful question, not to destroy the speaker but truly to understand what was said or its implications. But in attending colloquia, you can meet other people in the audience, and you also can meet the colloquium speaker. Often there is a reception after the colloquium, which provides you with an opportunity to make others' acquaintance and the acquaintance of the speaker.

SERVING ON A COLLOQUIUM COMMITTEE

As I mentioned in Chapter 9, serving on a colloquium committee is a no-brainer. You have the opportunity to meet scholars, often famous ones, from other departments. This is an opportunity a junior faculty member should not pass up.

PRESENTING OR ATTENDING WORKSHOPS

Sometimes professional meetings have workshops for people with specialized interests. The workshops may present statistical techniques, or therapeutic techniques, or new software. Presenting a workshop or even attending one gives you a chance to meet other people with interests very close to your own. Years ago, I attended a workshop on an advanced statistical technique. The workshop was terrible, and I would have said that I learned next to nothing from it. But in retrospect, I have kept meeting people over my career who say something like, "Hey, remember when we were together in that awful workshop on . . . ?" That awful workshop was a way to meet the colleagues and, even years later, to carry on conversations with them.

GOING TO PARTIES AT CONFERENCES

I have already told you I'm not much of one for parties. But when I was early in my career, I went to lots of them because it was a way to meet people in an informal setting. Even if you don't feel like going, go to some of them anyway. The parties at the very least will be a way of networking with other people. And you may even have a good time.

INTRODUCING YOURSELF TO FAMOUS OR NOT-SO-FAMOUS PEOPLE

When I was a junior faculty member, I missed the opportunity to get to know famous people because I was too shy to go up to them. But a lot of famous people are too shy, too. After a talk or colloquium, they may actually be standing by themselves or be occupied by a bore because others are afraid to initiate a conversation with them. Go for it. Chances are they would rather talk to you than stand by themselves or talk to a crashing bore.

WRITING TO FAMOUS OR NOT-SO-FAMOUS PEOPLE WITH AN INTELLIGENT QUESTION ABOUT THEIR WORK

If you read someone's work and are interested in it, consider writing the person with an intelligent question. Although I'm by no means super famous, I have gotten hundreds of letters from colleagues, including students, over the years, asking me questions. If the question is a bad one, the person has just made a stupid mistake. I now know that the person is a time waster.

But if I get an intelligent and thought-provoking question, I've learned that out there somewhere, I have a colleague who is reflective and thoughtful about my work. Sometimes I have corresponded with the questioner multiple times. Scholars, even famous ones, usually appreciate thoughtful questions sent their way. What they don't appreciate is foolish questions, such as one I've gotten repeatedly: "What do you think intelligence is?" I've felt like answering, "Something that you could use more of." Don't ask a question in correspondence as a substitute for reading a person's work. If you do, you are showing you are lazy and probably not very bright. Use the question as a chance to show the person that you have read the work and want to understand it even better than you do.

EDITING A BOOK

I have edited many books in my career. They are a way to get scholarly credit but also to meet the people, at least through correspondence, who write for your book. You might think that you have to know the people before you ask them to contribute to your edited book, but that is not the case at all. If your book looks like it will be a winner, people may be willing to contribute even if they don't know you. But if you want to increase the chances of positive responses, try to have a publisher lined up in advance, and try to have a few well-known people who have already said yes whom you can mention in your invitation letter as already having agreed to write.

EDITING A SPECIAL SECTION OR ISSUE OF A JOURNAL

Editing a special issue of a journal is much like editing a book. You get to meet, at least long distance, the people who agree to write. I have edited special sections and issues and have enjoyed getting to know people through interactions around their contributions to the special section or issue.

SUGGESTING COLLABORATIONS WITH PEOPLE YOU BARELY KNOW

It may seem like the height of egotism to write to someone you barely know or even don't know and suggest a collaborative project. I have done it, and others have done it with me. Usually, I would have at least to know of them, or to know something about them. But you would be surprised at how often such requests receive favorable responses. Many, if not most, scientists are opportunistic: They are looking for new opportunities, including ones they may not have thought ever would present themselves. So if you are given the opportunity to collaborate or if you create such an opportunity, you likely will create a new network of colleagues.

I do have one warning regarding such collaborations. There are scholars out there who do little more than try to associate themselves with famous people. You do not want to come across as such a person. And you certainly do not want to be one. Make sure that if you collaborate with someone, you know as much as you can about the person. This is especially hard with international collaborators but no less important. You don't want to get stuck with someone who is not trustworthy, or worse.

SIGNING CONSTRUCTIVE REVIEWS OF JOURNAL ARTICLES

Although the common practice is for reviews of journal articles to be blinded, I have always preferred to sign my reviews. I did so even when I was a junior faculty member, which put me at some risk. I have felt, however, that if I write an honest, constructive, and fair review, people will appreciate it even if the review is less than positive. I've never regretted signing.

There is one thing I cannot recommend, however, which is signing only positive reviews. I find such a practice hypocritical. If you want to sign reviews, you should be prepared to sign all or none of them, not just the ones that will serve to butter up the people whose work you have reviewed positively.

TELLING PEOPLE HOW MUCH YOU LIKE THEIR WORK

It may seem like gross flattery to go up to or write to someone just to tell them how much you like their work. But if you are sincere about it, go for it. Psychological scientists, even famous ones, get large amounts of negative feedback. Almost everyone is happy every once in a while to receive positive feedback, especially if it is specific and shows that the communicator is seriously acquainted with the work he or she is complimenting.

* * *

One way of networking is to give talks and lectures. How to optimize their effectiveness is the topic of the next chapter.

12

GIVING TALKS AND LECTURES

When you go to a conference, you ideally want to give a talk or some kind of lecture. As used here, a *talk* is any kind of oral presentation. A *lecture* is usually a somewhat formal kind of talk. The principles for giving good talks—informal or formal—are pretty much the same as for giving good presentations in classrooms.

TELL A STORY

Be a storyteller: The best talks tell a story. They hold listeners' attention because they start with a question, and the talk, like a good short story, becomes the unfolding of that story, from the beginning to the end, at which point the question is answered or at least answered in part. The answer to the initial question becomes the next question, with the answer to be given, hopefully, in next year's talk.

If a listener cannot figure out the story of your talk, you are doing something wrong. For example, I might ask a question such as, Are people who trust their romantic partner less jealous when there is a perceived threat to their relationship? I might then use the talk to tell what possible hypotheses there might be about the relationship between trust and jealousy, how I set about finding out the nature of this relationship, what I found out about the relationship, and then a conclusion or take-home story—what should listeners remember when they go home?

DON'T READ A TALK

Talks that are read rarely sound quite right. They sound stilted and artificial. The reason is partially just that the talk is read, but more that the kind of diction with which people speak is different from the kind with which they write. In other words, we do not speak the way we write.

SHOW SELF-CONFIDENCE

If you show a lack of confidence in yourself, how can you expect others to have confidence in you? You want to appear self-confident without appearing to be arrogant.

DRESS APPROPRIATELY

What constitutes appropriate dress depends on the setting. Dress may range from casual to a suit. Find out before you go to speak what the dress code is. You want to stand out for your talk, not your way of dressing.

START OFF CONCRETELY AND WITH EXCITEMENT

You typically have at most 30 seconds to grab the attention of an audience. If you don't capture them in the first half-minute or so, they're likely already thinking about something else—perhaps the next talk they will go to, or their significant other. So start off interestingly and with a story or a concrete example of what you will be talking about. You might open with a question from which your anecdote or story follows. Never start off with boring clichés like "Research has shown . . ." or "So-and-so (2011) found that . . ." Even if your research is interesting, the audience will have learned that you are what the English might call a "bloody bore."

DESIGN YOUR SLIDE SHOW

If you are using PowerPoint or more traditional slides, think carefully about how to design your presentation as a whole, as well as about individual slides. Make sure the order of slides tells your story. And make sure the slides are attractive and not too busy. Sometimes a good presentation can get lost in the bells and whistles of PowerPoint features. Make the talk about your work, not about your skill in using fancy features of PowerPoint.

PACE YOURSELF

You do not want to be in a situation in which you are rushing your talk at the end. Doing so annoys people and also often leaves them not understanding the most important part of the talk, namely the end. So have signposts for yourself that tell you where you should be at different points in the talk, and if you are falling behind, start catching up before you have to fly through at the end.

MAKE ALLOWANCES FOR AUDIENCES WHOSE FIRST LANGUAGE IS NOT ENGLISH

If you are giving a talk to a foreign audience or to others whose first language is not English, you must make allowances for the audience's English-language skills. Slow down. Avoid colloquialisms. Avoid jargon. Be very careful about telling jokes, which often are hard enough to understand in a first language. You may need to give a shorter talk to a foreign audience than to a domestic one—you just cannot expect to cover as much material.

PRESENT AN ADVANCE ORGANIZER

Have a slide early in your talk—not the first slide, but within the first few minutes—that outlines the topics you are going to cover and how they are organized. It will help your audience follow the remainder of your talk. Without such a slide, even if your presentation is well organized, the audience may have difficulty following the logic of the talk.

ORGANIZE YOUR TALK

The more organized your talk is, the easier it will be for audiences to follow it. So think carefully in advance about the story—its beginning, the development of its middle, and its end. Then tell your story in a clear, logical fashion that makes it effortless for the audience to understand.

EMPHASIZE IMPORTANT POINTS

No matter how many or few points you make, the audience will not remember all of the points. Most people probably won't remember even half of your points. So make sure to emphasize the points that you believe are most important. Say them louder. Say them slower. Use a larger font size or bold print. Just make sure people know what you believe is more important and what you believe is less important.

DON'T SWEAR, EVEN IF YOU ARE A SWEARER

OK, I tend to be a swearer. The words just come out. But I hope not in my talks. Some people are offended by swear words, no matter how well intentioned they are. Save yourself grief: Just don't say them.

BE AWARE OF AUDIENCE SENSITIVITIES

Different audiences have different sensitivities. Being aware of these sensitivities can greatly increase the impact of your talk. I have heard more than one job talk, for example, in which a candidate did not do his or her advance research. One stray remark, and the job was lost. The candidate of course had no clue. Sensitivities might be about the history of an institution or its locale, about behavior of past or present members of the department or university, about certain kinds of research that are valued or devalued in a place, or about social or moral issues. You do not want your talk to fail for reasons irrelevant to what you say. Therefore, avoid topics or suggestions that are likely to be highly offensive in a given context.

As an example, I have on multiple occasions given talks in fundamentalist Christian institutions. I avoid, to the extent possible, topics that are irrelevant to my presentation but that are likely to be offensive to some people in the audience. It's not that I'm afraid to speak my mind. It's that the issues have nothing to do with my talk, and if I'm going to antagonize people, I'd rather do so for good reason than for no reason at all.

USE CONCRETE EXAMPLES THROUGHOUT A TALK

The more concrete examples you can use in your talk, the better. Although concrete examples may seem to you to be a waste of time—you could give more data or more scholarly citations during the time you are providing the concrete example—I guarantee you, people will remember your concrete examples better than any data and also will better understand the data you do present if they are illustrated in terms of one or more concrete examples.

ASSUME THE AUDIENCE HAS LESS BACKGROUND KNOWLEDGE THAN YOU WOULD LIKE TO BELIEVE

We all tend to overestimate how much audiences know about our topic. We become so expert in our topic that we forget what it was like before we began to learn about the topic. So be sure to be very clear about what you are studying, what terms mean, and what the basic issues are. Avoid acronyms when possible, and assume the audience has general but not specific background on the details of what you are studying.

DON'T TALK DOWN TO YOUR AUDIENCE

Although you should assume audiences have less background knowledge than you might expect, you should not assume that they are children—unless, of course, they are. I was once attending a professional conference at which a highly eminent person was giving a keynote. The eminent person was a psychologist, and the conference was one of educational researchers. The psychologist must have decided that educational researchers are a bunch of dummies because his talk was at a level that would have been suitable for a high school audience. I could see that I was not the only one offended. He was talking to us as though we were children, and no one appreciated it. Although you are usually better off assuming less about audience background, this guy was ridiculous!

DO NOT CRAM TOO MUCH CONTENT INTO YOUR TALK

I know a psychologist who I think is a good researcher and who does interesting work. I long ago stopped going to his talks, however. His goal seems to be to cram as much as he can into whatever time period he has. I used to come out of his talks exhausted. I think most others were less tired—they just gave up on listening after the first few minutes. It's better to give a talk with less but clear information than one with more information that is beyond people's ability to grasp.

SHOW ENTHUSIASM

One of my former colleagues did some of the most interesting research of anyone I know. She deals with fundamental issues and always seems to have a new twist in her research. But if you hear her talk about her work, you would think that she is dying of boredom from what she is doing and wants you to know just how bored—and boring—she can be. I know she must be enthusiastic about her work, but that enthusiasm does not come through in her talks at all. Make sure it comes out in yours. Audiences may not share your enthusiasm if it is at a high level, but if you don't have any enthusiasm, they probably won't, either.

KNOW WHO YOUR AUDIENCE IS

What are the people in your audience interested in? What is their background? Why are they at your talk? The more you know about the backgrounds of the people in your audience, the better you can adjust your talk to fit their interests and needs.

A talk should always be geared to an audience. I never give exactly the same talk to different audiences. Know your audience, and speak to their knowledge and interests.

DO NOT BE DEFENSIVE IN ANSWERING QUESTIONS

Inevitably, the time will come when someone asks a question that you find offensive. Maybe the question was meant to offend you—maybe it wasn't. When you are under the stress of answering questions, you may find questions offensive that you would brush off if you were more relaxed. Never give a defensive answer—that is, one suggesting you are offended or that you are more interested in getting back at the questioner than you are in answering his or her question. Not only will the questioner be unimpressed, so will the rest of the audience. And worse, if the questioner did intend to offend you, the questioner will know he or she got to you.

PREPARE CAREFULLY

Especially after you have been giving talks for a while, or a particular talk for a while, don't start blowing off your preparation for a talk. You need to go in as prepared the fifth time as the first. I once went into a talk not very prepared, because I had given the talk multiple times before. I don't know what happened, but that evening (it was an evening talk) I couldn't seem to remember anything. I had failed to look over my slides, and it showed. I was embarrassed. I haven't repeated such an unprepared performance.

DON'T DRINK ALCOHOL BEFORE SPEAKING

Sometimes you might attend a dinner or a reception with alcohol before you give a talk. Your colleagues and friends at the dinner or reception may be having drinks, and you may wish to join them; they also may wish for you to join them. Don't. Wait until after the talk. If you're lucky, you may get through the talk OK. But you are setting yourself up to stumble on the questions. You just can't be at your sharpest if you have been drinking alcohol. Worse, you may not even realize you are not at your best. Others will. Only once have I had alcohol before a talk. And sure enough, I stumbled on questions. I just couldn't think clearly enough to answer the hard ones. I told myself "never again," and I've stuck to it.

DECIDE HOW YOU ARE GOING TO HANDLE QUESTIONS

There are different ways of handling questions. No one way is right and the others wrong. Some talks do not have time for questions. For example, keynotes often do not leave time for questions, or questions may be impractical because of the number of people in the audience. In such cases, questions are not an issue. But many talks do allow for questions. One option is to ask listeners to hold all questions until the end. The advantage of this option is that you can have a higher degree of confidence that you will get through your talk. What's more annoying than getting through only half a talk because of all the questions, many of which never should have been asked in the first place? But a disadvantage is that people who do not understand what you said or did may lose track of the talk from the point of nonunderstanding onward.

Another option, which I use, is to accept only questions of clarification during the talk, and then all other types of questions at the end. The advantage is that people who are confused can have their confusion resolved. And if one person is confused, the chances are good that others are as well. A third option is to allow all questions at any point in the talk. I do not recommend this option. If you have a chatty audience, you likely will not get through the talk, and may not even get through half of it!

PREPARE FOR THE UNEXPECTED

I have given thousands of talks in my day, and I can't count the number of things that have gone wrong. Microphones fail. PowerPoint setups don't work. Loud drilling noises intrude from outside. I thought the talk was on one topic and then I arrived at the colloquium and it was on another. I thought the talk was at one time and it was at another. I left lots of time to get to the talk, but I did not anticipate the major accident on the highway or the snowstorm that would clog traffic. I just cannot list all of the different kinds of things that can go wrong.

You can't prepare for every possible eventuality, but prepare for as many as possible. If you are planning to use PowerPoint, bring a paper copy of your talk, or bring your computer with the talk right on it. Check and double-check the time and place of the talk. Allow much more than ample time to get to the talk. Don't take the last flight out from your airport the night before, and certainly don't go the morning of the talk. The more eventualities you prepare for, the likelier you are to give the talk and see it go as you expected it to.

DON'T LET A QUESTIONER MONOPOLIZE THE QUESTION PERIOD

Occasionally, a questioner decides that he and his questions are just so important that the value of the occasion of your talk will be much reduced unless he asks all of the many questions he has in mind. Or you may answer her question, and then she responds, and then you respond, and then she responds to your response, and so on. You need to be ready to deal with a monopolizer. What I say to the person is that there are others in the room who appear to want to be heard as well, and I would be glad to continue the conversation with him or her after the talk or through e-mail. I then just call on someone else. There is a chance that the individual still may continue to talk. In that case, it will be up to a moderator to shut the individual up. Hope that you have a moderator who is willing to do so.

NEVER GIVE A FLIP RESPONSE TO A QUESTION

I have given a flip answer to a question from the audience only once. It was during my first job interview. The questioner, who looked like a graduate student, asked what I considered to be a really silly question. I gave what I considered to be an appropriate putdown. How was I supposed to know he was chair of the search committee? I didn't get the job. I sure never did that again!

SUMMARIZE THE MAIN POINTS AT THE END

As you finish your talk, summarize the main points that you want your audience to remember. Don't overdo it. Limit your summary to three to five points. Hit just the high points, no more. But make it clear to the audience that that is what you most want them to remember.

IF YOU SEE DURING YOUR TALK THAT YOU HAVE TOO MUCH MATERIAL, REJIGGER YOUR TALK

At one point or another, everyone mistimes a talk. They think it is a long talk, when in fact it is a short one. If, during a talk, you see that you underestimated how long it would take, think as you talk about how you can cut the talk. It's happened to me. Then just skip the topics or slides that are not essential to the talk. Audiences have occasionally seen me just skip some PowerPoint slides. I tell them the truth—that the points on those slides are not all that important and I would rather spend my time with them on points that are more important to my core themes. I've never gotten a bad reaction. Audiences appreciate not being barraged with details. And I'm always willing to send the PowerPoint if people request it, so they can see what they missed.

END WITH A POWERFUL TAKE-HOME MESSAGE

What do you want people to remember when they go home? What's the big finding? Or the big idea? I often try to end with an anecdote that brings home the main message of the talk I have given.

STAY WITHIN YOUR TIME CONSTRAINTS

Few things are more annoying than speakers who go over their time. Do they really think they and their talk are more important than anything else audience members might have to do? If you are going to go over time, at least ask the audience for permission to do so. But asking them puts them in an awkward position. Best by far is just staying within your allotted time. Or if you want to show that you just know you are more important than any of them or anything else they might have to do, keep talking. They will get the message that you are an insufferable egotist.

IF YOU MAKE A MISTAKE, ADMIT IT

If you make a mistake, don't try to get around it, or to evade responsibility, or to pretend it wasn't a mistake. Just admit it! People will respect you much more for admitting to a mistake than for trying to get out of it.

PRESENT AN E-MAIL OR WEB ADDRESS WHERE MORE INFORMATION IS AVAILABLE

I usually put my e-mail address on my first slide. A good idea is to repeat it at the end, inviting correspondence.

INVITE FEEDBACK

Tell people you would like to hear from them. Then, when you do, answer back. You may learn a lot and even make some new friends.

* * *

Now that we've discussed giving talks, let's discuss a related issue, writing articles.

13

WRITING ARTICLES

When you write articles, there are things you can keep in mind that will help make your articles the best they can be. This chapter lists some of them.

WHAT'S YOUR MESSAGE?

Before you even start writing, ask yourself why anyone should care about what you have to say. What is your message? What is interesting about it? How can you motivate readers to hear what you have to say? If you cannot summarize your message in a sentence or two, you are off to the wrong start. Excellent articles have a message. Not-so-good articles just go on and on, leaving readers to figure out what the author is trying to say. If you do not know what your message is, how are your readers going to know? Have the message in mind while you write, and try to ensure that the article is clearly working toward conveying that message.

---

http://dx.doi.org/10.1037/0000013-014
Starting Your Career in Academic Psychology, by R. J. Sternberg
Copyright © 2017 by the American Psychological Association. All rights reserved.

IF YOUR MESSAGE IS NEW AND DIFFERENT, HOW WILL YOU PERSUADE PEOPLE OF IT?

New ideas are a tough sell. People are used to thinking in certain ways. If you want them to think in a different way, then you need to lead them gradually from where they are in their thinking to where you want them to be. Do not assume that highly creative ideas just sell themselves. You need to think of a way to persuade people to give up their conventional ways of thinking.

WHAT STORY DO YOU WANT TO TELL?

The story is how people get from whatever they know and think to whatever you want them to know and think—that is, to an understanding and hopefully acceptance of your message. Just as in a talk, you need some sense of a beginning, middle, and end. The beginning is where the audience is now; the ending is where you want the audience to be. And what comes in between is to get the audience from where they are to where you want them to be. If you cannot figure out the story—a way to move people's thinking—then you are not ready to write the article.

WHO IS YOUR AUDIENCE?

A question you need to ask yourself before you even start writing is whom you are addressing. Are you writing for experts or novices? Are they generalists or specialists in your field? Are they people who are likely to agree with what you say, to have no opinion, or to disagree? The more you can figure out who your audience is, the more effectively you can write. If you do not know who your audience is, you are doing something wrong. You always should write with one or a few target journals in mind, journals that have similar although obviously not identical audiences. If you write to no audience in particular, no audience in particular will want to read your article.

WHAT'S NEW IN YOUR STORY AND YOUR DATA?

Whether your article is data based or theory based or a review of the literature, you need to think about what you have to say that is new. People want to know the news. Imagine watching a news program on television or on the Internet, and it turns out that all that is said is a rehash of what you already know. How interested will you be?

As I write this chapter, I am sitting on a plane next to my daughter, who is watching a children's movie she has watched before for the umpteenth time. She is 5. Maybe when you were 5, you were content to hear the same thing over and over again. But probably you no longer are. So emphasize what is new so that people will be intrigued by what you have to say. At the same time, to the extent possible, couch what is new in familiar language so that people will spend their effort figuring out what's new in your ideas or your data, not in how you tell about them.

IS THE STORY YOU HAVE TO TELL THE ONE YOU ORIGINALLY PLANNED TO TELL?

Sometimes we find that the story our literature review or our data leave us to tell is not the story we originally planned to write. That is, the story has changed. On the one hand, you owe it to your readers to tell them that the story the data have to tell is not the one you originally planned for. On the other hand, you do not want to obsess over the change. Emphasize the new story, simply indicating that the one you are now telling is not the one you originally planned to tell.

WILL GRADUATE STUDENTS UNDERSTAND WHAT YOU SAY?

No matter how sophisticated your intended audience is, try to write at a level intelligent beginning graduate students will understand. Sooner or later, if your article is successful, beginning graduate students will be reading it. And as they are the future of the profession, you want to be sure they can take what you have written and build on it. For certain articles, you will want to write at even a more basic level. I have edited three journals, and I would say that the Number 1 problem I have encountered is articles that are too hard to understand. The Number 2 problem is articles that appeal only to a very limited audience of readers.

WHO WILL DISAGREE WITH YOUR ARTICLE?

You want to write with your referees in mind, including ones who probably will not be inclined to agree with everything you say. Before submitting an article, ask yourself whether what you are saying is likely to be controversial. If there are obvious critiques of what you say, it is better to address them in the article before the article goes out for review rather than after. If there are obvious ambiguities in the interpretation of the data, address them. If your data support your interpretation but also might support someone else's, address how one might distinguish between the two interpretations, even if only in future research. Don't give hostile referees the pleasure of shooting you down. Instead, anticipate their arguments.

IF YOUR ARTICLE IS AN EMPIRICAL ONE, HOW DOES THE DESIGN TEST YOUR HYPOTHESES?

It may seem obvious to you how your study tests your proposed hypotheses, but it may not be obvious to your readers. So do not leave it to chance whether they can figure out how the design actually tests what you are hypothesizing. Make it clear. And if you cannot do so, don't expect your readers to be able to.

HAVE YOU POLISHED AND PROOFREAD?

Referees typically are not paid to review your work. They review as a service to the field and also, usually, because they are at least somewhat interested in what you have to say. What they are not interested in is correcting your spelling, grammatical, and diction errors. They are not grade school teachers who are there to correct obvious errors. If you do not treat them with respect—that is, polish and proofread your article before you send it out—how can you expect them to treat you with respect? My observation is that referees usually do not reject a submission because it has obvious typographical errors, but they will be less tolerant of other flaws in the article and hence more likely to recommend that the article be rejected if they find substantive errors or ambiguities in it.

DOES THE TITLE OF YOUR ARTICLE BRIEFLY CONVEY WHAT THE ARTICLE IS ABOUT AND, IF POSSIBLE, WHAT ITS MESSAGE IS?

There are far more journals and articles to read than ever before in the history of psychological science. No one can read everything. When scholars decide what to read, they usually start their decision-making process with the title. The title is, or at least should be, the key to what they will find in your article. If it is not, some people who should read the article will not read it because they will not realize it is relevant to their interests. Moreover, titles often are indexed. Having appropriate key words in the title thus can help ensure that the article will reach those who most will want to read it.

IS THE LENGTH OF YOUR ARTICLE PROPORTIONAL TO ITS NEW CONTRIBUTION?

Most journals have length limitations; some do not. But all journal editors expect that the longer an article is, the more new it should have to say. Put another way, if you do not have a whole lot new to say, keep your article short. If you do have a lot of new things to say, keep the article as short as you can, proportional to the contribution you believe it makes.

IS THE ABSTRACT AS INFORMATIVE AS POSSIBLE?

Of course, you want readers to read your whole article, not just your abstract. But for better or worse, in part because people are so busy, some people never will get beyond the abstract. For the sake of those readers, make sure that the abstract conveys the most important details about your study and its findings. You may feel that being comprehensive in the abstract risks giving away the rest of the article. That may be true. But people who are seriously interested in what you are doing will read the whole article anyway. People who are not seriously interested will stick with the abstract, and if you write a comprehensive abstract, they will know the gist of what you found.

HAVE YOU ACTIVELY SOUGHT AND TAKEN INTO ACCOUNT FEEDBACK?

The more you seek feedback on an article before submitting it, the better the article is likely to be. Your chances of an acceptance, initial or eventual, will be much higher if you actively seek feedback.

When you get feedback from referees, take it seriously. In my experience as a journal editor, when referees are sent a revision, nothing irritates them more than getting a revision that shows that the author was oblivious to the feedback he or she received. Even if you disagree with some of the feedback you received, do not just ignore it. State in a revision letter why you chose not to follow it. And when you do, show respect for the referee who made the suggestion. Do not just blow off steam and show how critical and disrespectful you can be of the referee. One other thing: Don't be defensive about feedback. Even if you disagree with it, be thankful to the person who provided it and take it seriously, even if you decide ultimately not to use it.

IF YOU ARE WRITING A LITERATURE REVIEW, DO YOU GO BEYOND JUST SUMMARIZING WHAT OTHER PEOPLE HAVE FOUND?

One of the journals I edited, *Psychological Bulletin*, was a journal of literature reviews. Some of the rejected submissions were nothing more than dissertation literature reviews, or might as well have been. What distinguished such reviews is that they reviewed literature without having any kind of strong organizing ideas or principles. They amounted to little more than "X said this" and "Y said that." This is not the kind of literature review you want to submit for publication. You want a literature review that presents compelling ideas for organizing a body of literature. As a result, a good literature review often has much of its action up front, when its organization is described, and at the end, when conclusions are drawn that are based on the organizing principles. If you are just summarizing, you are not ready for prime time.

WHAT'S YOUR TAKE-HOME MESSAGE?

A good article, like a good talk, has a take-home message. It does not just leave readers hanging or trying to figure out what they are supposed to have learned from what they read. If you cannot say in a few sentences what the readers are supposed to have learned that you want them to remember, you need to rethink what you have written. When you do not have a clear take-home message, readers may end up remembering little or nothing of what you have written.

HAVE YOU FOUND THE JOURNAL THAT'S THE RIGHT FIT FOR YOUR ARTICLE?

Journals typically take several months to make a decision on your submission. If you get an acceptance, great, and if you are given a chance to revise, well, good luck! But if you are rejected outright, you just wasted 2 or 3 months during which your article might have been on the way toward publication. At best, you will get feedback you can use to revise your article.

But at worst, the time simply will be lost. This is not, ideally, where you want to be. Your goal should be to try to choose a journal from which, at the very least, you can get a revise-and-resubmit action.

Here are some questions you can ask yourself before the submission: Is the topic of the article appropriate for the journal to which you plan to submit? Is the approach you have taken consistent with the mission of the journal? (For example, you don't want to submit a case study to an experimental journal.) Are there other articles the journal has published recently that are similar to yours in content and approach? Is the quality of the article appropriate for the competitiveness of the journal in accepting articles? Is the length appropriate? If you cannot answer yes to these questions, be sure to reconsider whether your choice of journal is appropriate.

HAVE YOU CONCRETELY RELATED WHAT YOU HAVE WRITTEN TO EVERYDAY EXPERIENCE?

Scientists of all kinds tend to write in abstract ways. The problem with this practice is that people often have trouble understanding abstractions. The more concrete you can make your presentation, and the more you can relate it to people's everyday experiences, the better people's comprehension of what you have written will be. Wherever you can, therefore, try to relate your presentation to things people know about and deal with in their everyday lives.

IS YOUR LITERATURE REVIEW TARGETED TO THE QUESTIONS YOU ASK IN YOUR WORK?

Most articles, whether empirical or not, have literature reviews. It is important in the literature review to cite relevant work. Indeed, this morning, when writing action letters on submissions to the journal I currently edit, I desk rejected (i.e., rejected without external review) an article whose literature review was so deficient that I did not even think it was worth the reviewers' time to read it. But almost as bad as a literature review that ignores large parts of the relevant literature is one that is unfocused—that just includes citations seemingly for the sake of including them, for padding the review. Keep the literature review focused on the questions you ask, rather than wandering and digressing so that the literature review seems as though it would have been relevant to almost anything anyone might have written on your topic.

IS YOUR USE OF QUOTATIONS CONSISTENT WITH YOUR NEED FOR QUOTATIONS?

Some writers, especially those who are just starting out, overquote. Their article seems to be more a string of quotations than a well-thought-through article. No one wants to read one long quote after another, as though the author is using quotes from others for lack of his or her own ideas. Use quotes when ideas are expressed in a particular way that is important to what you have to say. Otherwise, put things in your own words rather than directly quoting.

ARE YOU KEEPING THE IMPORTANCE OF YOUR WORK IN PERSPECTIVE?

No referee likes to read an article with fairly pedestrian findings that makes the findings sound as though they're the greatest thing since sliced bread. Do not oversell the importance of what you have found. Of course, you do not want to undersell it either, but in the end, it is overselling that most irritates referees. Put your work into a historical perspective, show what you have added to past work, and then let readers decide how important your ideas and data are, rather than vigorously reminding them.

HAVE YOU BEEN CURRENT AND GENEROUS IN YOUR CITATIONS?

Sometimes we get stale in our referencing. We get used to referencing certain sources and then start using the same references again and again. Sooner or later, usually sooner, the referencing becomes stale. So continually update your citations, and when in doubt, cite work that you think may be relevant. Also keep in mind that referees, when they receive articles to review, sometimes start at the end of the article rather than the beginning. That is, the referees look to see whether they are cited for work of their own they believe to be relevant. If they are not cited, they may tend to be less sympathetic to the article.

ARE YOU USING PRIMARY OR SECONDARY SOURCES?

When you write an article, cite primary sources whenever possible. That is, cite original articles rather than articles or books that cite the original articles. There are three reasons primary sources are important. First, you show readers that you are a serious scholar. Second, you do not replicate errors. More often than anyone would like, secondary sources misrepresent primary sources. As the secondary sources are cited again and again, the errors are replicated. Third, you will have the satisfaction of knowing that what you say is based on original documents, not possibly faulty summaries of them.

WHEN YOU WRITE UP RESULTS, DO YOU LET YOUR STORY GUIDE THEM RATHER THAN THE PARTICULAR DATA ANALYSES YOU DID?

Results sections should be in the service of the story the results tell. But what often happens is that the particular data analyses take over. Instead of the results section telling your story, the results tell the story of your particular progression of data analyses. How many times have you read a results section in which you lose any sense of what was done and why? You want ideas to guide the results section, not the data analyses you happened to do. That is, the data analyses should be in the service of ideas, not ends in themselves. Furthermore, don't overwhelm readers with data or data analyses. You should be able to justify each data analysis in terms of how it contributes to your story. If you cannot justify a data analysis, don't include it.

HAVE YOU BEEN FORTHCOMING IN ANY MANIPULATIONS YOU DID ON THE DATA?

No one likes to be played for a sucker. That is, no one wants to read your data analyses not knowing how you manipulated the data in the service of your analyses. Did you omit outliers? If so, how did you decide what constitutes an outlier? Did you have missing data? Did you have to throw away cases? If so, how many, and how do you know that the data left are representative of the original sample? Did you do any transformations on the data? Did you do other forms of cleaning? It's fine to do what you absolutely need to in order to make your data analyzable, but you must share with readers what you did.

DO YOUR CONCLUSIONS REALLY FOLLOW FROM YOUR DATA?

When we go into an empirical study, we usually have some idea regarding how we would like, or at least expect, our data to turn out. In my experience, the data often turn out almost any way except the way I initially expected.

Sometimes they turn out better, sometimes worse, and sometimes just different. But often we have trouble letting go of what we wanted to find. So we start seeing what we wanted to find, much as we see what we want to find in a Rorschach inkblots test. The difference is that the Rorschach inkblots truly have no meaning, whereas our data almost inevitably do have a meaning, although not necessarily one we can easily find. And it may take further research to make complete sense of the data. But in your discussion, go with what the data really say, not just with what you hoped they would say.

DOES YOUR DISCUSSION SECTION ACCOMPLISH WHAT IT NEEDS TO?

A good discussion section summarizes key results, but it also does more. It relates those results back to the original theory and hypotheses. It also discusses the limitations of the study and its data. What questions are answered, and what questions remain to be answered? How might those remaining questions be addressed? The discussion should have some kind of argument; that is, it should make one or more points. It should not be merely some kind of recounting.

IS YOUR ENDING STRONG?

You want your ending to make as strong a statement or set of statements as possible. And you want to end on a positive note. You might end with some kind of a story or with some kind of application to everyday life. Or you might want to end by relating your findings to what others have found. Here is what you do not want to do: You do not want to end with some kind of statement to the effect that "further research is needed." Further research is almost always needed. Really, how often does any study or even set of studies definitively end a line of research? Almost never. So ending by saying that further research is needed is sort of like ending by saying that the sun will come up tomorrow morning some time. Do people really need to be told what they already know? Also, do not end with something like, "So, in conclusion, no conclusive statement is possible." It is really rare in psychological research that anything truly is conclusive. Again, you don't have to tell people what they already know. And if truly there is nothing even vaguely conclusive in your data, you need to ask yourself whether you have enough to seek publication.

IF YOU ARE REJECTED WITH PREJUDICE (NO RESUBMISSION POSSIBLE), HOW DO YOU MOVE FORWARD?

If worst comes to worst, and you are rejected without possibility of resubmission (with prejudice), how do you move forward? You have several options. First, you can appeal to the editor that he or she reconsider and allow a resubmission. I do not recommend this course of action unless you seriously believe that a review or an editorial letter is just grossly unfair. In that case, you can write an appeal letter, indicating why you believe reconsideration is reasonable. Generally, you will need really strong arguments in order to get the reconsideration. And even if you have them, you would still be better off trying the journal that is your next option.

Second, you can resubmit to another, possibly less competitive journal. If you do, you will want to ensure that you have read the reviews carefully, figured out why your article was rejected, and fixed whatever it was that needed fixing. Otherwise, you are inviting a repeat performance of the rejection.

Third, you can wait until you have collected more data or reformulated a literature review and then submit to another journal. In other words, you do a resubmission, but not right away. You use the time in between to figure out how you can improve your chances of acceptance.

Fourth, you can abandon the article altogether. Although this is an extreme course of action, many of us who have been in the field a long time have had at least one submission that we have decided is best abandoned.

Fifth, you might try seeking a coauthor or a further coauthor who might have ideas about how to get your article to publication. If you have run out of steam on the article, sometimes someone else can see what you cannot and help you bring an article you thought was moribund back into the land of the living.

Whatever you decide, good luck! Nothing is more important to science than its becoming public, and when you publish, you help make your own science public for all to see.

*   *   *

I have discussed some of the nuts and bolts of succeeding as a new faculty member by writing articles. If you would like more detail, you might look at Sternberg (2000). Now let's turn to something less substantive but no less important: politics.

14

DEPARTMENTAL AND UNIVERSITY POLITICS

Departmental and university politics are an aspect of life in all departments. Some departmental and university politics are basically benign. You simply learn to live with them, and smile if you can. Other politics are anything but benign, and they may be malignant for the life of the department or university—and for your life, too. As a junior faculty member, your ability to intervene in departmental and university politics may be fairly minimal, and you may want to keep it that way. But at the very least, you should know what kinds of things you might expect to encounter.

Academics sometimes view departmental and university politics as a necessary evil. But they are not always evil. All functioning organizations have political give-and-take. That's largely how they get things done. So although you may cast a jaded or even cynical eye on departmental and university politics, remember that politics greases the wheels for progress to be made.

---

http://dx.doi.org/10.1037/0000013-015
Starting Your Career in Academic Psychology, by R. J. Sternberg
Copyright © 2017 by the American Psychological Association. All rights reserved.

All the quotes I've listed in this chapter are ones I have encountered at one time or another in my own career.

"THAT'S THE WAY THINGS ARE DONE AROUND HERE"

Basically, you're told to buzz off, or to put it another way, it's the department's way or the highway. This mentality is harmful for a department because it makes it very hard to effect meaningful change. Moreover, it assumes that the way things are done is the way they should be done. As a junior faculty member, you may not be able to make major changes in the way things are done, but you may be able to achieve work-arounds from time to time.

"LET'S LISTEN TO X, BECAUSE HE KNOWS BEST"

Every department has a preexisting power structure that was there long before you arrived. Part of this power structure is showing deference to the views or ways of the people who command power, if not respect, in the department. The problem, of course, is that X, whoever she is, may not know best. You should listen to X, and Y and Z, too, but in the end, you are now launching your own career, and you must decide for yourself what is true or false, right or wrong.

"IF X SAID IT, YOU KNOW IT'S NOT WORTH LISTENING TO"

Just as there are powerful people whose views command respect and often obedience, so are there people so low down on the totem pole that they are regarded as largely irrelevant to the department's power structure. Sometimes they truly are people whose views may not be worth much. More often they just are viewed as too young, too old, the wrong gender, the wrong race, the wrong political faction, or whatever. Decide for yourself who is worth listening to. In my experience, almost everyone has good things to say at least some of the time.

"LET'S HIRE MY FRIEND OR RELATIVE"

Everyone has someone for whom he or she wants to do a good turn. It may be a spouse, a child, a best friend, a colleague to whom one feels one owes something, or whomever. Departments that engage in this kind of nepotism or buildup of networks of friends usually find themselves on the road to mediocrity. It may be that the friend or relative is really the best person, but you almost never can tell without an open search. You may not be able to insist on an open search, but you certainly can support one.

"LET'S ADMIT MY UNDERGRADUATE RESEARCH ASSISTANT TO OUR GRADUATE PROGRAM"

It's hard to get good graduate students. Sometimes faculty members see a source of good graduate students in their current research assistants. By admitting the assistant as a graduate student, the faculty member is assured of having a student for whatever number of years are needed for the individual to complete the relevant graduate program. There are three problems with this approach. First, it may well be that there is someone who is a better candidate who just does not have the advantage of having come from the—or at least a—lab of a departmental faculty member. Second, it is often better for assistants to go for graduate study elsewhere so that they can be exposed to more diverse points of view. Third, departments that become ingrown—that make a lot of internal hires and student selections—often end up going downhill because they fail to be exposed to a diversity of types of people and perspectives.

"IF YOU WANT TENURE, JUST SHUT UP AND GET ON THE TRAIN"

I was once told that the train was leaving the station, and either I could get on it or stay off it. In other words, I either could go along with the particular (I thought, bad) policies that the department chair wanted to implement, or I could go my own way at my peril. I've never been good at that particular game. Like many academics, I went into academia to be myself, not to be a toady to someone else. I did not get on the train. I did get tenure. But I might not have. In that case, I would have gone elsewhere. That said, I was a high-level administrator at one point, and I also was essentially told to board the train or get off. I got off; I got out. I found myself a new job.

"THE TRAIN HAS ALREADY LEFT THE STATION"

In this case, you are told that it is too late for you to decide to get off the train because you are on it and it is running at full speed. And sometimes decisions truly have been made and it is too late to go back on them. But sometimes the train's having left is only an illusion. Maybe its engine is running but it has not yet started moving, or maybe it's moving but at a very slow speed. You need to decide for yourself whether you are on a moving train and, if so, whether it is possible to get off of it.

"THAT BELONGS TO X"

In departments, there always is individual property and shared property. Most property is actually owned by the college or university and merely loaned out to faculty members. But when people have been in a place for a long time, they begin to accrue resources, including ones they do not need. For example, I was in one department in which a faculty member who once had had an active lab was allocated a lot of space. That faculty member since had become much less active. Yet he still had the space. I actually spoke to the chair, who told me that he just did not want to get into a fight with the faculty member. He would rather wait things out and see whether the faculty member reactivated his research. I was thinking, "Fat chance."

A strong chair continually reevaluates and reallocates resources. A weaker one just leaves things as they are, even after the allocation has become outdated. Unfortunately, faculty members, even senior ones, may have relatively little say over those allocations.

"SHE'S MY STUDENT"

Students should be in colleges and universities to learn as much as they can from a diverse assortment of faculty members. Well, that's how things should be. The way they are, in practice, is that some faculty members become possessive of their students, or their imagined students, much as one would one's significant other. I do not believe in hoarding students. But I also have never figured out a way to make people who are jealous willing to share. The people who hoard students often are in it for themselves and view the students as an exclusive resource for the furtherance of their own careers. Students who are perceptive recognize who such faculty members are and look elsewhere for their advisers.

"IT'S NOT YOUR TURN YET"

When I was coming up for early tenure, at least one faculty member told me rather bluntly that it was not my turn yet. You might hear this from another faculty member who thinks that, in particular, it is his turn. Or you might hear it from a faculty member who herself had to wait and now would like to make sure that everyone else has to wait, too. Probably, the best thing to do is to talk with a lot of people and see whether you have enough support among your colleagues who matter to make it your turn, whether certain other people think it is or not.

"IF WE TOLD THE TRUTH, WE'D BE IN BIG TROUBLE"

Whichever shibboleth you fall for, don't let it be this one. When people lie, it often comes out. In my past experience as an administrator, when faculty members are punished, they are punished much more severely for a cover-up than they are for any original offense. You don't want to be party to a lie or any kind of scandal. If you sense one, get advice from a chair or dean as quickly as you can. But whatever you do, don't become part of it. Once you join a cover-up, you are in serious trouble, whether or not you originally were part of whatever it is that is now being covered up.

"WE MUST DO THIS, OR OUR BUDGET WILL BE CUT"

One way of trying to get compliance with a course of action is to present that course of action as the only one a department or group in a department can take to prevent its budget from being cut. This is another one to avoid. If something is wrong, it's wrong. Don't do something wrong or inadvisable because, allegedly, it will prevent a budget cut. You may get the budget cut anyway, and then be stuck with having done whatever it was that should not have been done in the first place.

"IT'S US OR THEM"

Sometimes departments become factionalized, as between the hard and the soft scientists, or the theorists and the experimentalists, or the scientists and the clinicians, or whatever. In the worst case, the factions become oppositional to each other or even seek actively to undermine each other. The best course of action is to stay away from such factionalism. Unfortunately, you are not always given a choice. You may be told, essentially, that you have to join up with one faction or another. If that's the position you are in and it's a position you do not want to be in, consider moving. You simply may be in a place that isn't right for you. It sure wouldn't be right for me. I would like to say that such factionalism is rare, but, unfortunately, it's not.

I'm not sure why academics fall for this stuff. They just do, even at some of the best places.

"YOU DO THIS FOR ME, AND I'LL DO THAT FOR YOU"

There is give-and-take in every department. That's no big deal. But if you are asked to participate in give-and-take, or tit for tat, make sure that you are going to want to give in response for taking. If you are being asked to do something you believe is wrong or unethical, don't buy into this false dichotomy. If you do, you may well regret it later.

"PEOPLE LIKE THAT REALLY DON'T FIT IN WELL HERE"

Some kinds of people really do not fit well into a given department or even institution. But when I have heard this line, it is more often than not a thinly veiled prejudice or bias. What it gets down to is an attempt to limit diversity so that like-minded or like-appearing people will be together without having to expose themselves to other types of people or ideas. Avoid social categories of "people like that." Judge each person on his or her individual merits.

"WELL, THAT'S WHAT I HEARD, ANYWAY"

Every department has its own rumor mill. In my experience, rumors serve a number of purposes, among which usually is not the dissemination of truth. A rumor might be started to show what important sources of information a person has, or how much power a person has, or how useful a person's information is, or just to undermine other people. They rarely are all so close to the truth. So if you hear rumors, view them as rumors, but do not just accept them at face value. If you need to know whether they are true, then follow up to the extent possible. But don't assume that because you have heard it, it's true.

"JUST DON'T TELL ME ABOUT IT"

Sometimes people prefer to turn a blind eye and a deaf ear rather than to be made aware of wrongdoing. You do not want to be one of those people. You can't help the way others are. But you have to take responsibility for what you think is right, and if something is wrong and you believe it to be a serious wrong, don't close your eyes and ears. Try to right whatever is wrong.

"DON'T YOU THINK YOU'RE WORKING TOO HARD?"

In some departments, the norm is to not work too hard or to not give too much of oneself. If one does work hard or show a high level of initiative, one may get pressure to lay off. You don't want to be in such a place. If it's one or two people, don't worry. If it's the culture of the place, get out. People assimilate to the culture they are in, often without even realizing it. This is not a culture into which you want to assimilate.

"THEY DON'T UNDERSTAND US"

"They don't understand us" is usually another way of saying how great we really are, if only people knew what to appreciate. Institutions that are mediocre—departments, universities, countries—usually blame outsiders. It's not their own fault. I've spent time in such a place. When people say, "They don't understand us," what they really are saying is that the place is mediocre and they like it that way. Some people may convince themselves that others really don't understand them. That usually means that they have been in a place so long that they have accepted mediocrity as meritorious. They just can't tell the difference between mediocrity and merit anymore.

"THEY'LL NEVER NOTICE"

Actually, yes, they will. Never go with "They'll never notice." When they notice, your career will be at best damaged and at worst, over.

"KEEP IT TO YOURSELF, IF YOU KNOW WHAT'S GOOD FOR YOU"

If you know what's good for you, don't keep it to yourself. When things are hidden, they usually come out, and never in a way that benefits the hiders.

"EVERYONE'S DOING IT"

The fact that everyone's doing it does not mean that you should be doing it. Decide for yourself what to do. That's why you became an academic. Don't do things just because others are. You may do what they do, but do so for your good reasons, not theirs.

"YOU HAVE NO CHOICE"

You have just become a participant in a modern-day Milgram experiment. Yes, you do have a choice. Whatever it is, get out. Leave the experiment.

"IF WE DON'T MAKE THIS HIRE, WE'LL LOSE THE SLOT"

Usually, failure to hire in a given year does not mean that a slot will be lost. But even if it is, do you really want to start filling slots with mediocre people just for the sake of filling them? If you are being forced to do this, you can hope that the administration turns over soon.

"WELL, THERE'S NOTHING REALLY WRONG WITH HIM; HE'S GOOD ENOUGH"

When making hires or selections for programs, don't pick people just because there is "nothing wrong" with them. Pick them as well because of all the things that are right with them. And if there aren't things that are right, don't select the person.

"WE JUST HAVE TO MAKE THIS HIRE"

In all likelihood, no, you don't.

"YOU HAVE NO CHANCE OF GETTING THAT"

You don't know until you try. Try. Then see whether you have a chance or not. Nothing ventured, nothing gained.

* * *

There you have it in a nutshell. These are not all the political issues that arise in a department. But these are many of them. And what to do in other cases, you already know: Do the right thing!

Now, let's put what we have learned together and talk about how to prepare for tenure and promotion.

15

PREPARING FOR TENURE AND PROMOTION

When you are a junior faculty member, a major goal is to be promoted to tenure, which usually (but certainly not always) comes with promotion to associate professor. Eventually, you probably will want to be promoted to full professor. I say "probably" because sometimes associate professors with tenure decide not to seek promotion to full professor, either because they have not been sufficiently productive or because they do not want to go through another major evaluation process.

Some factors regarding promotion to tenure are controllable; others are not. I consider both types of factors in this chapter. Some of the suggestions will elaborate on suggestions made earlier in the book. These are the suggestions that I believe are particularly important when it comes time for tenure or promotion.

---

http://dx.doi.org/10.1037/0000013-016
Starting Your Career in Academic Psychology, by R. J. Sternberg
Copyright © 2017 by the American Psychological Association. All rights reserved.

CONTROLLABLE FACTORS

Teaching

Most academics are required to teach. An evaluation of your teaching will constitute a part of your tenure or other promotion evaluation. In some institutions, teaching will be the major criterion for advancement. So you want to think early in your career about how to teach in a way that will facilitate, or at least not hinder, your promotion prospects.

How much the quality of teaching counts varies widely across colleges and universities. In a community college, it may be by far the most important factor underlying your promotion to tenure. In a 4-year liberal arts college, teaching will likely count a great deal, although other factors, such as research productivity, are likely to count as well. In a large research university, the quality of teaching is unlikely to get you tenure, although it may help. In such a university, teaching is more likely to prevent your promotion than to cause it. In other words, if you are a really bad teacher, your teaching may well sabotage your promotion. But if you are a really great teacher, your teaching is unlikely to cause you to be promoted.

Teaching is generally evaluated in one or more of three ways. Each of these ways can be helpful but is also problematic.

The first way of evaluating teaching is through student evaluations. Colleges and universities use such evaluations, even though they are of dubious validity. In particular, evaluations are heavily influenced by how easy a course is, how little work it requires, how high the assigned grades are, and how entertaining the course is. There is a systemic problem with an institution's counting such evaluations heavily, because doing so tends to lead to easier courses with less work and to more grade inflation. Oddly, then, the student evaluations may lead to outcomes that are largely opposed to those one would hope for in good teaching.

The second way of evaluating teaching is through peer observation. Other faculty members will come into your classroom, usually but not always on a prearranged day, and evaluate the quality of your teaching.

The third way in which your teaching may be evaluated is through your own self-study. You may be asked to provide your syllabi and also to answer questions about how you teach and what you do to maximize student learning.

If you are serious about improving your teaching, and thereby improving your chances of being promoted, don't wait until the end of a course to collect summative evaluations. Collect formative evaluations one third to half of the way through the course. What I do is, during class, to ask students to take a piece of paper and answer three questions: (a) "What do you like most about the class?" (b) "What do you like least about the class?" and

(c) "What would you most like to see changed in the class?" You may get some really good suggestions.

I have been teaching for 40 years. I do have one very general suggestion: Don't blame students for your own mistakes. In teaching, we all make mistakes. The test is too hard, the test is too easy, the grading was not what it should have been, we gave too much work, we gave too little work, and so forth. It is easy to blame students for our own mistakes, such as blaming them for not studying hard enough if almost everyone gets a low grade on a test. I've been at this for 40 years, and I still make mistakes. Just last semester, I gave a test that was too hard. Students generally got grades in the 70s, with a few in the 80s and a few in the 60s. This might not have been a problem were the scores not about 8 percentage points lower, on average, than for previous tests I had given. In the end, I made the somewhat painful decision to admit to the students that I had screwed up: The test just was too hard. I apologized and gave an optional makeup test. As teachers, we are under a lot of pressure. But so are students. Don't blame them if you make a mistake.

When your teaching is evaluated, much will be beyond your control—student evaluations, any faculty evaluations that may have come in, past syllabi. The one thing over which you may have some control is preparing a teaching statement and seeking endorsements from students you have advised or who have taken courses from you. If you are not asked to prepare a teaching statement, and you value teaching, ask if you can prepare one for the tenure or promotion committee. Then say something about your philosophy of teaching, what makes it special, how you have implemented it in your courses, and what indications you have of its success.

If you know there are some negative evaluations of your teaching, you may want to say something in your statement that you think would help counter the negative evaluations. Are you a tough grader? Do you assign a lot of work because you want students to learn? Do you test a lot? Be prepared to explain practices that might lead to lesser student evaluations that you believe show the strength rather than the weakness of your teaching practices.

Teaching strategies will be different based on whether you are teaching a large or small class, advising individual students, or leading a research group.

Large Lectures

Large lectures are a good way for lots of students to get to know you, but of course they are not a good way for you to get know lots of students. At least, you probably will not get to know them *well*. I make just a few suggestions to maximize your teaching effectiveness in large lectures:

- *Be super organized.* In a small section, students can question you if they lose track of where you are or what you are doing; this is much harder in a large lecture.

- *Include lots of real-world examples.* In a smaller class, these examples can come up through give-and-take between professor and student. In a large lecture, there is little or no give-and-take, so it is up to you to ensure that the concrete examples are there.
- *Be enthusiastic.* If you are not enthusiastic, the students won't be. And they will take it out on you in their evaluations of the course.
- *Consider multimedia presentations.* Can you use films or other videos? Recordings? Guest speakers?
- *Encourage active learning (even though the course is large).* Can you ask questions simply to stimulate thinking? Can you use clickers to have students register responses to questions? Can you have students divide into smaller groups?
- *Don't rush through your lectures.* There is almost always too much material to cover. Don't feel as though you have to cover all of it. That is what textbooks are for.
- *Focus on fairness, not easiness.* It's tempting to be an easy grader, just to get higher ratings. But do you really want to sell your soul for what may or may not yield higher ratings? Fairness means that every student has the same opportunity to succeed. There are all kinds of temptations to cut special deals (see Sternberg & Fiske, 2015). In almost every course I teach, at least one student requests a special deal, such as an extra-credit assignment to raise a grade. But if I give that student an extra-credit opportunity, I believe I need to give it to every student. Why reward only assertive students? How many other students would have liked the same deal but lacked the nerve to ask for it? It often is easier to just give in to this demand or that one, but it rarely is fair if you make a special deal with some students without giving the same opportunity to others. The only special deals I cut are for severe accidents or illnesses, serious personal distress, or similar documented events. And I would give these same details to all students confronting similar challenges.
- *Watch out for overlap with the textbook.* If your lectures overlap too much with the textbook, you are likely to lose students who think they just can learn what they need to learn by reading the textbook. If your lectures overlap too little with the textbook, students may feel overwhelmed and further feel that they need more of a sense of what material from the textbook you think is important. Hence you want to overlap with the text, but not too little or too much.
- *Never read a lecture.* As noted previously, reading a lecture sounds stilted and artificial.

- *Beware of unintentional plagiarism.* It may sound odd to warn teachers rather than students of plagiarism. But teachers often get material where they can. And these days, it is very easy to lift material off the Internet—for teachers as well as students—and you do not want to be in a position in which students come to realize that your material is lifted without attribution. Few things are as notable as plagiarism when it comes to killing off a career. (Sexual harassment is even more notable as a career killer.) Be very careful not to plagiarize—it never will be worth it.
- *Be careful of jokes.* I joke a lot. But these days, jokes are almost as likely to get you into trouble as to get you laughs. What is funny to one person often ends up being offensive to another.

Small Seminars

Small seminars are an excellent way of getting to know students. They also are, for many of us, the greatest fun of teaching. I always learn new things teaching seminars that I doubt I can learn in any other way.

- *Prepare assiduously.* Some professors think that discussions will just take off on their own. I have never found this to be the case. I always go in with a series of discussion questions. Sometimes, early in the course, I prepare all the discussion questions myself. Then, later in the course, I may invite students to prepare discussion questions as well and then turn them in to me in advance. I then prescreen the discussion questions, using just the ones that I think will help stimulate a good discussion. In my experience, if discussion questions are not prescreened, you will end up using duds from students who either did not understand the material or else understood it but did not think carefully about what to ask. On the whole, preparing a discussion class is about as much work as a lecture. What differs is the kind of work, not the amount.
- *Be sure to involve the whole class.* The greatest risk with a discussion section is that some students will say a lot and others will say little or nothing. The solution to this problem is to call on members of the class. When I find that a student is not speaking up, I call on him or her and ask the student to give an opinion. And don't always call on the same people. A risk with small seminars is that you will keep calling on the same students again and again, whether because they often have something to say or because they are willing to speak out even if they do not have much to say. You need to make sure the seminar is for the whole class, not just the assertive ones.

- *Balance the thinking skills your questions require.* You do not want to get into a situation in which all your questions have a single right or wrong answer. This is not a discussion; it is a recitation. Small classes provide an excellent opportunity to encourage students to think analytically, creatively, practically, wisely, ethically, and in other ways. But for that to happen, you have to ask questions that encourage the different kinds of thinking. Fact-based questions require use of memory for recall and recognition of facts. Analytical questions involve analyzing, evaluating, judging, critiquing, and comparing and contrasting. Creative questions involve creating, inventing, discovering, imagining, designing, and supposing. Practical questions involve applying, using, utilizing, implementing, putting into practice, and persuading. Wisdom-based questions involve thinking about how information can serve a common good over the long and short term.
- *Reward good but unexpected answers.* A risk in a discussion-based class is that we, as teachers, tell students we want them to think for themselves but then reward only responses that are the ones we hope for or expect. Students quickly learn that you only pretend to want them to think for themselves—what you really want is your preferred answer. So you need constantly to be on guard against yourself and your tendency, which we all have, to reward the answers that are the ones we would have come up with.
- *Do not monopolize the conversation.* Also, avoid the temptation to turn a discussion into a lecture. You may have many good things to say, but in a discussion, it is better if the good things come from the students rather than you. View your role as leading students to say good things rather than as being the one to say them yourself.

Advising

Advising is probably the best way to get to know students and their capabilities. It gives you a chance to learn about a student, his or her background, and his or her aspirations. Here are a few tips:

- *Set boundary conditions for yourself.* You need to think in advance about where your relationship with the advisee begins and where it ends. In other words, have boundaries clearly mapped out in advance, and then do not cross them.
- *Meet regularly.* Students are busy; you are busy. It's easy for meetings to be regular at first and then to peter out rather quickly. Make sure you have a regular time to meet with each advisee.

- *Give your advisees regular and honest feedback.* If you are advising a student and your opinion of the student is not very high, you need to let the student know that. You do not want a student to work with you, only later to find out that you have no confidence in his or her abilities. You owe it to your advisees to let them know where they stand in your eyes.
- *Do not exploit advisees.* Because of the unequal power relationship between students and advisers, advisers are in a position at times to exploit students for the adviser's own benefit. Students find out who the exploiters are. So, usually, do tenure and promotion committees. If you want to do what is best for yourself, do what is best for your advisees. What is particularly difficult in relations with students is that junior faculty members, like students, need to get somewhere fast. The students need to get into graduate school or to get a job; the junior faculty members need to get promoted. In my career, I have seen junior faculty members put themselves first, deciding their tenure is more important than students' job placement or graduate school placement. It's important that, if you advise a student, you put the student, not yourself, first and, for example, assign authorships based on actual conceptual and other contribution rather than your higher status as faculty.
- *Write all letters of recommendation with seriousness of purpose.* A burden on faculty is writing all the letters of recommendation students require. Sometimes, the letter writing never seems to end. It is easy to brush off letter writing as a time-consuming chore and to believe that your time could be better spent. But to your students, those letters are a major means to open doors. If you are not willing to put the time and care into writing letters of recommendation, don't agree to advise the students.
- *Recognize your responsibility to place students.* If you are an adviser, you have a responsibility to place students appropriately, in graduate school, medical school, jobs, or whatever. You must take this responsibility seriously.

Research Groups

Research groups are an excellent way to teach students about research. My own group meets once a week. Students learn not only from you but also from each other. Such meetings can facilitate their research and your own.

- *Make meetings required rather than optional.* Students always have something else to do. If you do not require attendance, chances are you will risk not getting much of it.

- *Let students guide the meetings as much as you do.* Do not turn a research group meeting into a lecture. Let students do much, if not most, of the talking.
- *Emphasize the importance of constructive criticism.* You want students to get constructive criticism on their research ideas. What you don't want is for everyone to be so polite that they are afraid to critique each other's work.

Research

Research is evaluated in a number of ways. One way, typically, is by the tenure and promotion committee members reading the research themselves. Sometimes, though, they are not fully qualified to evaluate the research, especially if it is outside their field.

A second way research is evaluated is for members of the candidate's department who are not actually on the tenure and promotion committee to read the research. In my experience, this is done more often in theory than in practice. Professors are busy and often view it as the tenure committee's responsibility to be intimately acquainted with the research.

A third way research is evaluated is through letters solicited from outside referees. Committees may write to typically between three and 10 scholars outside the home institution. They ask the scholars to evaluate the research (and teaching, if the referee is familiar with it) of the candidate. In my experience, these outside letters are usually weighed quite heavily in the tenure and promotion process.

A fourth way in which research is evaluated is through quantitative indexes. These indexes are available through the Web of Science or Google Scholar. Google Scholar provides a much more comprehensive database than does the Web of Science. Although there are a number of statistical indexes that may be used, there are four principal ones.

The first index is the number of citations to your work. *Number of citations* refers to the number of times you have been referenced in the field. Number of citations is a better indication of scholarly success than number of publications because your scholarly career is not taking off if you are publishing stuff that no one cites (or even reads). Number of citations shows impact, not just productivity. Tenure and promotion committees should recognize that number of citations will depend on your advancement in your career and on your field. Some fields just tend to have less activity than others.

The second index is h, which is the number of publications you have that have been cited at least h times. This index combines aspects of productivity (number of publications) with impact (number of citations). The more you publish, the higher your h index can be, but merely publishing a lot does not guarantee that you will have a high h index. As you go up the h scale, it gets harder and harder for your index to increase. For example, if your h index is 2, you need only three publications cited at least three times to raise your h index by 1. But if your h index is 100, you need 101 publications cited at least 101 times for your h index to go up to 101. Committees need to take into account seniority and field in interpreting h indexes. Other factors also can affect the index, such as whether you publish in English, whether your publications are referenced somewhere on the web, and so forth.

The third index is $i10$, which is the number of publications you have that have been cited at least 10 times. This index goes up if your work gets cited, even if no one work gets cited a lot of times.

The fourth index is any of the first three considered for only the past 5 years. The index for the past 5 years gives a sense of whether your impact on the field is on the rise or on the fall. Google Scholar shows the number of citations over a period of years, so it is possible to look at trends over time.

Any of these indexes is probably more revealing than sheer number of publications, although many tenure and promotion committees do count number of publications. Number of publications is not very meaningful because some publications may be significant and others may have little or no impact. For example, how does one count a book review versus a major theoretical article or an empirical article presenting a number of separate studies? The indexes were designed to help bypass the problems with sheer number of publications.

To maximize your chances of getting promoted, your best strategies depend on the type of publication you use to communicate your research.

Articles

For most psychologists, the main way of communicating research is through scientific articles. Tenure and promotion committees examining research tend to count these more than anything else.

- *Before submitting an article, check that the journal to which you submit is refereed.* Committees will not be impressed, for the most part, with articles published in journals that are not refereed.
- *Check the impact factor of the journal to which you submit.* Impact factors are determined by the extent to which articles in the journal are cited in the scientific literature. The higher the impact factor, in general, the harder it is to get an article into a journal. Some institutions, in considering promotions, take impact factors seriously.
- *Check the publication lag for the journal.* Some journals publish articles quickly after they are accepted. With other journals, you

may have to wait a year, 18 months, or even longer for the article to be published. Tenure and promotion committees generally count in-press articles as demonstrated achievements because the articles already have been accepted for publication. But you have to be careful, because part of what you want is that the article be cited, and in-press articles are far less likely to be cited than published ones. Especially if you are getting near tenure consideration, you may want to consider publishing in journals that have shorter publication lags.

- *Consider whether you want to publish open access.* Today, more and more of publishing is going to open access, meaning that the articles or books are available to users at no cost. Why would anyone not want to use open access publishing, given that more users will be able to read one's work? There are a few catches. First, someone has to pay for publication, so it usually ends up being the author or his or her university or funding agency. If you publish a fair amount, the costs can mount quickly. Second, some of the best journals are not open access or do not allow open access until a given amount of time has passed. Third, one has to be careful with open access journals. Some of them are high quality and highly desirable outlets for publication. But the rise of open access has given rise to a huge slew of journals that are not very well refereed or edited. Rather, publishers or others simply see them as a way to make money. The author or his or her representative pays to have an article published, and then it is published, but in such a way that few if any readers are likely ever to see the journal or the article. So you may end up with an article on your CV, but one that almost no one is likely ever to read. Finally, although some scholars view open access as the wave of the future, they are hedging their bets as to whether that future has arrived. In the past, there always were journals "for pay"; that is, there were less-than-first-rate journals that would publish almost anything so long as you paid a fee. Open access has not yet completely shed this stigma from the past.

Books

Very few junior faculty members in psychology write books, but some do. (I did.) Tenure and promotion committees vary in how they count books. Some are particularly impressed by a book; others may prefer refereed journal articles. It also depends on the kind of book you are writing or have written.

Scholarly books are likely to count toward tenure and promotion, textbooks may count less, and popular books may or may not count. If popular books are far away from your field, such as advice books or novelistic ventures, they actually could hurt you, as committee members may begin to question whether you are seriously committed to work in your scholarly field. The last thing the committee wants is to recommend tenure and then have you stop producing scholarly work.

Some of the most frequently cited works are books. But writing books takes a lot of time, and if you decide to write a book, make sure it does not detract too much from your publishing of refereed articles. You might want to consult with your department chair or dean to find out how a written book would be viewed in the tenure or promotion process.

Generally, you should write a proposal before you write a book and have the proposal approved by a publisher before you go ahead and produce the book. The last thing you want is to write a book and then discover no one is willing to publish it. If you have written a book and are ready to submit, it should be with a contract in hand. You need to realize that a book contract is not an ironclad guarantee that a publisher actually will publish the book. Virtually all book contracts have a clause in them that permits the publisher to cancel the contract if the book does not review well. But at least with a contract you will know that a publisher takes your work seriously and is willing to invest the considerable financial resources it takes to publish a book.

In seeking a book contract, try to get the best publisher and the best terms possible (see Sternberg & Sternberg, 2016). For scholarly work, the prestige of the publisher may matter more than the royalty rate. A prestigious publisher is better able to sell your book and get you a high level of royalties, even if the royalty level per book is lower.

Book Chapters

Book chapters generally count less than refereed empirical articles for tenure and promotion. Usually, they are not as rigorously refereed, and sometimes they hardly are refereed at all other than for stylistic conformity to the editorial style of the book. Book chapters can add heft to your CV, and in some cases they may gain considerable readership. But more often their readership is somewhat limited. I have done many book chapters myself and also have edited numerous books, but you should not rely on book chapters to put you over the top in getting tenure or promotion.

Submitted Presentations

Submitted presentations are an excellent way to start getting your name known. Even senior faculty members submit proposals for talks. Given that funds for travel usually are finite, you need to choose your venues for presentation with some care. In particular, make sure the conference will have a substantial number of people who are interested in your work, people whose opinions are important to you (or will be important to your tenure and promotion committee), and people who may want to follow up with you and become new members of your professional network. The problem, of course, is that one cannot always tell in advance which of these conditions will hold. Speak to more advanced faculty members in your area to get a sense of which conferences are worth presenting at.

Proposals for most submitted presentations are refereed. In writing a proposal for a conference presentation, keep in mind the tips from Chapter 12. You want to write a proposal that is engaging and will make sense to people who do not know your field well. You also want to assure the readers of the proposal that you really have the data in hand and are not merely banking on future data being good. You do not want to be in a position where you submit to present and then the data do not meet your expectations—or your audience's.

Invited Presentations

Invitations to present often are scarce in the very early years of a career unless one has had the good fortune to produce one or more early blockbuster publications. Invited presentations generally are better than submitted ones on a CV, but of course, it matters whom the invitation is from. (Your family may invite you to present to them, but really, who outside the family will care?) Invitations to present do not always just come out of the blue. If you know someone at a particular institution and would like to present there, you might want to drop a hint and see where it leads.

Posters

Posters are most often used by students and junior faculty and much less often by senior faculty. They can be a good way to get your name out. But typically, fewer people drop by a poster than will come to a talk. At the same time, if you end up in a dud session of a conference—the last one of the last day, for example, or one during the lunch hour, or one after dinner, or one with other papers that sound boring—you might be better off with a poster.

Uploads

There are now any number of databases provided by various services to which one can upload one's documents. These services provide a quick way for one's work to become available. The services are used by senior as well as by junior faculty.

There are a few important caveats to uploads. First, you must make sure that your publisher or potential publisher will allow the upload. Generally, it is your responsibility to ensure that you will not infringe on copyright or violate publisher policies. You may just assume that it is OK to upload your documents. Don't. You need to check. Second, because there are a number of different such services, you want to choose the one that is best in your particular area of endeavor. Third, be careful that the data in the upload are correct and will not be presented in a way later such that it looks like you have been fiddling with your data. Although your interpretation of the data may change later, be sure that the data don't, or if they do, be able to explain why they have changed. Fourth, never upload someone else's work without that person's written permission. Doing so could lead to charges of academic misconduct. Finally, do not accidentally compromise publication of your paper—that is, upload the paper and then find that your preferred journal will not publish it because it already was made available on the Internet.

Popular Press

The popular press can be an excellent place to get your ideas out. However, it probably behooves you first to publish in a scholarly journal any findings that are reported in the popular press. There are three reasons for this. First, that way you (and the public) will know for sure that the ideas or results you publish have been vetted for their scholarly integrity. Second, sometimes journals or book publishers may be hesitant to publish ideas or data that already have made it into the popular press. Third, tenure and promotion committees will be impressed that you value scholarly integrity more than just getting your name out there.

Blogs

Blogs can be a good way to publicize some of your ideas. Again, there are a few caveats. Although things may change in the future, postings on blogs generally are not viewed as truly important displays of scholarship. They therefore may not move you much forward for tenure and promotion. Second, you have to be really careful of what you say. It is amazing how easily people get incensed over comments that you may believe are totally innocent.

Service

The importance of service varies widely from one institution to another. Generally, expectations for service are higher for senior faculty members than for junior ones. Colleges and universities realize, or should realize, that you need time as a junior faculty member to establish your teaching and research. This idea sometimes is heeded more in principle than in practice. Senior faculty may view junior faculty as easily exploitable for service and require much of it from them. In general, try to find a small number of service activities in which you can engage and then do a really good job with them. Do not let yourself get pushed into one service activity after another. If you show willingness to do a lot of service, chances are good that you will be called on, as others may be more reluctant to do it. You may then find that the time you have available for teaching and research is diminished. If you are a minority or female faculty member, beware of becoming a token member of lots of different task forces or committees. The institution may be grateful, but they also may not always show their gratitude through a positive tenure or promotion decision.

Extension and Outreach

Extension and outreach apply only to some colleges and universities, especially land-grant ones. *Extension and outreach* refer to attempts to bring the work of the university to the population outside the university—say, to farmers or civil engineers or homemakers or whomever. The amounts of extension and outreach you do may be determined contractually. Make sure that you can document in writing the extension and outreach you do. You do not want to be in a position down the road in which you did your job but have no proof of it. In general, it is much harder to document extension and outreach than it is to document teaching and research. So you need to make sure that you keep proper documentation so there are no questions of validation later on.

Collegiality

Collegiality, as you can imagine, is very hard to define. One person's collegiality is another's displeasure. The best thing you can do in this area is to be amiable with others. You do not have to be at every party or every event. You do want to show that you care about others, their work, and their personal feelings. Avoid deeply personal fights with others. Faculty members most often get into trouble with respect to collegiality when they are egocentric or keenly unaware of how they affect others. Unfortunately, collegiality can be a catchall and sometimes is used to try to rid a department of people they just don't want to have around, for whatever reason, whether related to collegiality or not.

UNCONTROLLABLE FACTORS

There are some factors in a tenure or promotion decision over which you have little or, more likely, no control. You nevertheless should be aware of what these uncontrollable factors are.

Departmental Fit and Needs

Sometimes the perceived needs of a department change, whereby you are viewed as meeting the department's needs at the point of your being hired but are not perceived as meeting these needs when you come up for tenure or promotion. It may be that your interests changed, or the department's interests changed, or the kind of work you do is just not, or at least no longer, what the department wants. Or it may be that you personally are not seen as a good fit (see the preceding section on collegiality). Departments may or may not tell you that fit is an issue. Often evaluations try to pin perceived lack of fit on something else, such as inadequate service or mentoring. It behooves you, as a junior faculty member, every once in a while to talk with your chair and try to assess whether the direction you are taking in your work is one with which the department is satisfied.

Departmental or Institutional Politics

Sometimes tenure and promotion candidates get caught up in the politics of the department. One faction may try to sabotage candidates from another faction. Or one faction may take power from another and try to use any available slots to hire people more sympathetic to their ideology. Or it may be that you have made a powerful enemy, whether you know it or not. Or it may be that someone or someones simply want to hire someone, and they believe they need the slot you occupy to justify their proposed hire to the administration. No department is likely to officially acknowledge a role for politics in tenure and promotion decisions, but politics are always there, acknowledged or not.

Departmental Base Rates

Departments differ widely in their base rates for tenure—that is, in the average proportion of junior faculty they historically have tenured. Some departments tenure almost everyone. Some tenure half. Some tenure only a small percentage. Before you accept a position, know the base rate for tenure and realize that, when the time comes, the base rate is likely to affect your prospects.

Consolidations and Restructurings

Every once in a while, a college or university decides to restructure. Departments may be combined, or eliminated, or restructured. Your tenure or promotion chances may be affected by a restructuring if your unit is under threat or, alternatively, is chosen for expansion.

Budgets

Some colleges and universities reach points of financial exigency, which they may or may not announce. At such times, getting promoted or tenured may become difficult simply because the institution lacks the funds to tenure or promote everyone whom it expected to advance.

* * *

So now you have a good idea of some of the factors that affect tenure and promotion decisions. One of the factors is personal, and I have advised you to try to avoid serious interpersonal conflicts to the extent possible. In the next chapter, I talk about the kinds of conflicts one may encounter and how one can go about resolving them.

16
RESOLVING CONFLICTS

Inevitably, as a new faculty member, you will experience conflicts, virtually all of them unwanted. It is difficult to predict exactly what conflicts you will face. I have listed in this chapter some of those my colleagues and I have faced, along with steps toward solution. There are no "right" solutions to these conflicts. I merely suggest paths that may be helpful to you in reaching a resolution. For each conflict, I repeat what someone might say to you, and one or more ways in which you might respond.

CONFLICTS WITH STUDENTS

"I Deserved a Higher Grade on This Test [or Paper, or in This Course]"

You can be pretty confident that, sooner or later, a student will believe you undergraded him or her. The question is what to do.

When I am asked about a grade on a test or a paper, I always offer to regrade it. And well I should, because sometimes I do make mistakes. When one has a lot of materials to grade, mistakes are inevitable. This offer to regrade usually resolves the problem. Occasionally, a student may believe that you are somehow biased against his or her point of view or, worse, against him or her. This has happened to me a couple of times in my career. I then have offered to have another professor regrade the paper without the other professor's knowing the grade I gave the test or paper. I think that such an offer shows that I believe other professors would give the material a fresh and fair reading. If the other reader disagrees with me, I'm happy to use his or her grading—whether it is higher or lower. And what the student may not realize is that the grading of the other professor is as likely to be lower as higher.

If a student complains about a course grade, I simply offer to recompute it. Sometimes I need to explain to the student why he or she got the grade I gave. Some of these requests are a bit off the wall. I recently got a request for reconsideration of a grade of B+ from a student whose quiz grades were all in the B range and whose classwork was absolutely nothing special.

"I Did Not Plagiarize"

There is a pretty good chance that you will have a case of plagiarism, or at least what appears to be plagiarism. You may detect plagiarism through software such as Turnitin or through noticing that two students' tests papers or essay papers are remarkably similar to one another. Or you may remember having seen much the same content in a past year in which you taught the course.

With cases of suspected plagiarism, I strongly recommend that you not deal with them yourself. Rather, turn them over to the appropriate administrative body, such as the dean's office. There are three reasons for this recommendation. First, although the dean's office is likely to have had a lot of experience dealing with cases of alleged plagiarism, you are likely to have had little or no experience. They know more about handling such cases. Second, you have no way of knowing whether the student you suspect of plagiarism is a serial plagiarizer or perhaps has done it just this once. Don't bother to ask. What student will admit to being a serial plagiarizer? If all cases are reported to the dean's office, the dean's office then will be in a position to judge whether this is a one-time offense or part of a pattern. Third, accusations of plagiarism sometimes can take an ugly turn, such as when the student or the student's parents decide to hire a lawyer. Do you feel equipped, on your own, to handle a legal embroilment?

Because of the hassle involved in dealing with potential plagiarism cases, some faculty members try to dispose of them quickly by themselves. They give the student an F for the particular assignment or test, or they even fail the student for the course. But there is no way of handling such cases that is common across universities, and by turning it over to the dean's office, you ensure that the way of handling it will fit the norms of your own college or university. Bottom line: Turn cases of suspected plagiarism over to the appropriate authorities.

"I Did Not Cheat"

Cheating is even harder to judge than plagiarism. Did the student really look over at another student's work? What did she really do on that bathroom trip? Did he write answers on his hand? More often than not, evidence regarding cheating is less than conclusive. Occasionally you may get the case in which the cheater admits it or is caught red-handed. More often than not, however, you are relying either on your own imperfect observation or on reports of students who thought they saw something. I have handled accusations of cheating in the same way as accusations of plagiarism—I turn them over to the dean's office. I usually have no way of making a definitive determination, nor do I know whether there have been accusations of cheating before.

Some faculty are afraid to turn over cases to the dean's office because they fear the penalty will be either too light or too severe. That, I think, is a risk worth taking. At least the dean's office will have a great deal of experience dealing with these cases—you won't.

"I Need Extra Credit to Graduate"

Over the years, I have had some students come to me—usually at the last minute—to tell me that they need extra credit or at least a better grade in my course to graduate. They are not complaining that the grade is unfair, just that if I do not change their grade, their whole future is in jeopardy. I had one this past spring semester. Or a student may come and say that he is able to graduate but his medical school acceptance will be pulled by the medical school he plans to attend if his grade is as low as I plan to give him.

What strikes me in these cases is that, almost inevitably, the students wait until the last minute to address their alleged problem. As I said to one of these students this past fall, "Where were you the rest of the term when other students who were having trouble were coming to see me?"

I often allow an extra-credit option in my courses, but I make it available to all students, not just those who are assertive enough to ask for it. If you offer it only to those students who ask, you are essentially rewarding not good performance but assertiveness with respect to one's own interests. I do not think that assertiveness with respect to one's own interests ought to be a basis for a grade. Hence, if you are concerned that you will get some of these cases—which over the long term is not unlikely—offer an extra-credit option at the beginning of the term so that everyone can take advantage of it, not just students who are quick to assert their own interests.

"I Deserve to Be a Coauthor [or Senior Author]"

I'm sure it's a safe bet that you never want to get into an authorship dispute, most likely with a graduate student or postdoc but possibly with an undergraduate. The American Psychological Association (APA, 2016) guidelines give general principles for determining authorship, but they typically do not give sufficiently detailed guidance so that one can assign authorship on an individual paper. I have rarely had authorship disputes, maybe once or twice. I use the APA guidelines and suggest students read them; I also tend to err on the side of being generous to students. The best way to handle these problems is never to encounter them in the first place: Make clear to students from the start what your, and the field's, expectations are for coauthorship and priority of coauthorship.

"I Never Gave Informed Consent"

There is a very simple way to avoid a claim of not having given informed consent. First, always get informed consent in writing. Second, make sure your informed consent form will stand up to scrutiny. Normally, making sure of this is the job of the institutional review board (IRB), but you never know when someone will feel that he or she was not given sufficient information to decide whether to participate. Therefore, make sure you have confidence in the informed consent form. There are a lot of "standard" informed consent forms out there. Don't just use a standard form that does not take into account the particular circumstances of your research.

"I've Been Harmed by Your Experiment"

Imagine being in the Milgram experiment (see Milgram, 2009). Looking back, you realize that had the manipulation been a real one, you might have seriously injured or killed the learner to whom you thought you were giving painful shocks. Today such an experiment would not pass IRB review. You never know in advance exactly what will harm someone or be perceived as harming someone. If you get such a complaint, immediately report it to the IRB and to the department chair or dean. As long as you made a good-faith effort to protect participants, you most likely will be in the clear. But if you do not report what happened, you may get into trouble for not monitoring the safety of your research.

"I Feel Exploited"

If a student feels exploited, he or she may be more likely to tell others than to tell you. Although you do not want to hear this accusation, consider yourself lucky that the student is talking to you about it. Try to understand why the student feels exploited. If you can resolve the problem, again, consider yourself lucky. But if you cannot, seek mediation through a department chair or dean's office. You do not want accusations of exploitation hanging over your head. They get around.

"You Obviously Don't Like People of My Group"

An accusation of bias is yet another conversation that is likely to go nowhere. Assuming it is not true, you should deny the charge and then report the charge to your department chair or dean. If there is any chance it is true, you have to reexamine your behavior.

You may wonder why I keep suggesting that you report charges to the administration. The reason is that, although many charges never go anywhere, some do, and it is hard to predict in advance which will escalate and which will be forgotten as soon as they are made. Your reporting of charges is a way of protecting yourself. Figure it this way: Do you want the administrator to hear the charge from you, with your side of the story, or from the accuser, who likely will tell only his or her side of the story? You are much better off making sure that your side is heard up front, before the administrator starts making judgments on the basis of incomplete information.

"You Are Harassing Me"

A harassment accusation is serious. It may be valid or not. Don't argue. Arguing can make a bad situation worse. You cannot handle this kind of accusation on your own. Report the accusation immediately. See your department chair or appropriate dean. You also need to decide whether you are culpable, and whether the behavior in question was intentional or accidental.

Your college or university may refer you to an institutional attorney, who then will interview you regarding the accusation. There is one critical thing to keep in mind: The university lawyer represents the university, not you. The university may decide to fight for you—or against you—depending on what it perceives as the facts of the matter and its interests in the matter.

Therefore, if a formal accusation is made against you, get your own lawyer. Obviously, you did not go into academia to be hiring lawyers. But harassment accusations are serious and can have major consequences—not only dismissal but, if the case goes to court, financial penalties. Therefore, if such an accusation is made, take it seriously, even if you think the accusation is false or ill motivated. I have professional liability insurance in case I have any situation in which I need a lawyer to represent me. I never have used the insurance, but it's nice to know it's there in case I need it. It is quite inexpensive for an academic, although somewhat more expensive for a clinical psychologist who deals with clients.

CONFLICTS WITH OTHER FACULTY MEMBERS

"I Know You Reviewed My Article, and You Trashed It"

Reviews of articles are generally anonymous. The fact that reviews are anonymous does not stop authors from trying to guess who wrote those reviews. Inevitably, there will be an occasional article that you think is of inferior quality and not up to the standards of the journal to which the article was submitted. You have a professional responsibility to say what you think (hopefully, in a constructive way). But even if you try to be constructive, the recipient of the review may not interpret your comments as constructive. Moreover, sometimes an author will think it was you who gave the negative review when in fact it was someone else. The someone else may actually make it sound, intentionally or accidentally, like you were the reviewer! What do you do if you are accused of trashing an article that you may or may not have reviewed?

One option is to say you did not review the paper—whether or not you actually did review it. I do not suggest this option. First, you are accepting the accusation as worthy of a specific response. The accusation never should have been made in the first place. Second, there is no guarantee that whatever you say will be believed. Third, *trashed* and similar terms are a matter of perception. I would merely tell the individual that she knows that the comment is professionally inappropriate and you choose not to discuss it any further. There really is nothing you could say that likely would satisfy your critic. The critic has made up her mind without thinking things through, and you're not going to change that sort of person.

"Why Do You Always Ignore My Work in Your Talks and Publications?"

Someone once said this to me—a colleague whom I regarded as a friend. I was taken aback. The best response, I think, is to thank the individual for sharing his perception and assure him that, in the future, you will be open to all appropriate opportunities to cite his work. Then drop the subject.

"That's My Idea"

This conflict can arise either between you and a student or between you and another faculty member with whom you are collaborating. If you have an idea and you will want to claim credit for it, send it to yourself as an e-mail with a date and time stamp on it. Or if you want to communicate the idea to someone else, do so in a written way that ensures you will be recognized as having had the idea.

That said, you want to avoid these conflicts. Often it is hard to know who had what idea, especially when ideas arise in the give-and-take of conversation among members of a research group or among collaborators on a project. If someone outside a collaboration is claiming credit for an idea, you may want to ask the individual for documentation. Or you may suggest that you acknowledge their contribution in a footnote. If they are demanding coauthorship but you believe they have not contributed to a project, you may be able to work it out between yourselves. Otherwise, you can seek mediation through the chair's or dean's office or the office of the vice president of research. I would not grant coauthorship merely because someone demands it. For all you know, that person might do this regularly as a means of illegitimately accumulating publication credit.

"You've Sold Out"

There are several ways to sell out in academia, and a whole lot more ways to be perceived as having sold out. You could be perceived as having sold out to the administration of your institution, or to a granting agency, or to unreasonable demands of students, or to legislators, or really to almost whomever or whatever.

If you are accused of selling out, your first reaction may well be, "No, I haven't." After that first reaction, you may start thinking about why someone would think this way or whether there is a grain of truth in the accusation. That's the point at which you need to be brutally honest with yourself.

In one of my jobs as an administrator, some faculty accused me of selling out to members of the state legislature. Their thinking, in this case, was that if legislators believed something, it just couldn't be right. After all, what do legislators really know about education? In some cases, legislators may not know much. And then there may be other times in which a university does not want to see what legislators see about the way it goes about doing its business. So I asked myself, as will you, whether there might be any truth to the complaint. If so, perhaps you want to act on it. If not, you probably owe it to yourself to explain your actions to your accusers, and then you should go about your business. You never will convince everyone, and there is no reason you have to!

CONFLICTS WITH ADMINISTRATORS

Conflicts with administrators are presented in this section from the administrative point of view.

"So You Think You Deserve a Larger Raise"

If you believe you deserve a larger raise, you need first to consider carefully whether you want to bring it up with your department chair. Were other people's raises also low? Were there budget constraints this particular year? In general, I would not take the approach of "I deserve a larger raise." You are putting yourself in a position that is, or at least appears to be, antagonistic to the administration. You may end up getting a defensive response. A better approach might be to see your chair, mention that your raise was not all that you hoped for, and ask whether there are things you could do to improve your performance in subsequent years. Try to figure out exactly why the raise was not what you hoped for. Then follow the suggestions you receive. Administrators almost always appreciate being asked by faculty members how the faculty members can improve their performance. Such questions are not viewed as antagonistic but rather as genuine attempts to change for the better.

"You Appear to Have Misallocated Your Grant Money"

Misallocation of grant money means that money that was supposed to be spent on one thing was spent on another. Over the years, granting agencies have become increasingly vigilant in monitoring whether money that is supposed to be spent in a certain way actually is spent in that way. It therefore behooves you to track very carefully whether the expenses you make are allowable. In theory, the grants office of your institution is supposed to monitor expenditures, but they probably cannot monitor every expense on every grant in a thoroughly comprehensive way.

Misallocation of grant money is another one of those charges that is potentially serious. If misallocation of grant money is reported to a granting agency, the consequences can be dire. You may lose the grant, you may have to pay money back, you may be blackballed for future grants—well, you get the idea. You may get into trouble with your home institution as well as the granting institution.

The first thing to determine is whether a misallocation actually occurred. If it did and it was purposeful, good luck! I do not envy you your position. If you discover a misallocation that was accidental, report it and see what steps are necessary to rectify the situation. If you believe there was no misallocation, then make clear to the authorities why you believe the charges against you are incorrect. If the charges are for anything except minor expenditures, you may need a lawyer. Remember, as noted above, that university lawyers represent the university, not you. They will not look out for your best interests, but rather those of the university. Do not be fooled into believing they represent you!

"You Just Don't Fit in Here"

Hopefully, no administrator will ever tell you that you do not fit in with your institution. But it may happen. Realize that the administrator may seek to convey this message without actually directly telling you this. That is, the administrator may point out incompatibilities between expectations of the institution and what you seem to like to do, what you do best, or what you simply spend your time on.

Such happenings are more common than one would like to believe. It's happened to me: I was at one institution where I really did not fit. I thought I could help shape the institution to be one that would be a better fit. I might as well have tried to move a graveyard. Institutions are very slow to change, and for the most part, they resist change. I left voluntarily. Had I not left voluntarily, I might sooner or later have been asked to leave. Fit is really important.

I spent 30 years of my career at Yale University (which is not the institution to which I refer in the preceding paragraph!). For the large majority of those years, I felt like I fit in. At the end, I became less certain of my fit. I moved. These days, I'm at Cornell and feel like it is a good fit to who I am. Not fitting in is not a crime; it's not even a fault. If you care deeply about teaching and are in an institution that is research driven, you are in the wrong place. If you care mostly about your research and look at teaching as largely a distraction, you don't want to be at a 4-year liberal arts school. If you are at a large, impersonal university with huge classes and you crave meaningful individual relationships with your college students, you are in the wrong place. The point is that your best bet is not to wait to be told, in one way or another, that you don't fit in. If you find yourself a misfit, start looking for other employment before you are asked to do so.

"You Seem Only to Care About Yourself"

If you are accused of being self-centered, you need to take the accusation seriously. It is very easy for junior faculty to become self-centered. They are under the gun for tenure, and if they spend all their time thinking about other people, they will fall behind. The risk for a junior faculty member is that focusing on himself or herself becomes a dominating obsession and that other people notice it. If you are being perceived as being self-centered, whether you are or not, you may want to consider what you need to do to change other people's perceptions.

CONFLICTS WITH REVIEWERS OF JOURNAL ARTICLES

There are so many possible points of conflict between you and reviewers of your articles that I could not possibly go over all of them. Examples are (a) your data analyses are incorrect, (b) the results do not seem to support your conclusions, (c) the data do not make sense, (d) you failed to cite relevant past research, (e) you are seeing what you want to see in your data, (f) these data will never replicate, (g) your theory is awfully similar to X's but X is not cited, (h) your methods were inadequate to the problem, and so on.

If you are lucky, when you get reviews, you will agree with all or most of the points that the reviewers make. Good luck with that. I have found very few instances in which I looked at a review and was thankful for each and every comment. If you find yourself infuriated with the reviews or the editor's letter, do nothing for a few days. You need to cool down. The last thing you want to do is write a letter to the editor asking how he or she and the reviewers could be such fools. When you are ready, start revising, whether for the same journal or for another journal. Take each comment seriously, and then decide whether the change is one you are willing to make. Editors usually do not expect you to make every change that every reviewer has requested. You can argue. But do so respectfully and with dignity. Never get emotional in your response. Be cool and show, scientifically, why you disagree with a given point.

If you are going for another journal, you do not have to discuss the old reviews. But do not go to a new journal without seriously considering all the points in the old reviews. There are three reasons why it is essential that you take into account what the reviewers said.

First, if you do not take the points into account, you are likely to hear the same points again, or similar ones, in the next set of reviews. So you lost the opportunity to make the revisions that would have earned you an acceptance by the next journal.

Second, some of the same reviewers who reviewed the article the first time may review it a second time. Typically, reviewers will inform editors that they have reviewed the article before; the editors may nevertheless ask them to review it again. If the reviewers see you have not made the changes they requested, how happy do you expect them to be?

Third, often the comments that annoy you most are the ones that are most helpful. We all have a professional and usually deeply personal investment in our own work. So we need to be careful not to write off points that offend us personally but that might be useful in a revision.

* * *

There are so many possible points of conflict for junior faculty that it is not practicable to list them all here. I hope the samples in this chapter will give you some ideas about how to handle your own conflicts. Years ago, I did some research on conflict resolution (Sternberg & Soriano, 1984). We found that of the various ways of resolving conflicts we studied, by far the most effective was what we called "step-down." That is, try to defuse a conflict rather than blow it up. If you are angry, wait until you calm down to say your piece, or write your e-mail, or respond in any way. You will be more effective and more likely to resolve whatever the conflict is.

Now, let's consider mistakes you might make as a junior faculty member, whether with regard to conflicts or to anything else.

17

TWENTY-ONE COMMON MISTAKES JUNIOR FACULTY MAKE

In the days when I was in administration, I processed a large number of tenure and promotion cases. What struck me was how there were certain career mistakes that I saw not just once but again and again (see Sternberg, 2017b).

BEING UNABLE TO LEAVE GRADUATE SCHOOL OR A POSTDOC BEHIND

When you take a job, you are physically leaving graduate school behind. The question is whether you are leaving it psychologically as well. Most new faculty members make the transition well and thrive in their new careers. But there are temptations—to do one more collaborative project with your graduate adviser, to continue to work with your friends from graduate school,

---

http://dx.doi.org/10.1037/0000013-018
Starting Your Career in Academic Psychology, by R. J. Sternberg
Copyright © 2017 by the American Psychological Association. All rights reserved.

to stay on a grant from your own supervisor. One of the main achievements a tenure and promotion committee looks for is that you have started a new and independent career. This is not a trivial accomplishment: In graduate school and during a postdoc, you typically are in a more nurturing and supportive environment than when you start off on your own as an assistant professor.

Tenure and promotion committees often get nervous when they see continued collaborations from graduate school or a postdoc. This is not to say that you should never continue such collaborations. But make sure that they are a small proportion of your new research activities. No committee wants to recommend promotion for someone who is psychologically still a grad student or postdoc. After you have tenure, you pretty much can do as you please, but before you have it, make sure you show that you can make an independent start.

RUSHING THINGS INTO PRINT OR WAITING TOO LONG

Academics generally cannot afford to be perfectionists, at least in the early years of their career. If you are thinking that an article you are planning to submit is not the best it can be, know for sure that you are right. No article is ever the very best it can be. But when you start as an assistant professor, you have 5 or 6 years to prove yourself. Sometimes the tenure process starts during the 4th year. You just do not have time to perfect every, or really any, article you send out for publication. Obviously, you want your submissions to be of high quality and to reflect in the best possible way on your career and your career aspirations. But you cannot achieve such a goal if you are always waiting just a little bit longer before submitting. Part of being a junior faculty member is mastering the art of knowing when enough is enough.

The opposite problem, of course, is rushing to submit articles, which can be like offering a wine to drink before its time. The wine might have been good if only one had waited a bit longer to drink it. In my role as a journal editor, I was acting on an article recently for which a reviewer commented that there were an inordinate number of typographical errors. You do not want to be in this position. Reviewers get ticked off, editors get ticked off, and you will waste several months waiting to hear feedback on articles that possibly were doomed before you ever submitted them.

I cannot tell you exactly how long to wait on any given article before submitting it. You have to cultivate the art of knowing when to submit—no one can do it for you. But you need to do it, lest you lack publications either because you waited too long or because you were unwilling to wait long enough.

BEING RESISTANT TO FEEDBACK

Assistant professors often feel that they do not receive enough feedback; when they get it, they often are reluctant or even unwilling to follow it. In most institutions, you will receive at least one major feedback event before you come up for tenure, usually in the 2nd, 3rd, or at latest 4th year. If you do not, seek it out. You need feedback to know where your record is not developing as expected or to know that your record is developing exactly as hoped for.

If you get feedback from your department, you must take it seriously, even if you disagree with it. If you do disagree with it, discuss with your chair your disagreement and seek out his or her opinion. You really cannot afford to ignore departmental feedback if you want tenure in that department. If you believe that the feedback is seriously faulty, then think about applying for positions elsewhere. It is much better to find a new job before you are denied tenure than after.

Many departments provide counseling during the junior faculty years for people who will not make it through the tenure process. If you are receiving feedback suggesting that you are off track, you might even ask your chair whether you ought to be looking for a new position. If you look early, you will not have a tenure denial on your record, and you will have more time to look. After a tenure denial, chances are you will have at most a year. That's not a lot of time; moreover, you will have the denial on your record. So if it's not working out, get out while the getting is good.

FAILING TO FIND WAYS TO MAKE THE MOST OF WHAT YOU DO WELL

When I was an assistant professor, I had a senior faculty colleague whose reputation never quite matched what people expected of him. His career got off to a good start but then kind of faded. When I have thought about him, I've thought of him as someone who never quite figured out what he did well. He tried several areas of research, but after one or two initial hits, he just never had another hit.

Part of figuring out what you do well, sometimes, is giving up on dreams of who you had hoped to be. In my own case, I greatly admired my undergraduate and graduate advisers. Both were consummate scientists. Of course I wanted to be like them. As the years went by, I saw my career diverging more and more from their careers. Wherever I was going in my career, it was not where they had gone. At first, I found this realization depressing. I came to see that I never would be like them. As time went on, I came to see that my aspiration was unrealistic: I was not them; I never would be. I was finding my own path, reflecting the fact that my strengths were different from theirs.

There are lots of ways to have a distinguished career. You may think, when you start out, that the model of your adviser or some other professor whom you know should be the model for you. As you go through your career, recognize that there is no right model for you: You need to invent a new model that capitalizes on who you are as a person and as a professional. As I look back, I cannot say I have no regrets at all. I keep thinking that maybe I could be like me but still have become more like them. But it did not happen and never was going to happen. It didn't happen for me; it won't for you. Find yourself in yourself, not in your aspirations to be like someone else.

FAILING TO BE RESILIENT IN THE FACE OF LIFE AND CAREER CRISES

I have had a good career in many ways. I've published many well-cited articles, have won many awards, and even have been awarded some honorary doctorates. At the same time, I've had some stunning career crises. Sometimes research projects didn't work out, no matter how hard I tried to make them work out; sometimes I taught courses that got lousy ratings; I've had countless grant proposals turned down; I had one job that I never should have accepted and got out while I still could. I could go on and on. No matter how successful your career is on the whole, you will need to learn resilience in the face of failure. The question is not whether you will have crises, but rather how you will handle them.

When I was early in my career, I was starting out along with a large number of friends and colleagues in my cohort. In the early days, I heard about them and their work fairly often. But as the years went by, more and more of them somehow disappeared. They became invisible. What happened to them? Different things. Some failed to get tenure and just gave up. Some had strings of articles or grant proposals turned down and gave up. Some had severe personal crises—deaths, divorces, illnesses—and gave up. The common feature is that they gave up. There have been a number of times in my career when I have felt like giving up. Sometimes crises in my life have seemed so overwhelming that I thought I would be happy for a hole to open up in the ground so that I could just fall into it.

One not-so-big secret to having a successful career is to keep going, even when one feels like one is banging one's head against a wall. Eventually, the crises pass. But if you give up, that's it. You just bought the crisis as your permanent possession. In two words: Keep going.

TAKING ETHICAL SHORTCUTS

If you consider taking an ethical shortcut, don't. There will be plenty of opportunities: fixing data analyses, taking senior authorship on a paper with a student when you should be junior author, seeking double reimbursement for a trip (from a grant and from whoever invited you), giving a student a grade he or she does not deserve in exchange for who knows what, asking research assistants to do personal errands—the list really is endless.

There are three reasons you don't want to take ethical shortcuts. First, they are career destroyers. You can recover from a rejected paper or an unfunded grant proposal; it's really hard to recover your reputation after an ethical lapse. Second, when ethical shortcuts are discovered, as they usually are, the discovery often is public. In addition to any penalties you may face, you also have to face the shame. Third, if you are considering an ethical lapse, you most likely overestimate your cleverness in concealing it. You are new to the business, but there are people who have spent their careers digging out ethical lapses. You are almost certainly not a match for them.

PUTTING YOUR PERSONAL LIFE ON HOLD

This advice is something your department chair will never tell you. There always seem to be good reasons to put your personal life on hold. First you want to make sure you finish your dissertation; no sense going through all that work in graduate school to end up without completing your dissertation. Then there is waiting until you get the first job. Then, of course, there is the reappointment: You don't want the ignominy of being told to leave after only a year or 2 or 3. Then there is tenure: What's the point of it all if you'll be out on the street after 6 or 7 years? Then, of course, there is promotion to full professor: Do you really want to be a lifetime associate professor? And then there is the endowed chair: You know you deserve it and with just a little more work . . . By then, the person who has always put his or her life on hold has a string of failed relationships, no children or children who are maladjusted, and a life devoid of much beside his or her career.

You may wonder who I am to talk. Actually, I am an expert in this area. In the earlier years of my career, I was one of those who put his personal life on hold, and I have the scars to show for it. Fortunately, at this point I have a wonderful marriage and five terrific children. Had I continued on the path I was on, I would have neither. You can't put your life on hold forever. You may think you just need to get over the next hump, but after the next hump, there will be one just ahead of that one that you did not quite foresee. There always will be humps. The day you announce your retirement, someday way in the future, your professional friends and colleagues will start disappearing from your life. What will be left, if you planned your life right, is your family, the one, hopefully, you did not put on hold. They are the ones who will support you to the end. Once you are retired, all those publications can mean surprisingly little!

COVERING UP ERRORS

Of course, you will make errors. Everyone makes errors. That's not even up for question. The question is, what will you do after you make the errors, especially the real blunders? Look, everyone wants to cover up their blunders. If anyone tells you different, don't believe them. But should you cover them up?

This is a simple yes-or-no question with one correct answer: No. I've been in this business a long time, as a faculty member and administrator, and I'll say now, as I've said before: When people get into serious trouble, chances are it's for the cover-up and not for the original offense. These days, it's extremely hard to cover one's tracks. You say something, someone recorded it on a camera phone. You write something on your computer, it's forever somewhere on the web. You do something and there are records of it all over the place. If you make a mistake, admit it, pay the price, and move on. It's much better than sweating for some period of time whether you will be caught, only to find out later that you have been caught and now have two sins—the original one and the cover-up—to pay for.

ASSUMING GOSSIP WON'T GET BACK TO THE SUBJECT

For the most part, academics are incredible gossips. Why shouldn't they be? They trade in information, and gossip is information, although not always the most reliable information. It sometimes is said that knowledge is power, and part of the power of an academic is the juiciness of the gossip he or she has to share. The problem is that gossip has a nasty way of getting back to the person or persons it's about. Although we like to gossip about others, most of us don't like to be gossiped about ourselves, and if we do, we like only positive gossip. But how much of that is there? Who cares about positive gossip, anyway? When you gossip, ask yourself how the person would feel who is being gossiped about, knowing that the gossip came from you.

You may ask how your gossip possibly could get back. That's an easy one. Even if you know the people to whom you are gossiping, what you cannot know is who all their friends are and to whom they owe favors. You also don't know their motivations. You showed your power by handing them the bit of gossip, but you just gave them even more power over you if they should choose to transfer the gossip and its source back to the target of the gossip.

If you are in a situation in which people are gossiping, you don't have to walk out, but you also don't have to contribute actively. If you do, think about, for anything you say, how well it would go over if it got back to the target of the gossip.

NOT GETTING PROMISES IN WRITING

In academia, oral promises don't mean a whole lot. People forget what they have said, sometimes deliberately. Or the people who made the promises no longer have the power to execute them. Or what someone thought he promised is not what you heard, and what you heard is not what he thought he promised. In brief: Get it in writing. That way there will be no doubt about who said what, when, and how.

SHOOTING YOUR MOUTH OFF

There will be plenty of times when you hear things you don't want to hear or get e-mails you don't want to read. Your tendency may be to reply quickly and forcefully. Don't. Never reply when you feel the adrenalin racing through you. Wait. If you still feel the same way a day later, then do what you have to do. But a day later, you may see things in a very different way and save yourself the embarrassment of a response you will wish you never made.

FIGHTING THE WRONG BATTLES

In life, there are some things worth fighting for. But there are a lot that aren't. What has always puzzled me is how adept some scholars are at fighting for things that are not worth fighting for. Yesterday I read about an academic who was fired from a tenured associate professorship at a good university. He had claimed that the Newtown shootings a few years ago, as well as other mass publicized shootings, were a hoax perpetrated by the antigun lobby. Yikes! He even was reported to have harassed parents of a child victim of the Newtown shooting to prove that their child ever had existed. But that's not what he was fired for. He was fired for not filing, apparently for 3 years, required annual disclosures of conflict of interest. As an administrator, I fired scholars for repeatedly not submitting required annual reports. There was not one who academically deserved to be in his or her position. But they compounded the problem of being weak (or, in some cases, wacky) scholars with their insistence on not meeting the absolutely minimal requirements of the university for continued employment.

These are extreme examples of a more prevalent phenomenon. If you decide to engage in a battle, ask yourself whether it is a battle worth fighting. If so, why is it worth fighting? I've never been at an institution that didn't, in some way, tick me off. All institutions do things that are truly questionable. But with everything you have to get done, are any of those things worth fighting for? If they are, then go for it. But at least make sure that the battles are worthy ones.

How do you know whether a battle is worth fighting? Usually, you don't know for sure. But you can ask yourself the following questions: Is there a fundamental principle of academic freedom or integrity at stake? Am I fighting against a serious ethical violation? Have my own or someone else's rights been seriously infringed? You also should ask yourself what you would consider a reasonable resolution. If there is none, then what exactly are you fighting for?

EXPECTING THINGS TO BE FAIR

You've heard before that life isn't fair. Neither is academia. You might expect that because, in academic psychology, you are dealing mostly with scientists, there would be greater fairness. But there's not. Academic psychology shows all the strengths and weaknesses of the rest of life. Some people succeed and no one can figure out quite why; others fail for reasons that remain equally obscure. Some big names seem to have weak scientific records; other smaller names seem to have done outstanding work but never to have been fully recognized for it.

I could go on to give examples, but in a sense, the examples don't matter as much as the principle. When you start encountering the unfairness of academia—and you almost certainly will, sooner or later—don't despair because you are so disillusioned. That's pretty much the way all careers are, and perhaps the only surprise will be that academia is no exception and probably is worse than some others because so much in academia relies on purely subjective judgments of peers.

NOT FULLY LEARNING WHAT IS EXPECTED OF YOU

One thing no department chair wants to hear is, "I didn't know I was expected to do that," in which "that" can refer to almost anything—publishing extensively, teaching with excellence, getting grants, doing service, working amicably with graduate students, or whatever. Employment contracts usually state only minimal expectations for employment, for example, that you teach. They do not specify all the myriad tasks you really are expected to accomplish.

You need to find yourself a mentor absolutely as soon as possible. The department chair can be a mentor of a sort, but he or she generally has a bit of a conflict of interest because the chair has to represent the best interests of the department, and those interests may or may not correspond to yours. You need a mentor to convey to you the tacit or unspoken knowledge of the department—what is really expected of you and not just what people acknowledge publicly, whether orally or in writing. Ideally, find yourself a couple of mentors, perhaps one inside your institution and one outside it. My mentor as a junior faculty member, Wendell Garner, was extremely valuable to me. Yours will be, too. And if he or she is not, find another one. You need someone to teach you about the hidden ropes and hidden obstacles, and a mentor can help you learn those. Your junior colleagues also can be valuable to you, but usually they do not know a lot more than you do. So try to find someone senior who has been around for a while and who knows how things work in your institution.

DOING WORK THAT DOES NOT PERSONALLY EXCITE YOU

Many of us go into academia because it is a chance to have a job in which we can do what we gladly would do for free. Many of us so enjoy teaching or research or serving our department that it seems almost unfair to be paid for doing what we like so much. But if you are not doing work that personally excites you, it's time to take stock of your career. Research shows that you will do your best work if you are really excited about what you do (Sternberg & Lubart, 1995). So if you are not excited, something is wrong. You need to reassess. What can you change? Can you change your teaching? Your research? Your service? Your life? Many of us, when we chose academia, chose a lower salary for a more exciting job. If your job is not exciting, try to figure out a way to make it so. If you can't figure out a way, ask yourself whether you are in the wrong institution, or perhaps even the wrong job.

BUDGETING TIME POORLY

As an academic, your time is going to be very limited. You cannot afford to be a time squanderer. You probably know yourself well enough to know whether you are someone who budgets time well. If you are, congratulations—you will need your time management skills. But if you are a poor time manager, try to get someone to help you—a significant other or a research assistant, perhaps. Do not wait until you are well advanced in your early career to recognize that you are behind in doing the things you needed to get done to be promoted and now are running out of time.

FOCUSING TOO MUCH ON LONG- OR SHORT-TERM GOALS

In academia, you need both sensible long- and short-term goals. As a junior faculty member, you cannot concentrate too much on either. You need short-term goals to get you to your tenure promotion. But you need long-term goals to get you to be a well-recognized success. Those who set only short-term goals may get through the first reappointment or first promotion but then drift aimlessly. Those who set only long-term goals may have the prospect of a successful career in front of them, but they do not do the short-term work to ensure that they ever will get to the long term.

When I was a junior faculty member, I wrote many articles. But I also worked on some long-term book projects. The articles got me to tenure; the books became my most widely cited work. You may be different. But what will not be different is the need for both long- and short-term goals and the recognition that they are not the same thing.

SPREADING YOURSELF THIN

This one is simple: If you agree to undertake a project, make sure you have time to complete it, to complete it well, and to do so without sabotaging your other work. Lots of unfinished projects do not tenure make.

BEING UNPROGRAMMATIC IN YOUR RESEARCH

Especially if you are in a research-intensive environment, you are expected not only to do research but also to do research that is programmatic—that has a theme and a sense of direction. If you find yourself doing a lot of basically unrelated projects, you are on the wrong track, at least in a research-intensive university. It's fine to have a couple of fliers, but you will need to demonstrate, for tenure, that you have a program of research and that it is leading somewhere. There should be coherence and direction to the research, rather than just a number of scarcely related projects.

TALKING THE TALK, NOT WALKING THE WALK

There are some people who try to talk their way through their careers. And some people are even good at it. But people in academia are watched pretty closely, especially junior faculty members. If you talk the talk, but don't walk the walk, people will notice. Here is an extreme case: When I was a junior faculty member, a colleague told me he was working on two books. That was almost 40 years ago. When I saw him more recently, he said he was working on two books. We're all still waiting.

NOT KNOWING WHEN TO FOLD

There is an expression from the song "The Gambler" that says you have to know when to hold 'em, and you have to know when to fold 'em. The same applies to careers.

If your career is not going the way you want, don't wait around, hoping it will get better. Try to figure out what is wrong and correct it. But if you cannot figure out a way to correct it, and you've given it all you've got, consider doing something else. In my experience, too many academics invest huge amounts of their self-esteem in a particular career aspiration. I once did the same myself. Many of us never quite reach that career aspiration. Some of us even find we are in the wrong career.

Some of my former graduate students of whom I am most proud are ones who decided not to pursue an academic career, or they started an academic career and decided it was not for them. There is nothing magical about any one kind of career. There are all kinds of ways to conceive of intelligence (Sternberg, 1990). I have argued that the best way to conceive of intelligence is as figuring out what you want from life, and then doing all you can to achieve it (Sternberg, 1984). But if you do not achieve it, then you need to think flexibly about other options. The smartest people in the room are not the ones who choose a goal and then stick to it, come hell or high water, but rather the ones who, having really tried but failed to achieve one goal, then move on to formulate a new and personally better goal. I've done it many times in my own life, and I hope you will, too!

EPILOGUE

Well, time to wrap this all up with one last piece of advice: You can't do it all on your own. Academics and, especially often, scientists, have a predisposition to be loners. But you just cannot make your career a success on your own. You will be teaching and will need the support of the many students who do student evaluations on you. You will be mentoring and will need the support of your mentees. You will be doing research, and almost certainly some of it will be collaborative. You will need the support of your collaborators. You will serve on committees with others. You will need to get along with your chair and with the other members of your department. If you have a grant, you may have assistants with whom you have to work. And most of all, you will need the support of your family.

To make a musical analogy, view yourself as the conductor of a large orchestra in your career; do not view yourself as a soloist in that orchestra. You will be an unusual conductor because you will have composed much of the music you play. But you cannot make your career work unless you can get

http://dx.doi.org/10.1037/0000013-019
Starting Your Career in Academic Psychology, by R. J. Sternberg
Copyright © 2017 by the American Psychological Association. All rights reserved.

all the players of the orchestra to work in harmony with you and hopefully with each other. So good luck on your symphonic venture, and remember that even conductors sometimes allow wrong notes. But if they are good conductors, they keep going, and over time, as they work more and more with an orchestra, the musical sounds only keep getting better and better.

When I was in college, I took a course in developmental psychology. My course, like other courses at the time, ended in adolescence. The assumption back in the early 1970s was that development more or less ended with the end of adolescence. One then was an adult—end of story. Today we know better, and one of the courses I teach today is "Life Span Development." I show in the course how development not only does not end with the end of adolescence, it hardly has begun! So as you move into your career, do not make the mistake of believing that your development as a professional has ended, perhaps with the end of graduate school or the end of your postdoctoral training.

When I started out as an assistant professor, I falsely believed that I was fully formed. I figured that the kind of work I was doing would be the kind of work I would be doing throughout my career. Wow, was I wrong! I still value the work I did when I was 25, but my work today does not resemble at all what I was doing then. Part of the reason is that I realized that mentorship and collaboration continue throughout one's career. My undergraduate mentor, Endel Tulving, and my graduate mentor, Gordon Bower, remain advisers to me today, more than 40 years after I got my PhD. Moreover, my faculty mentor, Wendell Garner, advised me almost up to his death. Over the years, I have had more than 50 graduate student and postdoctoral collaborators, and many more faculty collaborators. I cannot even count the number of undergraduate collaborators (at this moment, I have 12). Science is a collaborative enterprise, from the beginning of your career to the end. Much of your success, as has been true for much of mine, will not be just about what you have done, but also about your skill in choosing and working with collaborators.

I hope you have found this book useful. If you have any questions or comments, I welcome hearing from you. You can write to me at robert.sternberg@cornell.edu. There also are other sources you can consult to learn more about careers in psychology (e.g., Darley, Zanna, & Roediger, 2004; Prinstein, 2013; Sternberg, 2004b, 2017b; Sternberg & Sternberg, 2010, 2016). Good luck to you, and please be in touch if you would like to be!

REFERENCES

American Psychological Association. (2010). Crediting sources. In *Publication manual of the American Psychological Association* (6th ed., pp. 169–192). Washington, DC: Author.

American Psychological Association. (2016). *Tips for determining authorship credit.* Retrieved from http://www.apa.org/science/leadership/students/authorship-paper.aspx

Bandura, A. (1997). *Self-efficacy: The exercise of control.* New York, NY: Worth.

Baumrind, D. (1991). Parenting styles and adolescent development. In R. M. Lerner, A. C. Petersen, & J. Brooks-Gunn (Eds.), *Encyclopedia of adolescence* (pp. 746–758). New York, NY: Garland.

Borich, G. D. (2013). *Effective teaching methods: Research-based practice* (8th ed.). New York, NY: Pearson.

Brown, P. C., Roediger, H. L., III, & McDaniel, M. A. (2014). *Make it stick: The science of successful learning.* Cambridge, MA: Belknap. http://dx.doi.org/10.4159/9780674419377

Buskist, W., & Davis, S. F. (Eds.). (2005). *Handbook of the teaching of psychology.* New York, NY: Wiley-Blackwell.

Darley, J. M., Zanna, M. P., & Roediger, H. L., III. (2004). *The compleat academic: A career guide* (2nd ed.). Washington, DC: American Psychological Association.

Detterman, D. K., & Sternberg, R. J. (Eds.). (1982). *How and how much can intelligence be increased?* Norwood, NJ: Ablex.

Frensch, P. A., & Sternberg, R. J. (1989). Expertise and intelligent thinking: When is it worse to know better? In R. J. Sternberg (Ed.), *Advances in the psychology of human intelligence* (Vol. 5, pp. 157–188). Hillsdale, NJ: Lawrence Erlbaum.

García Márquez, G. (2007). *Love in the time of cholera* (E. Grossman, Trans.). New York, NY: Vintage.

Goodman, N. (1983). *Fact, fiction, and forecast* (4th ed.). Cambridge, MA: Harvard University Press.

Gorsevski, E. W. (2015). *Writing successful grant proposals.* Rotterdam, the Netherlands: Sense.

Janis, I. L. (1972). *Victims of groupthink.* Boston, MA: Houghton-Mifflin.

Kaufman, J. C., & Sternberg, R. J. (Eds.). (2010). *Cambridge handbook of creativity.* New York, NY: Cambridge University Press. http://dx.doi.org/10.1017/CBO9780511763205

Komarraju, M., Karau, S. J., Schmeck, R. R., & Avdic, A. (2011). The Big Five personality traits, learning styles, and academic achievement. *Personality and Individual Differences, 51,* 472–477. http://dx.doi.org/10.1016/j.paid.2011.04.019

Landrum, R. E., & McCarthy, M. A. (Eds.). (2012). *Teaching ethically: Challenges and opportunities*. Washington, DC: American Psychological Association. http://dx.doi.org/10.1037/13496-000

Lubart, T. I., & Sternberg, R. J. (1988). Creativity: The individual, the systems, the approach. *Creativity Research Journal, 1*, 63–67. http://dx.doi.org/10.1080/10400418809534288

Marzano, R. J. (2007). *The art and science of teaching: A comprehensive framework for effective instruction*. Alexandria, VA: Association for Supervision and Curriculum Development.

Milgram, S. (2009). *Obedience to authority: An experimental view*. New York, NY: Harper Perennial.

Mischel, W. (2015). *The marshmallow test*. New York, NY: Back Bay.

Popper, K. (2002). *The logic of scientific discovery* (2nd ed.). New York, NY: Routledge.

Prinstein, M. J. (Ed.). (2013). *The portable mentor: Expert guide to a successful career in psychology* (2nd ed.). New York, NY: Springer. http://dx.doi.org/10.1007/978-1-4614-3994-3

Ray, J., & Kafka, S. (2014). *Life in college matters for life after college*. Washington, DC: Gallup. Retrieved from http://www.gallup.com/poll/168848/life-college-matters-life-college.aspx

Roediger, H. L., & McDermott, K. B. (1995). Creating false memories: Remembering words not presented in lists. *Journal of Experimental Psychology: Learning, Memory, and Cognition, 21*, 803–814. http://dx.doi.org/10.1037/0278-7393.21.4.803

Rogers, D. T. (2015). Further validation of the Learning Alliance Inventory: The roles of working alliance, rapport, and immediacy in student learning. *Teaching of Psychology, 42*, 19–25. http://dx.doi.org/10.1177/0098628314562673

Rowe, M. B. (1972, April). *Wait-time and rewards as instructional variables: Their influence in language, logical, and fate control*. Paper presented at the conference of the National Association for Research in Science Teaching, Chicago, IL.

Spear, L. C., & Sternberg, R. J. (1987). Teaching styles: Staff development for teaching thinking. *Journal of Staff Development, 8*(3), 35–39.

Sternberg, R. J. (1984). What should intelligence tests test? Implications of a triarchic theory of intelligence for intelligence testing. *Educational Researcher, 13*, 5–15. http://dx.doi.org/10.3102/0013189X013001005

Sternberg, R. J. (1987). Liking versus loving: A comparative evaluation of theories. *Psychological Bulletin, 102*, 331–345. http://dx.doi.org/10.1037/0033-2909.102.3.331

Sternberg, R. J. (1990). *Metaphors of mind: Conceptions of the nature of intelligence*. New York, NY: Cambridge University Press.

Sternberg, R. J. (Ed.). (1997). *Teaching introductory psychology*. Washington, DC: American Psychological Association.

Sternberg, R. J. (1998a). *Cupid's arrow: The course of love through time*. New York, NY: Cambridge University Press.

Sternberg, R. J. (1998b). *Love is a story.* New York, NY: Oxford University Press.

Sternberg, R. J. (Ed.). (2000). *Guide to publishing in psychology journals.* New York, NY: Cambridge University Press. http://dx.doi.org/10.1017/CBO9780511807862

Sternberg, R. J. (Ed.). (2002). *Why smart people can be so stupid.* New Haven, CT: Yale University Press.

Sternberg, R. J. (2003). *Wisdom, intelligence, and creativity synthesized.* New York, NY: Cambridge University Press. http://dx.doi.org/10.1017/CBO9780511509612

Sternberg, R. J. (2004a). Obtaining a research grant: The view from the applicant. In J. M. Darley, M. P. Zanna, & H. L. Roediger (Eds.), *The compleat academic: A career guide* (2nd ed., pp. 169–184). Washington, DC: American Psychological Association.

Sternberg, R. J. (2004b). *Psychology 101 1/2: The unspoken rules for success in academia.* Washington, DC: American Psychological Association.

Sternberg, R. J. (Ed.). (2007). *Career paths in psychology* (2nd ed.). Washington, DC: American Psychological Association.

Sternberg, R. J. (2012). Ethical drift. *Liberal Education, 98*(3), 60.

Sternberg, R. J. (2013a). Securing a research grant. In R. J. Sternberg (Ed.), *Writing successful grant proposals from the top down and the bottom up* (pp. 3–24). Newbury Park, CA: Sage.

Sternberg, R. J. (Ed.). (2013b). *Writing successful grant proposals from the top down and the bottom up.* Newbury Park, CA: Sage.

Sternberg, R. J. (Ed.). (2017a). *Career paths in psychology* (3rd ed.). Washington, DC: American Psychological Association.

Sternberg, R. J. (2017b). *Psychology 101 1/2: The unspoken rules for success in academia* (2nd ed.). Washington, DC: American Psychological Association.

Sternberg, R. J., & Bower, G. H. (1974). Transfer in part–whole and whole–part free recall: A comparative evaluation of theories. *Journal of Verbal Learning & Verbal Behavior, 13,* 1–26. http://dx.doi.org/10.1016/S0022-5371(74)80026-5

Sternberg, R. J., & Fiske, S. T. (Eds.). (2015). *Ethical challenges in the behavioral and brain sciences.* New York, NY: Cambridge University Press. http://dx.doi.org/10.1017/CBO9781139626491

Sternberg, R. J., Fiske, S. T., & Foss, D. J. (Eds.). (2016). *Psychologists making a difference.* New York, NY: Cambridge University Press.

Sternberg, R. J., & Grigorenko, E. L. (2001). A capsule history of theory and research on styles. In R. J. Sternberg & L. F. Zhang (Eds.), *Perspectives on thinking, learning, and cognitive styles* (pp. 1–21). Mahwah, NJ: Lawrence Erlbaum.

Sternberg, R. J., & Grigorenko, E. L. (2007). *Teaching for successful intelligence* (2nd ed.). Thousand Oaks, CA: Corwin Press.

Sternberg, R. J., Grigorenko, E. L., & Kidd, K. K. (2005). Intelligence, race, and genetics. *American Psychologist, 60,* 46–59.

Sternberg, R. J., Kaufman, J. C., & Pretz, J. E. (2002). *The creativity conundrum: A propulsion model of kinds of creative contributions*. New York, NY: Psychology Press.

Sternberg, R. J., & Lubart, T. I. (1995). *Defying the crowd: Cultivating creativity in a culture of conformity*. New York, NY: Free Press.

Sternberg, R. J., Nokes, K., Geissler, P. W., Prince, R., Okatcha, F., Bundy, D. A., & Grigorenko, E. L. (2001). The relationship between academic and practical intelligence: A case study in Kenya. *Intelligence, 29*, 401–418. http://dx.doi.org/10.1016/S0160-2896(01)00065-4

Sternberg, R. J., & Soriano, L. J. (1984). Styles of conflict resolution. *Journal of Personality and Social Psychology, 47*, 115–126. http://dx.doi.org/10.1037/0022-3514.47.1.115

Sternberg, R. J., & Sternberg, K. (2010). *The psychologist's companion* (5th ed.). New York, NY: Cambridge University Press. http://dx.doi.org/10.1017/CBO9780511762024

Sternberg, R. J., & Sternberg, K. (2016). *The psychologist's companion* (6th ed.). New York, NY: Cambridge University Press.

Sternberg, R. J., & Weil, E. M. (1980). An aptitude–strategy interaction in linear syllogistic reasoning. *Journal of Educational Psychology, 72*, 226–239. http://dx.doi.org/10.1037/0022-0663.72.2.226

Svinicki, M., & McKeachie, W. J. (2013). *McKeachie's teaching tips* (14th ed.). Belmont, CA: Wadsworth.

Vygotsky, L. S. (1978). *Mind in society: The development of higher psychological processes*. Cambridge, MA: Harvard University Press.

Williams, W. M., & Ceci, S. J. (1997). How'm I doing? *Change, 29*(5), 12–23. http://dx.doi.org/10.1080/00091389709602331

INDEX

AAUP (American Association of University Professors), 150
Abstracts, 193
Academic articles, 189–199
    abstracts of, 193
    audiences of, 190
    citations and sources in, 196–197
    conclusion sections of, 197–198
    conflicts with reviewers of, 230, 234–235
    critiques of, 178, 191–192
    discussion sections of, 198
    distribution of your, 174
    endings of, 198
    and everyday experience, 195
    as factors in tenure and promotion, 217–218
    feedback on, 193–194
    and historical perspective, 196
    hypotheses in, 192
    intelligibility of, 191
    and journal fit, 194–195
    journal rejections of, 199
    length of, 193
    literature reviews of, 194, 195
    messages of, 189–190, 192–194
    novelty in, 190–191
    polishing and proofreading of, 192
    quotations in, 196
    research ideas generated by, 78
    results sections of, 197
    stories told in, 190, 191
    titles of, 192–193
    transparency in, 197
Academic careers, 25–36
    getting set up for, 33–36
    interim activities before, 30–33
    job offers for, 22, 25–30
Academic integrity, 43
Academic journals, 159–161
    associate editors on, 161
    consulting editors on, 160–161
    fit of academic articles with, 194–195
    journal editors on, 161
    and networking, 172, 177–178
    publication lags of, 217–218
    reviewers on, 159–160
    special issues of, 177
Academic misconduct, 15
Academic politics, 201–208
    and acting independently, 207
    and admissions for graduate students, 203
    agency in, 208
    and budgets, 205
    cover-ups in, 205
    and existing policies, 202
    factionalism in, 205–206
    give-and-take in, 206
    gossip in, 206
    and hiring, 208
    and nepotism, 202–203
    and power structures, 202
    prejudice in, 206
    and putting in effort, 207, 208
    and resources, 204
    and sharing students, 204
    of tenure and promotion, 203–205, 223
    and turning a blind eye, 206, 207
Academic psychology departments, 16. *See also specific headings*
Academic standards committee, 153
Acquisition editors, 171
Acronyms, 183
Active learning, 212
Ad hoc committees, 153, 157
Administrators, 232–234
Advising, 214–215
Alcohol use, 185
American Association of University Professors (AAUP), 150
American Educational Research Association, 163
American Psychological Association (APA)
    divisional representatives of, 163
    guidelines for authorship, 65, 108, 228
    and service work, 159, 162
Analytical questions, 46, 214

APA. *See* American Psychological Association
APS (Association for Psychological Science), 159
Articles. *See* Academic articles
Assessment (classroom testing), 52–54
Associate department chairs, 147
Associate editors, 161, 172
Association for Psychological Science (APS), 159
Associative errors, 77
Attire, 180
Authoritarian style, 60–61
Authoritative style, 60–61
Authorship, 65–66, 108–109, 228

Background checks, 64–65, 100, 115
Backing up data files, 33–34, 84
Base rates, 223
Benefits, employee, 35–36, 96, 131
Bias, 50, 206, 229
Big-picture thinking, 82
Blogging, 164, 173, 221
Book exhibits, 171
Books
    editing of, 177
    as factors in tenure and promotion, 218–219
    organization of, 33–34
    prepublication review of, 161–162
    publishing chapters in, 10
    research ideas generated by, 78
Boundaries, 62–63, 214
Bower, Gordon, 63–64, 125, 128, 250
Budgets
    and academic politics, 205
    as factors in tenure and promotion, 224
    institutional, 152
    justifications in, 94–95
    overspending of, 80–81

Calendars, 98–99
Ceci, Stephen, 48
Cell phones, 52
Chairs, department. *See* Department chairs
Cheating, academic, 43, 152, 227
Children, 28, 36
Citations, 196–197
Class observations, 56

Classroom testing, 52–54
Class size, 39–40
Coauthors, 199
Collaboration(s), 105–116
    background checks in, 115
    and committee decisions, 114–115
    and common good, 110
    and cultural differences, 111–112
    data checking in, 115
    deadlines for, 115–116
    division of resources in, 110–111
    from graduate school and postdocs, 237–238
    grant funding for, 116
    leadership in, 113
    and networking, 177–178
    new, 106
    with other departments and schools, 107, 109
    with other research labs, 101–102
    procedural agreements in, 107–108
    sharing credit in, 108–109
    and social loafing, 112–113
    student. *See* Student collaboration
    termination of, 113–114
    transparency in, 116
College counseling centers, 70
Collegiality, 222
Colloquia, 175
Commercial consulting, 165
Commercial ventures, 165
Committee decisions, 114–115
Committees. *See specific committees*
Community relations committees, 155
Compensation committees, 154–155
Competitive offers, 22, 97–98
Computers, 4, 99
Computer techs, 34
Conclusion section (academic articles), 197–198
Conferences
    and networking at parties, 176
    relevance of, 220
    reviewers for, 160
Conflict resolution, 225–235
    with administrators, 232–234
    with other faculty members, 230–231
    with reviewers of academic articles, 230, 234–235
    with students, 225–230

Consolidations, institutional, 224
Constructive criticism, 178, 216
Consulting editors, 160–161, 172
Consulting work, 160–161, 165
Contracts, 124, 245
Conventions, 171
Copyeditors, 171
Corporate research funding, 123
Course evaluations, 48
Course load, 26–27
Cover-ups, 205
Creative thinking, 46, 54, 91–92, 214
Credit (authorship), 65–66, 108–109
Credit, extra, 43, 212, 227
Critical thinking, 46
Cultural differences, 111–112
Cursing, 182
CVs, 20–21

Data
    backing up, 33–34, 84
    checking of, 115
    novelty of, 190
    raw, 85–86
Day care, 36
Deadlines, 42, 115–116
Deans
    meetings with, 20, 35
    and start-up grants, 95
Defensiveness, 184
Delayed gratification, 71
Departmental base rates, 223
Departmental colloquium committee, 151
Departmental consolidations and restructurings, 224
Departmental directors of transfer students, 146–147
Departmental fit, 223, 233
Departmental politics. *See* Academic politics
Department chairs
    and academic politics, 204
    and budgets, 95
    and forensic work, 164
    meetings with, 35
    and service work, 147
Department executive committees, 148
Department honors advisers, 155
Developmental editors, 171

DGS (directors of graduate studies), 145–146
Dinners, 18
Directors of graduate studies (DGS), 145–146
Directors of undergraduate studies (DUS), 144–145
Disability accommodations, 43
Disciplinary committees, 152–153
Discussion questions, 45–46, 214
Discussion section (academic articles), 198
Dissertations
    completion of, 30, 241
    literature reviews in, 194
    publishing of, 10
Durocher, Leo, 110
DUS (directors of undergraduate studies), 144–145

Educational curriculum committees, 149
Effort, 207, 208
Electronic devices, 52
Elevator speeches, 15–16, 82, 87
E-mail, 51, 188
Empirical papers, 10, 192. *See also* Academic articles
Employment contracts, 245
English as a second language, 69, 181
Enthusiasm, 47–48, 81, 184, 212
Ethics
    and collaboration, 72, 109, 114
    and institutional review boards, 156
    shortcuts in, 241
Examination textbooks, 41
Expectations, 244–245
Exploitation, 65, 215, 229
Extension and outreach, 222
External grant evaluation, 133
Extra credit, 43, 212, 227–228
Extramural (external) grants, 120–123

Facebook, 173–174
Fact-based questions, 214
Factionalism, 205–206
Faculty
    conflicts with, 230–231
    meeting with other, 34
Faculty compensation committees, 154–155

Faculty search committees, 150–151
Faculty senates/councils, 150
Fairness, 212, 244
Fallback plans, 95–96
Famous people, 176–178
Federation of Associations in Behavioral and Brain Sciences, 162
Feedback, 132, 188, 193–194, 215, 239
Felonies, 15
Flattery, 178
fMRI (functional magnetic resonance imaging) research, 100
Forensic service work, 164–165
Foundations, 122–123
Free recall, 77
Functional magnetic resonance imaging (fMRI) research, 100
Funding. *See also* Grants
    internal sources of, 83
    for research lab expenses, 98–101. *See also* Start-up grants

García Márquez, G., 78
Garner, Wendell, 245, 250
Goals, 246
Goodman, Nelson, 78
Google Scholar, 216
Gossip, 206, 242–243
Government organizations, 120–122
Grading, 42–43, 225–226
Graduate admissions committees, 148–149
Graduate school, 9–12, 145–146, 237–238
Graduate students, 62, 191, 203
Grants, 117–139
    for collaborative projects, 116
    contracts vs., 124
    and frame of mind, 135–138
    function of, 118–119
    and institutional review boards, 76
    misallocation of funds from, 232–233
    and organizational meetings, 174
    organizations behind, 120–123
    overview, 26
    panels for, 172
    preparation for applications to, 124–126
    proposals for, 32–33, 101, 126–135
    start-up, 28–29, 93–98

Grants.gov, 121
Gratification, delayed, 71
Groupthink, 114

Harassment, 213, 229–230
Health benefits, 35–36
H index, 216–217
Hiring processes, 208
Honorary degrees committees, 156
Honors advisers, 155
Housing, 31–32
Humor, 56, 213
Hypotheses, 88, 129, 192

$I10$ index, 217
Iconix, 4
Impact factors, 217
Informational technology (IT) consultants/liaisons, 151
Informed consent, 228
Institutional review boards (IRBs), 75–76, 156, 228
Insurance, liability, 230
Intelligence, 12, 247
Internal grant evaluation, 133
Intramural (internal) grants, 120
IRBs (institutional review boards), 75–76, 156, 228
IT (informational technology) consultants/liaisons, 151

James S. McDonnell Foundation, 122, 123
Job interviews
    elements of, 15–22
    following up with, 22–23
    preparation for, 13–15
    technology failures during, 17, 44–45
Job offers
    competitive, 22, 97–98
    elements of, 25–30
Job searches, 13
Job talks. *See* Job interviews
John Templeton Foundation, 122
Jokes, 56, 213
Journal articles. *See* Academic articles
Judicial committees, 152–153
Junior faculty
    and academic politics, 201
    common mistakes of, 237–247

and disciplinary committees, 152–153
and power structures, 16
and self-centeredness, 233

Labs. *See* Research labs
Laissez-faire style, 60–61
Laptop computers, 99
Leadership in, 113
Lecture courses, 211–213
Lecture notes, 45, 47
Lectures. *See* Talks and lectures
Lesson planning, 43–46
Letters of recommendation
    sources for, 11–12
    for student advisees, 215
Liability insurance, 230
Library liaisons, 152
Literature reviews, 10, 128–129, 194, 195
Long-term goals, 246

MacArthur Foundation, 122
Media, 78–79
Memory, 54
Milgram, S., 228
Military organizations, 120
Minorities, 12
Mischel, W., 71
Mistakes, 54–55, 188, 211, 242
Multi-institution collaborations, 109
Multimedia presentations, 212
Multiple-choice testing, 53

National Institutes of Health (NIH)
    grants offered by, 120, 121, 125, 132, 134
    serving on grants panel of, 172
National Science Foundation (NSF), 120, 121, 125, 134, 172
Nepotism, 202–203
Networking, 169–178
    and academic journals, 172, 177, 178
    with book editing, 177
    and collaborations, 177–178
    and colloquia, 175
    on committees of your college or institution, 171
    at conference parties, 176
    at convention book exhibits, 171
    by distribution of articles, 174
    with famous people, 176–178
    and flattery, 178
    on grants panels, 172
    at meetings of granting organizations, 174
    online, 173–174
    with print media, 174–175
    with professional associations, 171, 172
    at professional meetings, 170
    by students, 67–68
    with workshops, 176
Newsletters, 174–175
Newspapers, 174–175
NIH. *See* National Institutes of Health
Nondisclosure policies, 123
Nongovernmental organizations, 122
Nonprofit organizations, 165
Nonverbal feedback, 48
North Atlantic Treaty Organization, 122
NSF. *See* National Science Foundation
Number of citations index, 216

Office hours, 42
Offices
    setting up, 33–34
    spaces for, 29
Online networking, 173–174
Open access publishing, 218
Overhead costs, 96, 130–131

Pacing, 181
Papers, 87–92. *See also* Academic articles
Parenting styles, 60
Parties, 176
Partner accommodations, 22, 30
Partnership for Child Development, 123
Personal life, 241–242
Plagiarism, 152, 153, 213, 226–227
Politics, academic. *See* Academic politics
Popular press, 221
Postdocs, 10, 237–238
Poster presentations, 220
PowerPoint presentations, 17, 44, 47, 181
Power structures, 16, 202
Practical thinking, 54, 214
Pregnancy, 28

Prejudice, 206
Preproposals, 126
Prepublication book review, 161–162
Presentations, 219–210. *See also* PowerPoint presentations; Talks and lectures
Presidents (professional associations), 163–164
Primary sources, 196–197
Print media, 174–175
Procedural agreements, 107–108
Production editors, 171
Professional advancement. *See specific headings, e.g.:* Networking
Professional associations, 162–164
    board members of, 163
    committee members of, 162
    council members of, 162–163
    divisional presidents and vice presidents of, 163–164
    networking with, 171, 172
    presidents and vice presidents of, 164
    secretaries of, 163
    treasurers of, 163
Professional conferences. *See* Conferences
Professional meetings, 170
Promotion. *See* Tenure and promotion
Promotion committees, 171
Proofreading, 89–90, 131–132, 192
Psychological Bulletin, 194
Publication lags, 217–218
Publishing
    of dissertation, 10
    and nondisclosure policies, 123
    open access, 218
    opportunities for student involvement in, 67
    rushing into, 238

Quotations, 196

Raw data, 85–86
Reactance, 97
Reading material (coursework), 46–47
Real-world examples, 212
Reputation, 13, 119
Research, 75–93
    evaluation of, 216–217
    execution of, 84–87
    as factor in tenure and promotion, 216–221
    in graduate school, 9–10
    guidelines for, 75–81
    planning of, 32, 81–84
    trendy, 12
    unprogrammatic, 246
    writing papers on, 87–92
Research assistants, 100, 203
Research equipment, 99
Research grants. *See* Grants
Research groups, 215–216
Research labs, 93–104
    collaboration with other, 101–102
    setting up, 35
    spaces for, 29, 97–98
    start-up grants for, 93–98
Resilience, 70–71, 240
Restructurings, institutional, 224
Results sections (academic articles), 197
Retirement funds, 35–36
Reviewers, journal, 234–235
Risk-taking, 68, 82, 101
Roediger, Henry, III, 77, 78
Rowe, M. B., 50
Royalties, 219
Rumors, 206

Sacco, Justine, 173
Salaries
    and conflicts with administrators, 232
    and overhead costs, 131
    overview, 25–26, 35–36
    summer, 26, 119
Search committees, 16
Secondary sources, 196–197
Secretaries, of professional associations, 163
Self-centeredness, 233–234
Self-confidence, 180
Self-doubt, 70
Self-efficacy, 70
Self-presentation, 69
Seminars, 51, 213–214
Service courses, 27
Service work, 143–157
    as AAUP representative, 150
    on academic journals, 159–161
    on academic standards committee, 153

on ad hoc committee, 153, 157
as associate department chair, 147
as book proposal reviewer, 161–162
in commercial and nonprofit consulting, 165
and commercial ventures, 165
on community relations committee, 155
on departmental colloquium committee, 151
as departmental director of transfer students, 146–147
as department chair, 147
on department executive committee, 148
as department honors adviser, 155
as department IT consultant or liaison, 151
as director of graduate studies, 145–146
as director of undergraduate studies, 144–145
on disciplinary/judicial committee, 152–153
on diversity committee, 154
on educational curriculum committee, 149
as factor in tenure and promotion, 221–222
on faculty compensation committee, 154–155
on faculty search committee, 150–151
on faculty senate/council, 150
forensic, 164–165
on graduate admissions committee, 148–149
on honorary degrees committee, 156
on institutional review boards, 156
as library liaison, 152
in professional associations, 162–164
and professional conference proposal reviews, 160
requirements for, 29
on social media, 164
as union representative/steward, 149
on university athletics committee, 153–154
on university capital construction committee, 156–157
on university technology transfer committee, 157
on work–life balance committee, 157
Sexual harassment, 213
Short-term goals, 246
Simon, Herbert, 77
Slideshows. *See* PowerPoint presentations
Social distance, 111
Social loafing, 112–113
Social media, 164, 173–174
Sources (research), 196–197
Spear-Swerling, Louise, 46
Spencer Foundation, 122
Spousal accommodations, 22, 30
Start-up grants, 28–29, 93–98
Storytelling, 179–180, 191
Student advising, 214–215
Student collaboration, 59–72
    administrative help with, 66–67
    authoritative style in, 60–61
    and background checks, 64–65
    boundaries in, 62–63
    and delay of gratification, 71
    enthusiasm in, 64
    and ethics, 72
    and exploitation, 65
    financial support for, 119
    and guidelines for assigning credit, 65–66
    modeling behavior in, 72
    networking and publishing with, 67
    and openness to ideas, 63–64
    opportunities for, 107
    on research, 100, 103
    risk-taking in, 68
    and sharing students with other labs, 66
    and student resilience, 70–71
    and student self-efficacy, 70
    and students' zones of proximal development, 61–62
    teaching roles in, 68–69
    time devoted to, 63
    with undergraduate vs. graduate students, 62
    win-win situations with, 60
Student conflicts, 225–230
Student evaluations, 146
Summer salaries, 26, 119
Syllabi, 42–43

Tablets, 52
Tachistoscopes, 4
Talks and lectures, 179–188
    alcohol use prior to, 185
    amount of content in, 183–184, 187
    answering questions in, 184–187
    attire for, 180
    and audience knowledge, 183
    and audience sensitivities, 182
    capturing audiences in, 180–181
    concrete examples in, 183
    and cursing, 182
    and defensiveness, 184
    endings of, 187–188
    and English as a second language, 181
    enthusiasm in, 184
    as factors in tenure and promotion, 219–220
    important points in, 182
    and knowing your audience, 184
    mistakes made in, 188
    outlines for, 181
    pacing of, 181
    preparation for, 185, 186
    at professional meetings, 170
    and self-confidence, 180
    slideshows in, 181
    and sounding natural, 180
    storytelling with, 179–180
    structure of, 182
    summaries in, 187
    time constraints with, 188
Taxes, 155
Teaching, 39–57
    and agreements in writing, 30
    and backing up files, 84
    and course load, 26–27
    and developing courses, 39–43
    and discussion questions, 45–46
    and electronic device use, 52
    as factor in tenure and promotion, 210–216
    flexibility in, 19
    in graduate school, 9–10
    guidelines for behavior while, 55–56
    and individual lesson planning, 43–46
    and lab space, 29
    mistakes made while, 54–55
    and office space, 29
    principles of, 46–52
    service requirements with, 29
    spousal accommodations with, 30
    start dates for, 27–28
    startup grants for, 28–29
    and testing, 52–54
    and types of courses, 27
Teaching evaluations, 210–211
Technology
    failures with, 17, 44–45, 186
    student use of, 52
Technology transfer committees, 157
Tenure and promotion, 209–224
    academic politics of, 203–205, 223
    budgetary factors in, 224
    and collaborations from graduate school and postdocs, 238
    and collegiality, 222
    and consolidations/restructurings, 224
    denial of, 239
    and departmental base rates, 223
    and departmental fit, 223
    extension and outreach factors in, 222
    research factors in, 216–221
    service factors in, 221–222
    as source of conflict with administrators, 232
    teaching factors in, 210–216
Tenure committees, 171
Testing, 52–54
Textbooks, 41, 90–91, 212
Thank-you notes, 22
Theory papers, 10
Time management, 245–246
Titles, article, 192–193
Transfer students, 146–147
Transparency, 116, 197
Treasurers, of professional associations, 163
Tulving, Endel, 77, 78, 250
Turnitin, 226
Twitter, 164, 173

Undergraduate programs, 144–145
Undergraduate students, 62
Union representatives and stewards, 149
University athletics committees, 153–154

University capital construction committees, 156–157
University politics. *See* Academic politics
University technology transfer committees, 157
Uploads, research, 220–221
U.S. Department of Education, 120

Vice presidents (professional associations), 164

W. T. Grant Foundation, 122
Web addresses, 188
Web of Science, 216
Williams, Wendy, 48
Wisdom, 54, 214
Work–life balance committees, 157
Workshops, 176
World Bank, 122
World Health Organization, 122
Writing
  of research papers, 87–92
  skills for, 69
Written agreements, 30, 99, 243

Zones of proximal development, 61–62

ABOUT THE AUTHOR

Robert J. Sternberg, PhD, received his BA from Yale and his PhD from Stanford. He also is the recipient of 13 honorary doctorates. He is a professor of human development at Cornell University and honorary professor of psychology at the University of Heidelberg, Germany. He previously served as a university dean, provost, and president. Earlier, he was IBM Professor of Psychology and Education in the Department of Psychology at Yale University and director of the Yale Center for the Psychology of Abilities, Competencies, and Expertise (PACE Center).

He was the 2003 president of the American Psychological Association and the 2012–2013 president of the Federation of Associations in Behavioral and Brain Sciences. He is editor of *Perspectives on Psychological Science* and previously was editor of *The APA Review of Books: Contemporary Psychology* and *Psychological Bulletin*. He has won many awards, including the James McKeen Cattell (1999) and Williams James (2017) Awards of the Association for Psychological Science.

Dr. Sternberg is a member of the American Academy of Arts and Sciences and the National Academy of Education and a fellow of the American Psychological Association, Association for Psychological Science, American Educational Research Association, and American Association for the Advancement of Science. His work has been cited in professional literature more than 115,000 times.